St. Teresa of Avila Convent
560 Sterling Place
Brooklyn 38, N. Y.

Gift of Sister Marie Bellarmine to

Carmel - Saranac Lake - 1963

MADAME DE CHANTAL

Also by Elisabeth Stopp
(*Translation and Introduction*)

ST FRANCIS DE SALES: SELECTED LETTERS

Madame de Chantal in a widow's habit. Miniature of about 1604
Musée Historique Lorrain, Nancy

MADAME DE CHANTAL

Portrait of a Saint

―⊸∘◉∘⊂―

ELISABETH STOPP

THE NEWMAN PRESS

Westminster, Maryland

1963

NIHIL OBSTAT: JOANNES M. T. BARTON, S.T.D., L.S.S.
CENSOR DEPUTATUS
IMPRIMATUR: E. MORROGH BERNARD
VICARIUS GENERALIS
WESTMONASTERII, DIE 31 JULII, 1962
The Nihil Obstat *and* Imprimatur *are a declaration that a book
or pamphlet is considered to be free from doctrinal or moral error.
It is not implied that those who have granted the* Nihil Obstat *and*
Imprimatur *agree with the contents, opinions or statements expressed.*

Printed in Great Britain

MATRI SORORIBUSQUE

CONTENTS

ILLUSTRATIONS

PREFACE

―――――⋺∘◉∘⋞―――――

THIS book is an attempt to portray the personal and spiritual development of a saint and to set the portrait against its background in time and place. A detailed account of Madame de Chantal's spiritual teaching, and of the work connected specifically with the organization of her own order in later years, is not within my competence; what chiefly attracted me was the story of her life and the actual process by which a not very unusual young married woman of the world gradually turned into a saint.

For the narrative of events I have followed the long chronicle written immediately after Madame de Chantal's death by a younger member of her own order, Françoise-Madeleine de Chaugy. I have drawn on the saint's published letters and writings, on original, unpublished material in the Visitation archives, and on my own knowledge of the places where she lived. No detail of my narrative and exposition is without historical foundation, though it would, of course, have been impossible to give footnote references for every statement. On the very rare occasions when I have had to resort to conjecture, this is clear from the formulation of the text.

The Christian names of St Jane Frances de Chantal and St Francis de Sales have been given in the form in which they are current in the English calendar and spiritual tradition. Other names are given in their French form. It has been quite deliberate, and in accordance with the whole trend of this book, to refer to St Jane Frances as 'Madame de Chantal' even after she had entered religion. The name is, moreover, historically accurate, as this was how, by right of her rank as a baroness, she continued to be known to the end by her contemporaries outside the cloister.

Throughout my work I have received invaluable support from St Chantal's order, the Order of the Visitation. I owe grateful thanks to the First Monastery at Annecy for allowing me to work in the archives, to consult and photograph manuscripts and early printed works concerning the founders. The First Visitation in Paris and the monastery in Angers also put archive material at my disposal, while Saint Pierre d'Albigny, Thurnfeld, Turin and Vif allowed me to use or take photographs of portraits in their possession. The Visitation in Waldron, Sussex, lent me prints and assisted me loyally throughout in many ways.

I should also like to thank the Reverend Stephen Rigby for unfailing encouragement and help, the Superior of the Canonesses of St Augustine, Cambridge, for telling me about the miniature of St Chantal at Nancy, Mr T. S. Wyatt for letting me have one of his photographs of Annecy, M.l'Abbé Roger Devos, *directeur* and librarian at the Grand Séminaire, Annecy, for generously allowing me to use some of the photographic material he assembled for the 1960 St Francis de Sales Exhibition in Annecy. I acknowledge permission given to use photographs supplied by the Bibliothèque Publique, Dijon, and the Musée Historique Lorrain, Nancy. Finally I want to thank my husband who supplied stringent criticism and skilled photography.

ELISABETH STOPP

Cambridge, 29 January 1962

a passive prisoner, but
was now to learn that
it was possible to temper
personal initiative
with patient readiness

Part I

PREPARATION

Chapter 1

BEGINNINGS AT DIJON

1572-1592

⸻◦◉◦⸻

Jeanne-Françoise Frémyot was born in Dijon on Tuesday, 23 January 1572. She was baptized the same day and given her first name after the saint whose feast day it happened to be: St John the Almoner, remembered especially for his charity to the sick and the poor. Her second name was added at the time of her confirmation, in honour of St Francis of Assisi.

Jane was the second daughter of Bénigne Frémyot, councillor and afterwards president of the parliament of Dijon. Her mother was Marguerite de Berbisey and the only recorded fact about her is that her ancestors belonged to the family of Burgundy's greatest saint, St Bernard of Clairvaux. Their first daughter, Marguerite, was about two years older than Jane; a son, André, was born in July 1573, and his mother died in giving birth to him. Frémyot married again, a widow of whom nothing is known except that her name was Claire Jousset and whom the children remembered no better than their own mother. It is presumed that she died within a short time of the marriage. The children were brought up under the immediate care of their father and with the help of an aunt.

Very little is known about Jane's childhood, that is, exactly as little as she herself chose to tell of it in later years, generally with the intention of illustrating something she was trying to teach or explain. In an instruction to her novices[1] she describes herself in

---

[1] *Sainte Jeanne-Françoise Frémyot de Chantal. Sa vie et ses Oeuvres.* Edition authentique publiée par les soins des Religieuses du Premier Monastère de la Visitation Sainte-Marie d'Annecy. Eight vols., Paris 1874–9. Vol. 2, p. 514. Arabic numerals in brackets after a quotation in the text, thus (2, 514), refer to this edition.

a little aside as having been '*fille à toute folie*', 'ready for any mischief'; though what follows—she used to tease her tame starlings by holding out bits of sugar to them as she dashed up and down the stairs and all over the house—is nothing more than normal high spirits. She seems to have been an alert child, lively and very intelligent. Her intelligence was inherited from her father and fostered by him; he allowed his motherless children to spend a good deal of time in his company and to join in the general conversation even when he had important visitors.

One day when a huguenot nobleman was engaged in an after-dinner argument with Frémyot, the five-year-old Jane listened intently, and escaping from her nurse at the other side of the room, made a vigorous statement of what she had been taught:

'Sir, you've got to believe that Jesus Christ is in the Blessed Sacrament because he himself said so. If you don't believe it you're calling him a liar.'

The visitor, impressed in spite of himself by her earnestness but also not a little amused, offered her a dish of sugared almonds as being something more suited to her age than theological controversy about the Real Presence. But Jane, the lawyer's daughter, was ready to turn the point in support of her argument, and holding out her apron to take the sweets, at once tipped the whole lot into the large fire burning on the open hearth. It was an object-lesson to illustrate the fiery fate of heretics in the next world.

'This', she said, 'is what happens to people who don't believe what our Lord says.'

It seems, however, that the two remained good friends, and during the guest's stay she often went up to him to see if she could make any further progress with his conversion. Her mind continued to work along the same drastic lines:

'If you called the king a liar my father would have you hanged.'

She did not as yet know, comments the biographer, that noblemen have the honour of having their head cut off when it comes to execution. Pointing to a large oil-painting of St Peter and St Paul she said:

'You see these two great presidents? They'll have you hanged if you keep on denying our Lord the way you do.'

Her father, the president, was her ideal; his authority, his work, or what she understood of it, filled her horizon. The development of her personality in later years clearly bears the imprint of this close and positive relationship as it perhaps also reflects the lack of a mother's influence during the formative years of her childhood. '*Madame de Chantal est une grande sainte et un grand homme,*' said the lady-in-waiting of Queen Anne of Austria when she returned to court one day after an interview with Mère de Chantal at the Paris Visitation convent many years later. When circumstances demanded it, Jane was ready and able to act as she knew her father would have done.

Bénigne Frémyot was a man of absolute integrity, brave, clear-sighted and just. He came of a family of parliamentarians, wealthy lawyers concerned not only with the local government of their city but reaching out to the wider sphere of national politics. Dijon, the capital of Burgundy, had had a powerful ducal court until 1477 and was compensated for the loss of its court when the king appointed it to be one of the twelve regional parliaments which worked in conjunction with Paris. Parliament soon drew to itself by purchasable and hereditary offices all the ablest men, indeed many of the nobility who had in former days served at the court. The de Berbisey family, that of Jane's mother, was one of this kind, originally springing from wealthy mercantile stock. They had gained a patent of nobility at about the beginning of the fifteenth century after intermarriage with a branch of the de Normands, the family of St Bernard. Over the past hundred years the rich lawyer parliamentarians had begun to form a special kind of élite, the *noblesse de robe*, whose members rose still further in the social scale by intermarriage with the *noblesse d'épée*, or hereditary nobility, and by the purchase of property outside the town.

The revenue of the aristocracy proper came from the land, from their peasants over whom they still ruled as landed gentry in essentially feudal ownership. Their profession was that of arms. The baron's duty was to furnish the king with soldiers in time of war and to lead his men. When his sword was not needed the nobleman lived as a gentleman farmer, also administering local justice, entertaining his friends and hunting, this last being the exclusive privilege of the nobility. The member of the *noblesse de robe*, on the other hand, actually earned his own living by the use of professional and academic training. It was in the course of the sixteenth century that these two groups began to be less rigidly separate in the social realm. Jane's uncle, Claude Frémyot, the eldest of the family, was one of the richest landowners of the district, having acquired the seigneurie of Is-sur-Tille, near Dijon. He married the sister of Jane's mother, the same aunt that helped to look after the children. Jane's father owned the smaller commune of Thostes and often retired to the manor house there with his family. It is a village on a little hill at the edge of a wide plain overlooking the forest of the castle of Bourbilly where Jane lived after her marriage.

These new parliamentarian landowners were in no sense *bourgeois gentilshommes*, although their purchase of land was all part of the gradual and insidious movement of the expropriation of the countryside by the town. They were simply shrewd investors in landed property. Though it was natural that they should seek to raise their family status by intermarriage with the titled families whose interests coincided most closely with their own, they had too many civic virtues to be mere social climbers. As president Frémyot had himself married into the nobility he made sure that his daughters did the same; he deliberately educated them towards this end so that they could fill their place as ladies of the manor. The wife played an important part in the local baron's life, for she was left in charge during his absence at the wars and usually acted as steward. A rich, clever girl with a capacity for hard work, possessing high ethical standards of service in the bourgeois tradition and yet having a strain of nobility, was obviously a most desirable match.

Frémyot had his children educated at home by visiting tutors who taught them what was considered essential for girls at this time: reading, writing, dancing, playing musical instruments and singing part-songs in harmony. Nurse and aunt taught them sewing and embroidery, an art for which Jane showed exceptional talent. The girls also learnt spinning and weaving which a lady had to understand, but rather in order to supervise her maids than to put her own hand to the task. Later in life, however, Jane used her spindle (the spinning wheel was as yet a novelty) as an instrument of humble work, spinning thread for clothes for the poor, for her children, for her director's purple soutanes. In the convent, at recreation, her spindle was always in her hand. Frémyot himself also taught the children; his teaching, mainly on historical, moral or religious subjects, took the form of a regular series of talks to his family, morning and evening. The president was a learned man; humanist culture and educational ideals had not left a city of the size and importance of Dijon untouched. There was perhaps a little resemblance in this household to that far more brilliant circle by the river Thames in Chelsea where earlier in the century Sir Thomas More had instructed his daughters. The brave stand which Frémyot made in later years on a matter of conscience is also not unworthy of comparison with the heroism of the statesman, lawyer and saint. The Frémyot girls assimilated from their father a sound knowledge of their own country, its history and institutions, a reasoned grasp of their faith, a balanced judgment of people and things in general, all qualities without which Madame de Chantal's work as a foundress and administrator would have been unthinkable. It was to her father that she owed her sense of leadership.

The patriarchal atmosphere of her home, the insistence on the importance of the family unit and family traditions, did its share towards making her a fit instrument for the work she was to do. For a woman of her time she had wide vision. From childhood on she had been privileged to see the world through her father's eyes, looking out from the shelter of a cultured home to the community of the city in which her family played a leading part, and beyond that to the province of Burgundy, which took an important place in France as a whole. But the burning contemporary issue in this country and in the wider European fellowship of nations was that of religious allegiance, and the struggle for the victory, in France at any rate, of the catholic cause. It is no wonder, then, that the first recorded story of Jane's life is one concerning just this issue. Her grandfather, Jean Frémyot, who died a patriarchal death in the presence of his assembled family while mass was being celebrated in his room, used to address his household regularly to give them instruction on the new tenets put forward by Luther and Calvin. He actually taught them to counter arguments, not only so as to make them apostles for the truth in their own town where Calvinism had considerable support, but so as to fortify them within against the pull and fascination of what he considered heresy. This was the sort of intellectual atmosphere in which the Frémyot children grew up.

Dijon was a wealthy city, the capital of a rich, wine-growing province. Lying in the very centre of France it occupied a position of strategic importance at the meeting place of rivers and the intersection of main roads: from Italy and the south to Paris, from Germany and the east to Lyons, the second city of the land. Because it was a stronghold against invasion from the Rhine, the town was heavily fortified, its dense population crowded into a narrow space within high walls and the natural rampart of rocky hills. At the time when Jane was growing up there were about 3,600 hearths in the city on which tax was payable, from which it is estimated that there were some 2,000 houses and up to a hundred streets. Thirty or more churches were the pride of the city. It was a place of incessant noise. From the very early morning, narrow cobbled streets echoed to the din of carts on their way to the daily market held at the cross-roads and in the little squares. Horse-drawn traffic rumbled unceasingly to and from the many hostelries for which Dijon was famous. The natural cordiality and liveliness of the citizens fitted in well with the hotel trade and gave scope to the native love of good food and even better wine, as also to their commercial astuteness. Sellers cried their wares, innumerable bells chimed the hours, children played and shouted, talk between neighbours was endless and loud. The Dijonnais is very sociable, loves a good joke, is avid for news; at the same time his judgment is shrewd, he is a realist by nature, a conservative by instinct. He has a reputation for thrift in matters of money and of feeling but he is not niggardly. He just knows how to expend both wisely.

Jane, a true Dijonnaise, grew up in the very centre of this city and all its hubbub. Because there was so little room within the town walls, good and bad houses jostled side by side, the new having been sandwiched in as the old were gradually pulled down. There were no select quarters, and although the Frémyots were not of the people they lived right among them. The house in which she was born no longer exists.[1] It is certain, however, that

[1] A plaque commemorating the saint's birthplace is now fixed to the wall of 5, rue du Palais opposite the former parliamentary building which is still the central law-court of Dijon. The striking Renaissance façade with its

her father lived practically opposite the Palais de Justice, the seat of the parliament of Burgundy. She grew up in the shadow of this building and of the public service it stood for. Together with the parish church and her own home, it formed the psychological centre of her young life.

Her home was a *hôtel*, that is, a house of some consequence and built of stone, while most of the others were only built of wood, having thatched roofs instead of slates. But it did not belong to Frémyot, who was a younger brother. This rented house was built on the simple pattern common to city dwellings of the time: an entrance hall which served as a reception room and opened out into a large communal room—the great chamber adjoining the kitchen. A staircase led straight from the chamber to the bedrooms on the first floor and to the servants' attics at the top of the house. Lessons took place in the large living-room, the family and their guests dined there, while both children and grown-ups spent a good part of their time in the kitchen, a warm, friendly meeting place which even among the nobility of the sixteenth century bore none of the social stigma it was later to acquire. The girls learnt the art of household management from its very foundations, and they were also taught in the most natural manner possible to understand servants and to relate to them. It was testified in her canonization process that in the eight years of her married life Madame de Chantal found it necessary to dismiss only two servants. This was perhaps not exclusively due to sanctity.

In the summer months, when the crowded city with its primitive drainage became too insalubrious—little canals into which all the rubbish was thrown trickled down the centre of the narrow streets to join a sluggish, marsh-bound river outside the town—Frémyot sent his children to the country, either to his own house at Thostes, or to their uncle. They had many friends where there were children of their own age, notably the family of President Bourgeois de Crépy, whose country mansion was at Vic-en-Chassenay, close to Thostes and Bourbilly. His daughters, later

---

portico and corinthian columns remains unchanged except that the statues have disappeared from their niches and the lions from their pedestals. The assembly hall of Frémyot's day is now the *Salle des Pas Perdus*. Behind a magnificent carved screen at the far end there is a chapel dedicated to the Holy Ghost where mass used to be said before parliamentary sessions.

to become Madame Brûlart and the Abbess du Puys d'Orbe, and correspondents of St Francis de Sales, were the special friends of the Frémyot sisters. They also visited at the castle of Époisses close by which is still in excellent preservation today, giving a good idea of the manorial architecture of the time. It stands right in the middle of the village, with great round towers flanking the castle walls, with a chapel, a mansion and farm buildings complete with a large pigeonry, standing as a tower apart. Encircling all, there is a moat with a massive drawbridge. The children loved the freedom of the country and the forests after the winter in the city. As for Jane, '*fille à toute folie*', she was roaming in the meadows and forests which were later to be her own domain, while Époisses became her parish, its baron her husband's overlord.

Towards the end of the year 1587, when Jane was nearly sixteen, her sister married Jean-Jacques de Neufchèzes, Baron des Francs, who lived in the west, near Poitiers. He belonged to a family famous in the military and political history of Burgundy and of all France. It was considered a brilliant match and it came at a time when the president was well pleased to know at least one of his daughters settled at a safe distance from Dijon where civil war was threatening. For her greater safety Jane was sent to accompany her sister and live with her for the time being, while André, then thirteen years old, stayed with his father. There were other reasons for this decision originally put forward by Jane's brother-in-law: he felt that at seventeen his young wife needed a companion from home to begin with. Marguerite herself wanted it.

This was the first long journey that Jane had ever undertaken and the excitement of it made up to some extent for her reluctance to leave her father at a critical moment. She was old enough to understand something of his great responsibility and the dangers he might well run in the course of his work. She surely did not expect the separation to last so long; because of the dangerous situation at Dijon her father did not recall her until four years later when she was nearly twenty. These impressionable years must have been of great importance in her development but little is known about them. Her biographer concentrates on two main episodes, both told to illustrate her fortitude against the temptations that confronted her in this new and much freer life. It was her own memory that later on selected these particular incidents in a crowded period of four years. They speak significantly of what perhaps mattered most to her even then and certainly later —her faith. They also tell of her whole cast of mind, her thoughtfulness, her strength of will and independence, a certain solitariness even at that age.

Jane's formal education was now considered complete and for the next few years she shared the life of her sister with its daily round of entertainment, visiting, hunting parties—she was an expert rider from her youth upwards—dancing and singing. It does not appear that Marguerite was given any considerable share of domestic responsibility such as fell to Jane's own lot at Bourbilly later on, but the sisters did not allow themselves to be completely absorbed by the social round. Two children were born to Marguerite, and throughout her stay Jane found her role as aunt an absorbing one.

Their new environment gave the sisters pause for thought and even grief. The castle of Brun-Buisson where they lived was close to Poitiers. During the religious wars the whole of this region as well as the neighbouring provinces of Anjou and the Touraine had been in control of the huguenots until quite recently; churches, monastic buildings, wayside shrines had been devastated in the course of the fighting. Contemporary engravings show scenes of the kind familiar to those who have seen bombed cities. When Jane walked or rode past such places she grieved over the desolation and emptiness where there had once been worship and the Blessed Sacrament. This sense of loss made such an impression on her that she often spoke about it to her nuns many years later. She was moved to tears at the sight, and when she joined the others, having lingered to walk in a ruined church or look at some cross or statue which lay shattered and half hidden in the long grass by the roadside, she did not dare remove her velvet mask as she would normally have done when she returned home.[1] She was afraid her host would see that she had

---

[1] At this period ladies only went out with either a black velvet mask or a veil to hide their face. Judging by contemporary prints Jane would also have worn a felt hat rather like a Trilby, a white starched lace collar standing up to frame her face, a riding coat of wide circular cut à la cloche and decorated with silver chains and buttons. She rode side saddle.

been weeping and would wonder if his guest were feeling miserable or had any complaints to make of the way she was being entertained. The first time she heard and understood in the liturgy for Maundy Thursday the passage from the Lamentations of Jeremias: 'How doth the city sit solitary that was full of people . . . The ways of Sion mourn because there are none that come to the solemn feast: all her gates are broken down: her priests sigh'[1] her mind at once went back to these rides near Poitiers and she remembered her grief. Later on she asked one of her nuns with a gift for rhyming to compose a hymn based on these verses and she said: 'If I had had this song when I was young I should have sung it every day' (1, 343).

Her life in Poitou widened her experience in other ways. In the retinue at Brun-Buisson there was an elderly lady-in-waiting of the kind that often features in historical romances: an intriguer, insinuating, superstitious, avid to procure for others by fair means or foul the excitements and pleasures she was no longer able to enjoy herself. She was a corrupter of youth, and because she brewed love potions and also appears to have acted as a sort of Elizabeth Arden of her day by the manufacture of creams, powder and rouge, she was suspected of being a witch. It is to Jane's credit and speaks not only for the special protection of grace but also for her sound judgment that the old lady was unable to make any headway with her. On the contrary, Jane tried to get her dismissed; but as the temptress was clever and smooth-tongued both Marguerite and her husband were taken in, refusing to heed Jane's warning until, in the end, the woman was shown up.

A further incident points to the fact that her hosts were perhaps in some way lacking in insight and that during her years at Brun-Buisson she had to a great extent to rely on herself and fight her own battles. She appeared a good deal in company, she was an attractive person, well connected and known to have a rich dowry. Suitors soon came forward. The newly married couple were ardent match-makers and soon put forward definite proposals for Jane. They concerned a close friend of the baron's, a young nobleman who had apparently everything to recommend him and who pressed his suit with great determination. But he was in secret a huguenot, a fact which he hid from everyone and

[1] Lam. Jer. I, 1 and 4.

especially from Jane, knowing her to be a devout catholic. Her innocent eye was not deceived. She repelled his suit with equal persistence, pleading that her father would not have heard of such a match. The baron and his wife, however, disagreed with Jane, refused to believe that the suitor was not a catholic and made life difficult for her by persisting with the idea. It was hard for Jane as a guest to stand out independently against her hosts and against the judgment of people older than herself. She had always looked upon her sister as being in charge of her like a mother and had made a point of obeying her. Her relatives were evidently far more worldly and casual than she was, and although her firmness was impressive, they must at times have found her passionate candour rather disconcerting:

'If I were forced to choose', she declared, 'I should prefer to be locked up in prison for life rather than live in the house of a huguenot, and I would rather face death a thousand times over than be bound in marriage to any enemy of the church.' (1, 15)

This incident, naturally enough, caused some little coolness to spring up between the sisters, but when the time came for Jane's return home—her father sent for her in 1591—they parted firm friends again. Jane's ultimatum had made her suitor declare himself in his true colours, admit openly that he was, in fact, a huguenot, and withdraw his suit. The baron was no doubt sufficiently human not to relish having been wrong about a close friend, but it appears that he had the magnanimity not to let his sister-in-law feel this. He was one of the witnesses and guests at her own wedding about a year afterwards and they always remained on good terms. Jane must have been glad in future years to think that a rift had been avoided, for her sister died in childbirth two years later at Semur in Burgundy, where she was staying with her father. The baron himself only survived Marguerite by a few years and Jane looked after the three small children for a time at Bourbilly.[1]

Jane returned home in 1591 and was now for a time her father's

[1] She watched over her nephews in later years, especially Jacques who took orders and later became Bishop of Châlons, cf Ch. 10, p. 210. The elder nephew died in battle shortly before Madame de Chantal's own son was killed in 1627.

only companion at home. André, then a boy of eighteen, had been sent to Paris for his studies. Letters must of course have passed between father and daughter, but it is unlikely that she realized what grave dangers both he and André had had to face.

The religious struggles in France, lasting from about 1559 for some forty years, were marked by a greater ferocity than elsewhere in Counter Reformation Europe. Calvin was a Frenchman; his doctrine was well understood by his compatriots, and men with minds of a logical cast similar to his own either passionately acclaimed or else fiercely opposed his arguments. Armed combat followed close upon ideological conflict, the cleavage went right through families and towns, throughout the country as a whole and as far as the monarchy. The direct heir of the childless Henri III being his huguenot cousin, Henri of Bearn and Navarre, a political association known as the League had been formed with the consent of king and pope. Its object was to ensure a catholic succession to the throne of France and it was, to begin with, a legitimate association joined by most of the local parliaments, including Dijon. But as the years passed and no solution was found while the king's own manner of life became increasingly evil, the League turned against the crown. The majority of the members of the Dijon parliament refused to continue allegiance to Henri III, but Frémyot, with a small band of followers, kept a clear hold on the underlying principle, refusing to be disloyal even to a bad king. In spite of the risk of a protestant succession, he continued to put his whole trust in the principle of kingship which he saw as an integral part of the catholic cause. He hoped that this cause would triumph, as in the end it did, but at the same time he took a long view of the situation and refused to allow himself to be dazzled by an immediate advantage which might lead to the eventual overthrow of a just conception of monarchy. The decision was a hard one but once he had made up his mind he took radical action. In the spring of 1589 he left Dijon with his few supporters, and going into voluntary exile, he formed a rival parliament which he and of course the court at Paris claimed as the legitimate one. The seat of this parliament was at first Flavigny, and then the heavily fortified town of Semur, close to Bourbilly and to his own estate at Thostes. This town, some thirty miles distant from Dijon, still preserves its ancient aspect, standing on the granite promontory of a high plateau round which a river forms a natural barrier while towering ramparts reinforce its impregnable position in the plain. A castle and a church of cathedral-like proportions dominate the town. It was to this place that Jane returned to live with her father who had gained the support of local landowners, among them Baron Guy de Chantal.

The following March an attempt was made to intimidate Frémyot. His house in Dijon was pillaged, his thirteen-year old son, André, who had been left in his uncle's charge was seized and imprisoned as a hostage in the fortress at Dijon. This same uncle was sent as an ambassador to the rival headquarters to parley with his younger brother and to make him relinquish his position and return. At the same time Frémyot was told that if he refused to submit, his son's head would be sent to him in a sack. In answer to this threat he wrote an impassioned letter stating his own position and inviting his former friends and colleagues to reconsider theirs.[1] The lawyer in Frémyot so effectively pleaded his case that he won, if not a complete victory, at least a moral one. The threat was not carried out, a time of truce set in between the rival parliaments, and Frémyot remained where he was. In the letter he said that because he loved his son he would rather see him die honourably now than let him live to know that his father had turned traitor, acting against his honour and his duty as a Christian gentleman. At the same time he himself preferred death now to life dishonoured and a family name tarnished for ever. In August of that same year Henri III was assassinated and this brought the whole question to a head. Consistent to his principles but also to his faith, Fréymot decided to acknowledge the lawful succession of the huguenot Henri of Navarre; on the other hand, he was prepared to die defending his town unless the new king were converted so that the French monarchy remained catholic.

The League disputes in Dijon were more than a regional affair, for Burgundy was an important province, France one of the great powers of Europe and of Christendom. The stand made by men like Jane's father had effects of far-reaching consequence. It is not possible to conceive of the great resurgence of religious culture

[1] The original of this letter can be seen in the municipal archives of the city of Dijon.

in seventeenth-century France under a monarchy from which it was divided in faith. The rapid rise and spread of the Order of the Visitation was a part of the spiritual revival after the Counter Reformation, and the order rightly pays tribute to the courage and integrity of men like the father of their own foundress.

Fréymot acted as the king's adviser in his dealings with the rebel parliament, and it was largely owing to his diplomatic skill that a solution was found which upheld the monarchy without ruining Dijon. The decisive factor, however, was the king's solemn abjuration in July 1593 when he was anointed as the catholic monarch of France. Henri IV marched into Dijon on a state visit about two years later, and when it came to meting out reward and punishment, Fréymot again showed the spirit that moved him: he pleaded for his former enemies and refused the honour of being nominated head of the parliament. Instead, he spoke to the king of his intention of retiring from public life and taking holy orders, a plan he had long been meditating. The king rewarded him by the gift of an ecclesiastical benefice, that of the abbey church of St Etienne, so that Fréymot could set up a new home in the abbot's lodge, long vacant. He also conferred on him the important see of the town of Bourges. As Fréymot was unable to become a priest through a canonical impediment from which he could not get dispensation (he was twice widowed, and in his second marriage had married a widow), the benefice of Bourges was later passed on to his son André who was at this time a student in Paris.

The part that Fréymot played in the League Wars is to a large extent the common property of history but some of the details of these years have only been preserved through his daughter's account of him. She spoke of him often. She said it was her conviction that she had all her life proved herself unworthy of such a father; at the same time she knew that it was his example that spurred her on to every new effort. As she had not known her mother her affection was wholly fixed on him: his image dominated her youthful imagination, he set the ideal standard of which she, a woman, was always bound to fall short. Her whole character and her later psychological development bear out her strong and positive tie to her father. Perhaps this tie also accounts for some of the tension and inner strain that were often a feature of her life.

She could never, as she imagined, live up to such a father.

Long before the situation in Dijon was finally settled, life had again become sufficiently normal in the president's makeshift home out of town for him to look forward to Jane's return and to consider her future. She had grown up during her absence. The Dijon portrait, painted when she was twenty, gives some idea of her appearance at this time, while the description given from hearsay by her first biographer to some extent supplements the picture. Perhaps the most significant thing about this portrait is the attitude in which she chose to be painted. She is kneeling in prayer. The other striking thing is the plainness of her dress and the complete absence of any sort of jewellery at a time when ladies of rank revelled in over-decorated, rich clothes, pearls, golden chains and feathers; new sumptuary laws against undue luxury were continually being issued. Her brown dress trimmed with velvet is becoming in its almost puritan simplicity, the neat white guimp, the velvet head-dress with its white rim shows up her fine forehead and the light brown colour of her hair. The starched lace of her cuffs forms a fitting frame for her beautiful hands. It is, however, obvious that this modesty was not an affectation, a mere parade of piety; her air of recollection belies this, and the contrast of such simplicity to the high state in which girls were usually decked for a pre-marriage portrait is too great. She is described as a handsome girl, friendly and completely unaffected yet at the same time having much natural dignity. Her good looks owed nothing to contrivance, her charm nothing to concessive weakness. She was lively and gay, and at the same time her intelligence was clear, quick and incisive, her judgment sound; she was consistent and steady in her behaviour. 'In short', concludes her biographer, 'she was such as to be called *la dame parfaite*.' (1, 16)

The marriage of a girl of her standing could in no sense be a matter of chance in those days. The plans of the two families concerned were probably already formed when she returned from Poitiers but the free consent of the two people concerned was considered essential. She continued to appear a good deal in company, staying for the present with her relatives in Dijon. Although she was much sought after in marriage, it seems that she behaved suitably in the face of her popularity and in any case found the young man of her father's choice entirely to her taste. This was not only a matter of obedience on her part, for Baron Christophe de Rabutin-Chantal was an attractive person of a kind to win her love, respect and loyalty. His father, Guy de Chantal, whose lands lay within a few miles of Semur, had been one of the president's most useful supporters in the defence of this town. Christophe had himself been captain of the troops stationed at Semur so that the president had had a chance of getting to know him and of recognizing his worth.

According to the contemporary accounts this young officer of twenty-eight was not only, like his father, a good soldier and an expert swordsman—he had many duels to his credit—but there was also a different side to his nature: he had read widely, he was interested in the arts, he valued intelligent conversation and himself wrote poetry. He seems to have combined the toughness and valour of a sixteenth-century warrior with an intellectual refinement more common in the nobleman of the seventeenth century. He was also a man of staunch faith, though no fanatic upholder of punctuality where church-going was concerned: his wife told of him that he was a real slug-a-bed when it came to going out to mass in the morning. The only way to rouse him on dark winter days was to wave a lighted taper very close to his sleep-held eyes. He had been brought up in the forest solitude of the castle of Bourbilly by a mother whose memory he continued to mourn. While this had fostered the more withdrawn side of his character, he had also been much in company when at court in Paris. The sociable, brilliant side of him was drawn to a wife who could appear to advantage in company, where he could be proud of her beauty and intelligence; the other side of him appreciated her deeper qualities, her understanding, her devout cast of mind, her goodness. He would not have been human had he not also valued her rich dowry and sensed her capacity to be a good manager, for he was heavily in debt. She for her part had the joy of realizing that by obeying her father she was able to fulfil her own happiness. It was a good match.

Their war-time marriage took place at the fortified castle of Bourbilly; the civil strife was not yet over and the president's only home was the country house at Thostes which was not capable of defence in an emergency. The civil contract, drawn up

Palais de Justice, Dijon (*see p. 23*)
Bibliothèque Publique, Dijon

Jeanne-Françoise Frémyot in 1592. The Dijon Portrait

at Thostes, is dated just after Christmas, on 28 December 1592, and the religious ceremony followed immediately at the chapel of St Marguerite at the castle. It was conducted by her uncle, one of the gifted Frémyot brothers who was prior of a Cistercian abbey not far from Dijon. Her sister and brother-in-law made the long journey from Poitiers so as to be with her, but André was away in Paris and her uncle Claude was unable to get a safe conduct from Dijon to join them. Guests came from the neighbouring castles; it was mid-winter, there was time for a little relaxation and feasting and the war was no longer quite so close to their gates as it had been during the past few years. It was a happy time for a wedding.

The visitor who goes to Bourbilly today sees nothing of the old castle, now replaced by a nineteenth-century reconstruction; but the site of the new chapel is the same as that of the old, and its entrance, a lofty gothic arch, is the only architectural remnant of Madame de Chantal's time. It was in this chapel that nuptial mass was offered, and it was here that she knelt next to Christophe under the long white veil extended over them both according to the ancient liturgical rite still then in use in her diocese. After the *Pater Noster* she heard her uncle's voice saying for her the prayer still said today, and which in so far as it depended on her was perfectly fulfilled in her life:

'May the yoke of peace and love be upon her, may she marry faithful and chaste in Christ, ever follow the example of holy women, be dear to her husband like Rachel, wise like Rebecca, long-lived and faithful like Sarah. May the author of lies not work his evil deeds within her, may she cleave to the faith and the commandments, be true to one husband and fly from forbidden approaches; may she fortify her weakness by strong discipline, may she be distinguished for her propriety, honoured for her modesty, learned in heavenly lore, fruitful in offspring, good and sinless, may she win through to the repose of the blessed and to the kingdom of heaven. May they both see their children's children unto the third and fourth generation, and may they reach old age together.'

Providence withheld this last blessing.

Chapter 2

MARRIAGE AND WIDOWHOOD
1592-1604

⟶ ∘◦⊙◦∘ ⟵

T he castle of Bourbilly, newly rebuilt now on its ancient
site, stands at the head of a densely wooded valley widening out into meadowland. The river Serein comes in a
cascade down the rocky, forested slopes guarding the back of the
castle, then waters the moat and flows on a curving course across
the pastures which gradually narrow towards a point where a
saw-mill marks the end of the Bourbilly clearing. Beyond the mill
the forest closes in again while beeches and pines cover the slopes
on either side of the valley. No direct highway leads to the castle,
just a descending track which leaves the hilly forest road skirting
the valley. From this approach and from any other, except when
the trees are bare, Bourbilly is completely hidden from the outer
world. It is hard to imagine a place more remote, the skyline
bounded on every side by trees, no village close by, no sign of
habitation except the house by the mill. There is just sky, forest,
and the meadows where the cattle stand grazing by the river.

Jane had grown up in a city, and though she was not unused
to the country, the remoteness of Bourbilly was a new experience
for her. But there was plenty of hard work and much to learn
while she had her husband's company for the first two or three
months. Then the spring weather brought the renewal of fighting
and he had to join the king in the campaign which culminated at
the decisive battle of Fontaine-Française in June 1593. Before he
left he instructed her in all she had to do for the management of
the estates which had in past years been much neglected. His
father was more interested in fighting than in farming, his mother,

34

who had managed the lands with devotion and competence, had died ten years previously, he himself had had to incur debts during the war, both to pay a personal ransom and for the upkeep of his men. The house and the lands were still in good condition and brought in considerable revenues, but stewards and farmers had got into the habit of cheating their absentee landlord, the servants did what they liked and ruled the household. Christophe himself knew what to do but could not stay there to do it. It was a formidable task for a young woman without experience of estate management, and not unnaturally she fought shy of it at first. Her biographer tells how Jane and her husband had a long talk about the matter as they walked up and down the avenue in the castle grounds, and how he unfolded to her the story of his mother's courage in carrying out this same task for years in face of the unendurable pain of her long drawn-out illness. She had been brought up at court in Paris and had even less experience of country life than Jane. The example of her constancy so impressed Jane that she at once decided to shoulder the burden wholeheartedly; it was work for which she had considerable aptitude but no natural liking whatever. In a certain sense this burden was never lifted, for in later years the responsibility for organizing and administering a great order fell on her; she never liked it any better than she had done at the beginning—she was always quite frank on this point—but she did it, and did it supremely well.

The first thing she did was to establish a routine and to give the day at Bourbilly a definite shape and framework. Since the death of Christophe's mother the daily foundation mass at the house chapel had lapsed. Jane re-established it by drawing a resident chaplain to the castle, and had it said very early so that even the servants who were going to work in the fields a long way off could get to it. Her biographer makes a point of the fact that she did not appear specially devout at this stage and that this was not an unusually pious move on her part. Daily mass was the rule at the home of the sixteenth-century gentleman who himself attended it together with his family, his guests and his servants, even at harvest time or before the early start of a hunting expedition. She just saw to it that a good habit was restored to its rightful position in the daily life of the castle and herself set an example. On Sundays she went to mass at the local parish church some miles away.

The baron thought this a little excessive and pointed out that they were fulfilling their obligation perfectly well at home; but she generally got her way, putting forward the argument of good example, and because, as she put it, 'it gave her a very special sort of satisfaction to worship God together with all the faithful' (1, 22).

Servants, labourers and stewards had to come to her every morning for their orders which were generally given in writing to those who could read, for then there could be no argument. In this way she gradually managed to prevent disorder instead of having to remedy and punish it afterwards. This always remained her method of approach. In the morning she supervised the work, often by riding out to the fields herself, and then in the afternoon by taking her own spinning to the maids' room. There she would sit talking to them so as to get to know them and also to entertain them, leading their thoughts to matters other than the personal gossip of a small, isolated community. She also read to them, sometimes from the *Annales de France*, a popular chronicle-history full of exciting anecdotes, sometimes from the lives of the saints. This would take the form of a collection of stories, and was very probably the *Golden Legend*. There was quite a considerable library at the castle, for her husband was a reader; together they had inspected the shelves on her arrival and she had been allowed to exercise censorship and make a clean sweep of the bad or indifferent books that had found their way there. She herself supervised the accounts, and gradually over the years set aside the money to pay off their debts. If she had not learnt how to do all this planning and arithmetic, she wrote to her newly married daughter in later years (5, 415), they would inevitably have been ruined. Her father, who had at one time administered the finances of Dijon, had no doubt initiated her into the art of domestic book-keeping.

The pattern of the wise administrator can be discerned in the very first year of her marriage: she was beginning to qualify for the lesson that was destined to be read at the mass for her feast day in later centuries:

'Who shall find a valiant woman? Far and from the uttermost coasts is the price of her . . . the heart of her husband trusteth in her . . . she hath considered a field and bought it . . . she hath put out her hand to strong things and her fingers have taken hold of the spindle . . . she hath looked well to the paths of her house and hath not eaten her bread idle . . . she hath opened her hand to the needy, and stretched out her hands to the poor.'[1]

There is little first-hand evidence about the eight years of Madame de Chantal's married life, but the most striking feature of it in the eyes of all was her charity to the poor. This was the natural duty of the chatelaine in the days before organized public assistance, but she seems to have excelled in compassion and generosity from the beginning. Her charity is the subject of most of the accounts of the witnesses of Bourbilly in the canonization process. This document, the original of which with the signature or mark of all the people concerned, is in the archives at the Visitation at Annecy.[2] It dates from 1684, that is, forty-three years after the saint's death. The information was collected in the surrounding villages by the chaplain of Bourbilly himself who was at the same time priest at the Visitation convent of Semur. The idea came from the superior of the convent. Fr Poussy went round the villages with a notary and took down authenticated accounts while there was yet time. It was already almost too late: eighty years since Madame de Chantal had left Bourbilly, over forty years since her death; yet it was better than nothing at all. Jeanne Pouthiot, widow of Sebastian, a mason, was one of the most valuable witnesses. At the age of ninety she was described as being in excellent health and with all her wits about her; she remembered seeing Madame de Chantal when she was a child. Then there was a widow of seventy, Brigide Baubis, daughter-in-law of her personal maid, Marguerite Potot, who knew her as well as anyone and was devoted to her. The memory of these old people picked out what had most impressed them and what had been thought worth while handing down from generation to generation.

All the witnesses repeat the same thing with slight variations in circumstance: she made herself the servant of the poor and the sick in the villages and her bounty in giving alms or food knew no limits. This was at a time when she herself was forced to cut down on expenses and was wearing wool and linen instead of a

[1] Prov. xxxi. (Douay).
[2] Canonization Process. Vol. II, Part II, folio 649 ff. Ms., Visitation Archives, Annecy.

noblewoman's velvet and silk, making do with her wedding dress for great occasions. Almsgiving, she said, gave her more confidence to ask God for what she herself needed, and when people pointed out that the poor often abused her kindness she was quite unperturbed. She kept a sort of permanent hot-pot going in an outdoor soup-kitchen at the back of the castle in time of famine. Beggars lined up with their bowls and came in at the castle gate, filed past her to have their bowls filled, and were then given a hunk of bread which she herself had cut and put ready in baskets. Then they walked out at a specified side-gate so as not to break up the one-way traffic. Once outside, some of them ate up quickly and presented themselves again with clean and empty bowls. Madame de Chantal was not deceived but remained unruffled: did she not present herself at the gate of heaven over and over again, just like these beggars, and God looked mercifully upon her every time? Who was she to turn away God's creatures? (1, 23)

She was also a skilled and compassionate nurse, no disease was too revolting for her, no sick person too abject. Together with her servant she went to the cottages and washed neglected old people, dressed wounds, helped women in labour, saw to it that their family got something to eat. It was quite a pleasure to be ill, said the villagers, because that meant the joy of a visit from '*la sainte baronne*'. During the famine she not only had a special bread-oven built out of doors for the poor; she cleared a large room indoors where she gathered together nursing mothers and their children, keeping them till they could fend for themselves and sending bread to those who were left at home. What is striking is her capacity to organize this sort of relief work in the best possible way and on a large scale; all the witnesses mention details which point to her exceptional practical competence. Then again, over the years she learnt a great deal about the art of healing and the lore of herbs and medicines. She had a proper little apothecary's room later on, and in her letters to her convents in future years she often gave medical advice, telling sick sisters just what they were to do and take, especially when they could not afford to call in the doctor.

The witnesses say little, naturally enough, about her prayer and her interior life, for to them, and also to her, this was her prayer, this was the form of devotion most suited to a married woman:

charity to the poor in God's name. She dedicated herself to the penance of hard work. She had read the life of Elizabeth of Hungary, a saint whom she often mentions—wife, mother and widow. It did not need this great example, however, to show her what lay close to hand for her and to set about doing it. As for prayer that was not action, at the beginning of her married life, when her husband was away, she took to saying all kinds of special prayers, but left off when he returned. Her one idea then was just to do her best by him and her household and so she let the spiritual exercises lapse. In any case her prayers centred mostly on him, and she says that she really could not imagine what else there might be to pray about. Her stage of spiritual development was unprecocious: she found God in a primarily active way through service to her neighbour. The spirit in which she served her neighbour is, however, clear from many details. On one occasion, reports Jeanne Pouthiot, she had spent most of the day helping a woman in labour. The child was still unborn when she had to leave, but later on in the small hours when all was well and the husband chanced to open his door to look out into the night, he found the baroness kneeling in prayer close by his threshold. She had returned to pray for his wife's safe delivery and to be at hand in case she were again needed. This kind of story bears the stamp of absolute authenticity. Her especial tenderness for young mothers was perhaps not unconnected with the fact that she herself lost two children almost as soon as they were born and that during the first four years of her marriage she had no child of her own to care for, the grief of personal loss to overcome.

Another point on which there was no divergence between the witnesses is that there were never any quarrels between husband and wife, a matter which servants are in a good position to observe. She herself said later on that there was scarcely even any difference of opinion. They were completely sure of one another and found constant mutual support in their happy relationship. She was left alone a great deal in the early years of her marriage, which is why she was able to devote herself so largely to good works; at the same time these long absences left her exposed to difficulties of various kinds: she was so attractive that certain of her husband's friends wanted to tempt her from the path of virtue. She had the skill, the '*sainte finesse*', to put them off without allowing them to see that she had guessed their intention and so without shaming them out of her friendship. This, it seems, is the point of the anecdote the biographer tells (1, 27) about a friend of her husband's entertained alone by her all day, who refused to move off when night fell and began to make complimentary speeches. Excusing herself by saying that she had to visit a neighbour and that she was in any case no sort of company when depressed by her husband's absence, she told him that all arrangements had been made for him to spend the night in comfort at Bourbilly. With that she swung herself on her horse and rode off into the darkness.

Christophe was sociable and loved good company, games, hunting parties. Both of them had many friends in the neighbouring estates so that in the winter they entertained freely and also paid their own visits. At such times Madame de Chantal put off her homespun garments and appeared in state. She wore the fine clothes she had kept carefully from earlier days, and on the greatest occasions, for instance the civic rejoicing after the king's solemn entry into Dijon on 4 June 1595, she put on her silk wedding dress, ornamented with gold and jewels. The portrait facing p. 81, painted a few years later, shows her in grand gala clothes. According to a reliable account of her at this time she was an excellent hostess and her conversation was amusing: her lively imagination and her vivid way of talking lent interest to every little detail. She had a sense of fun, but knew exactly where to stop and how to stop others. Her ability to entertain remained with her all her life; recreations fell flat when Mère de Chantal was absent, but when she was there, enlivening every story, drawing people out and making them give of their best for the recreation of the community, then everything went with a swing. She herself no doubt enjoyed social gatherings in her younger days, but when one thinks of the lively hostess of Bourbilly against the background, perhaps only dimly realized by her guests, of her work among the poor, it seems likely that some part of this continued hospitality was perhaps only another field for the exercise of her growing universal charity.

In 1596 she had a son who lived. Celse-Bénigne was followed two years later by Marie-Aymée, Françoise was born the next year

40

and Charlotte in 1601. At the beginning of this last year the baron, then thirty-five years old, retired from active service at court, partly on a matter of principle which involved a difficult decision of conscience and a refusal to obey an order he considered unjust; partly it was because during his last campaign he had fallen seriously ill of dysentery. He wrote a poem of farewell to the ladies of the court telling them that the charms of solitude with his beloved wife at Bourbilly far outweighed anything they might have to offer, a poem which Madame de Chantal kept when she became a nun and which her biographer had seen. For the next few months the couple lived in retirement while she was expecting her last child and nursing her husband back to health after his illness. They enjoyed one another's company in peace and it seemed to be the beginning of a calmer and more secluded stage in their life together.

In the first realization of his young middle age, Christophe's thoughts often turned towards death during the time of his slow convalescence. But it was not a subject on which Jane could bear to dwell, and when he suggested that whichever of them survived the other should promise to consecrate the remaining years to God, she brushed the idea aside, hoping that her brisk confidence would soon get the better of a sick man's imaginative musings. Her common sense, however, was not entirely proof against the atmosphere. One morning he told her that he had had a vivid dream in which he had seen how the coat he was wearing was being gradually dyed scarlet until in the end he saw himself robed as a cardinal—an interesting fusion of his waking thoughts on death and religious dedication, with a disappointed courtier's ambition for office. In his dream fantasy he saw himself as a religious of high rank and at the same time as a martyr to his principles. When he explained the dream as a portent of another injury in battle, she refused to take him seriously, for her mind, says her biographer, was above such idle fancies. And yet she could not resist telling him that she too had had a dream, only one to be despised, of course. She had seen herself dressed up in a great black veil like a widow; quite a natural result, she said, of all the terrors she had suffered for him during his illness. But now he was better, so there was no need to worry.

About a fortnight after Charlotte's birth when Madame de

Chantal was still something of an invalid while Christophe was better and getting impatient of his indoor existence, a cousin and good friend of his from a neighbouring estate, Monsieur d'Anlezy, called to congratulate him on his recovery and his wife on the birth of a daughter. It was a fine spell in early autumn; he talked about the good effects of fresh air and exercise, suggesting a walk with the dogs and some deer-stalking out in the woods. Christophe at once agreed and soon after dawn the next morning they set out. They walked up the forested hill at the back of the castle towards a dense wood in the direction of Vic-en-Chassenay, accompanied by five or six servants but carrying their own loaded guns. The dogs were for the moment held in leash. The two men were advancing slowly through the underwood in a coppice, by this time probably flat on the ground, a method of deer-stalking described by a sportsman in a contemporary account:

> *A peine puis-je entrer dedans la taille forte*
> *Il m'y fault toutefois trainer en quelque sorte*
> *A peine je me baisse et, contraint quelquefois*
> *Je lache mon limier dans l'espesseur du bois*
> *Et moy de pieds et mains, non sans quelque accrochage*
> *Je me traine attravers le plus fort du boscage*
> *Pour le suivre de pretz.*[1]

They were making for a clearing in the wood, crawling at some little distance from one another through dense undergrowth at this the most exciting moment of the chase when Christophe, looking round, called softly to warn his friend behind him against getting the strap of his arquebus caught on a branch (*'non sans quelque accrochage'*). Then suddenly a shot rang out, the dogs barked wildly and the servants following on some way behind heard a cry. D'Anlezy's gun had gone off and the scattered shot had embedded itself deep in Christophe's thigh and in his body. In one account it is stated that d'Anlezy actually aimed at his friend, mistaking his fawn coloured cloak for a deer. In view of

---

[1] 'I can hardly push my way into the dense coppice; all the same I manage to crawl in somehow. I can barely stoop and am forced at times to let go of my dog in the bushy underwood; and on all fours, not without getting caught up at times, I drag myself along to the thickest part of the copse so as to follow close on the dog's track.' Claude Gauchet, *Le Plaisir des Champs*, Paris, 1583, p. 182.

their method of stalking as it is described in the poem, and of the particular point which the hunt had reached, this seems unlikely. Christophe, coming to, at once realized that the injury was fatal. He showed the presence of mind of an old campaigner who has often been at close quarters to death. Telling his friend that he was not to blame and that he fully forgave him for his share in the accident, he asked for a priest, and so as to make sure of getting one, he sent four servants off to four different parishes, a fifth was sent to Bourbilly to his wife, but with strict instructions to say it was nothing serious. She was not deceived: '*On me dore la pillule!*' she cried as her maids helped her dress, for she had not yet been up and out of bed since Charlotte was born.

She found her husband in the end cottage of the hamlet, still close to the forest to-day, where he had been carried on an improvised stretcher. He spoke to her of death and of resignation to God's will, she countered with hope and life. He would not allow her to say a word against d'Anlezy whose despair was such that he was tempted to suicide. Christophe tried to console him, spoke to the priest who had meanwhile arrived, and after making his confession, asked him to inscribe his formal pardon of d'Anlezy in the parish records. The doctors had him moved back to Bourbilly but he was so badly wounded that they did not dare to risk an operation for the removal of the shot; an infection followed and he lay over a week dying, in great pain but in full possession of his faculties. He put all his affairs in order and made his will, inserting a clause disinheriting any of his family who should attempt to avenge him in true Renaissance style.

Christophe's chief effort went towards trying to comfort his wife and make her resign herself to the inevitable, as he had done. But she refused to the last to believe that his death was certain. When it came to the point and he was waiting for her to say 'yes', she slipped from the room, ran out all alone into the woods and cried aloud to God to save him: 'Take all I have, my children, everything, but leave me my husband!' She fought for his life as any wife would have done, and her desperate prayer while there was any hope left cannot be called a lack of resignation, except by a harsh critic, such as she always was to her own self. Christophe turned his thoughts entirely to God, received the last sacraments and died peacefully nine days after the accident. This was the point at which his wife said her *fiat*.

Resignation did not lessen her grief but it helped to turn it gradually into a means of closer union with God whose will she was striving to accept. She lived through months of mourning, courteously receiving the friends who came to try and console her, going about her daily work as bravely as she could. Her nights were spent in a vigil of prayer and weeping, either in her own room or out in the woods where she was more certain of solitude. In an account which she wrote later in answer to questions put to her by her nuns she describes her state of mind at this time. Her loss, her desolation became a bridge to God. She was then twenty-eight, her children were small, the eldest being five years old, and her life seemed to her to have only just begun. But she thought she now saw the happiness of this world in its true colours as a thing of little importance that passes swiftly. What remained was God and serving and loving him in a spirit of complete dedication, as she had loved her husband. She made a vow of chastity, an action which seemed to correspond to her growing desire to belong to God more absolutely. Not that she fully understood her own state of mind at the time; a passionate longing to know God's will for her more clearly filled her mind and heart. If it had not been for her responsibility towards her children she would have liked to escape alone and unknown, to end her days in the Holy Land, a concrete symbol which her imagination put before her, as before crusader and pilgrim, to signify a closer approach to God in this life. Having read the lives of the saints, she tried to imitate them by taking the discipline and manufacturing herself a hairshirt to wear in secret. Heart and soul, with a beginner's fervour and imprudence, she threw herself into the spiritual life as in her country solitude she understood it. Yet she sensed that direction was essential, though according to her account she had only the vaguest notion of what this really implied. Violent temptations of all kinds—she does not specify them—which wore her out far more than her actual grief, began to assault her. Yet at times there was also a kind of bliss to surprise her spirit in the face of all her misery. She was caught up in a paradox of pain and joy.

In the last year of her life in an interview in Paris with the Archbishop of Sens whose testimony is one of the most moving in the canonization process, she told him that from the first she had felt both grief and joy after her husband's death.[1] Without really understanding what she meant, she heard herself repeating to God over and over again the words: '*Vous avez rompu mes liens et je vous offrirai un sacrifice de louange*'—'You have broken my bonds and I shall offer you a sacrifice of praise.' Another phrase that kept repeating itself in her mind was: '*Dieu fait tout en sa miséricorde*'—'God does all in his mercy'. She longed to have someone to advise her and to explain what was happening to her spiritually. But she was alone. Her desire was so great that she even saw it concretely before her in a vision remembered as clearly after thirty-five years as if it had been the same day.

She was riding home one afternoon and approaching Bourbilly across the wide valley from the direction of the saw-mill along the path upstream beside the river. Not far past the outbuildings of the mill where the stream begins to hurry towards the falls, a rocky, wooded copse known as the Bois Thomas rises sharply to the left of the path. Just skirting the foot of this little hill some way ahead of her and about to disappear from her line of vision, she caught sight of someone walking in the direction of Bourbilly. It was a man of more than average height and in clerical dress. He was wearing a black soutane with a white surplice, his biretta was on his head; that is to say, he was robed ready as though he were just about to step into the pulpit to preach. He turned round and for a moment she saw his face. Joy swept over her, and a great certainty that God had heard her prayer. A voice said within her: 'This is the man beloved of God and among men into whose hands you are to commit your conscience.' (1, 39) The vision faded and she rode home alone but comforted.[2]

After that she turned resolutely to action. She ordered her household on a smaller footing with fewer servants, she gave her husband's state clothes and most of her own as well as much of her jewellery to the neighbouring churches for vestments and revenue. Her vow of chastity was followed up by another: she

---

[1] Canonization Process, Vol. II, folios 672–6. Deposition of Mgr Octave de Bellegarde, Archbishop of Sens.

[2] The exact place where this vision occurred is clearly discernible to-day, the saw-mill, rebuilt, is still in use for cutting up the wood from the Bourbilly forests.

promised to give all the spare-time work of her hands to the poor
or to the churches, making a rule of life for the use of her time,
devoting every possible moment to prayer and to good works.
At the same time she gave herself more than ever before and in a
more personal way to her children, teaching and caring for them
herself with little help. A few months of this strict routine combined with her state of inner tension soon told on her appearance;
her aunts in Dijon decided that it was high time she were taken
out of herself. It was the last thing she wanted. However, after a
family council her father invited her to come to town with the
children. She got there towards the end of March in 1602, about
six months after her husband's death.

The topic uppermost in her mind, and probably little suspected
by her relatives, was her need for advice on the spiritual difficulties
that were now overwhelming her. She describes how her prayer
on this subject really ran away with her and how she found herself
asking God for something she scarcely understood, in words and
phrases that were not of her own prompting; she spoke to God
urgently as though he were there, visibly, before her eyes. Walking alone in the forests of her home she had spoken to him out
aloud, begging for help and promising to obey to the letter whatever her guide, should she find him, were to ask of her. She says
that she had no idea what a director was—not consciously, perhaps, especially when looking back later on her confused state of
mind. But had she not read the story of Elizabeth of Hungary
whose devotion to the poor and whose fate in some ways so
closely resembled her own? This princess had been left a widow
with small children when her husband whom she loved died on
his way to the crusades. Her mourning, her longing to give herself
completely to God, were as great as Madame de Chantal's. But
Elizabeth had a director, chosen for her by papal agreement and
with her husband's approval; she saw God in him and allowed
herself to be moulded as he commanded. Conrad von Marburg
wanted to make a great saint of Elizabeth but it is perhaps true to
say that although he was a good man with noble intentions, he
only succeeded in spite of himself. What in the end made a saint
of her was her unconditional obedience to a scheme of sanctity
into which she did not really fit. Unconsciously, Madame de

46

Chantal seems to have been impelled in the same direction and to the same sort of guide.

She spent a good deal of time making the round of the churches in Dijon and she also went on the local pilgrimages. The most important of these was the shrine of Notre Dame d'Étang on a rocky plateau some way outside the town.[1] There, in the country church which took her back in some measure to the peace of Bourbilly, she was introduced to a friar, certainly not, as she well realized, the man she had seen in her vision. Some pious ladies who were themselves his penitents and who appeared to flourish happily under his direction encouraged her to talk to him.

The spiritual food which Madame de Chantal was then given was, to say the least of it, unsuitable. The friar was both devout and learned, but instead of realizing that Madame de Chantal was the kind of person who was best protected from her own ardour and calmed down, he was delighted with her excessive piety and allowed her to go on with her stern routine of austerity, penance and interminable prayers. He even increased them, sincerely believing that in this way she would give still greater glory to God. But when, naturally enough, her temptations grew worse and her anxiety overwhelming, he tried to counter this by further spiritual violence. He made her bind herself to the person of her director by four vows, a measure which only a soul of her calibre could have borne. She did not, in fact, bear it unscathed; a certain compulsive element remained in her psychological make-up for many years if not for the rest of her life. Her personality before her widowhood gives no indication of any tendency to anxiety states, and though the full blame for them does not rest on her first director, he at least did nothing to counteract the effects of circumstance on her psychological state. She was to obey him, never leave his direction, keep secret all that he told her and not speak to anyone except himself about her spiritual affairs. These were the

[1] The pilgrimage of Notre Dame d'Étang (not: 'de l'Étang', as in Mère de Chaugy), closely linked with the religious life of Dijon, still exists at Velars-sur-Ouche, a village six miles outside the town on the N5 to Paris. The actual shrine, centering round a very small ancient 'black' Madonna, has now been removed from the plateau of St Joseph to the village church in the valley. The present (1962) curator of the shrine and parish priest is Pierre du Jeu, the son of Vicomte Emmanuel du Jeu whose biography of Madame de Chantal is the best of the more recent French ones.

four vows and Madame de Chantal agreed to burden her conscience with them all, thinking that her aversion came from her lack of virtue, not from her common sense. The door was thrown wide open to scruples.

For two and a half years she battled on under this direction and it did not break her spirit; on the contrary, she had in a sense found what she was looking for: discipline and obedience to an external authority. An essential part of her confused spiritual state was that she did not know exactly what she was looking for and what was good or bad for her. She could not see the wood for the trees, but trial and error under obedience did her little harm precisely because she was obedient. In an interior locution she had at this time, God seemed to draw her to himself with her whole being, and she heard the words: '*Comme mon fils Jésus a été obéissant, je vous destine à être obéissante*'—'Even as my Son Jesus was obedient, your destiny too is obedience.' Though it brought her no peace this direction served as a trial-run for the real thing. Her biographer comments that she went on languishing for a God whom she could not find because she was not following the particular road by which he wanted to communicate himself to her. But she was doing his will as she saw it and beginning to learn that in practice, finding God simply meant uniting herself with his will as she saw it from moment to moment. In this sense she had already found him, and as the years went on, she realized ever more clearly that whatever marvellous things she may have been expecting in her confused spiritual state, there was no other way of union for her except in a whole-hearted co-operation with God in the circumstances of her life. Clarity of insight and the ensuing peace of soul that comes with understanding—this is what eluded her under her first director. But the essentials were there.

She had not been in Dijon long when a letter arrived from her father-in-law: if she and her children did not come and live with him at Monthelon he would disinherit the children. It is not known whether any argument preceded this letter; it seems unlikely. He appears to have been the sort of person who communicated his wishes by means of an ultimatum. He was seventy-five by this time, too old for warfare, which was the only way of life he really understood, grieving for the loss of his only son, unwilling to move back to Bourbilly which by now had tragic

Bourbilly

Baron Christophe de Rabutin-Chantal
Cabinet des Estampes, Bibliothèque Nationale

associations for him and was in any case a large place to manage. On his son's marriage he had retired to a much smaller castle not far from Autun and about forty miles distant from his former home. He felt disinclined to move. He had also allowed himself to get into the grip of a scheming housekeeper by whom he had a number of illegitimate children. It is possible that he was in fact summoning his daughter-in-law in an attempt to solve his domestic problem, although on the face of it this did not appear. He supported the servant against her and allowed her to go on ruling the house, wasting his substance by extravagant entertaining, which he liked, and inefficient land management, which he unwillingly condoned. He wanted to gain without giving up: Madame de Chantal was to be there, also his grandson with his sisters, so that he could have a more dignified family life in his old age, but at the same time the servant was to stay and do as she liked. It was his daughter-in-law who bore the brunt of this situation. The next seven and a half years provided her with a training in the exercise of patience and humility which were of a kind to make the strictest religious novitiate appear plain sailing.

Monthelon was a gloomy place, square and squat, little more than a fortified country house standing isolated in a plain. It had four look-out towers without which it would not have qualified as a castle, a small house chapel, a moat. There was no central court. A gallery ran along the first floor on the southern or entrance side of the castle, overlooking what was in effect a farmyard. Above the door at the top of the entrance steps were the baron's arms carved in stone and surrounded by his Grand Cordon of the Order of St Michael, conferred on him for brave war service under Henri IV. Above the arms was his device in Latin and French:

VIRTUS VULNERE VIRESCIT.

LA VERTU S'ACCROIT PAR LES PLAIES.

'Virtue'—or that indefinable blending of valour, goodness and resolution in difficulties implied by the Latin word—'grows by wounds'. As Madame de Chantal and her children walked up these steps in the early autumn of 1602, just about a year after her husband's death, the stage seemed set for the next act, the motto found.

Unlike Bourbilly, Monthelon has survived almost unchanged,

and, one is tempted to think, complete with its air of dilapidation. It is now partly a museum, partly a convenient store-house for the neighbouring farm and even a sort of parish hall for the village about half a mile away. To the left of the steps there is a small chapel, still the same structure as in the sixteenth century. The steps themselves lead straight into the great chamber, and from there one passes to the kitchen at the back. There is a twisting staircase leading first to Madame de Chantal's room above the great chamber and also to the baron's next door. Both rooms have a door out to the gallery and a window front and back, though not a large one, so that there seems to be little light. In the corner of her room there is a vast stone fireplace with a carved crest, still exactly as it was in her time. A door at the end of the gallery immediately next to her room opens on a small attic above the chapel.

The attic was the only place where she was allowed to reign undisturbed, for she managed to get permission to use it as a little hospital and dispensary. The people who came there mostly had such repellent diseases—lepers are freely mentioned in the local tradition—that everyone fled at their approach. It says a great deal for her persevering tact that she managed to get her measures tolerated in this household, and it also speaks well for the old baron; for looking to the needs of the poor and the sick must have been far more disturbing to the family at such close quarters than in the large courts and halls of Bourbilly. Nevertheless she did it, and her early biographies are filled with long and circumstantial accounts of her nursing. She was not allowed any share in the running of the house, she even had to ask permission when she wanted to give a glass of wine to the messenger who brought her letters. She therefore turned to those things which were within her reach. She prevailed on her father-in-law to have the foundation mass from Bourbilly transferred to Monthelon so as to set the framework for her own life, for her children and for any others of the household who could be persuaded to follow her example. The patients in the attic were not to be excluded either. She had the ingenious idea of having a number of gratings made in the attic floor which was also the chapel ceiling, and through these four openings, one leper to each grating, explains the old farmer who now acts as caretaker to the castle, they could watch and hear mass. Strength for her active work came from there, and like her makeshift hospital, her own heart lay open to grace.

She avenged herself on the servant by repaying evil with good. Her subordinate position after years of independence made her feel all the more keenly the loss of status which widowhood brought with it, and her patience was continually on trial by the day-to-day bickering inherent in this kind of situation. Judging by the impression her character makes before it became overlaid with the commonplaces of hagiographers, she was not naturally patient, indeed according to her own account, she was inclined to be imperious. Moreover, the sight of what was going on around her must have tried to the utmost her innate sense of justice and order. If she had done no more than avoid open retaliation this would in itself have been a remarkable achievement. But she did far more than keep the peace, turning, as always, to practical and positive action. Gathering together all the children in the castle, her own and the servant's, she herself gave them regular lessons. All were taught to read, write and count, and daily catechism with prayers well learnt and recited were soon the rule. The children were also allowed, as a privilege, to help her carry food to the sick and to visit the poor when the hovels where they lived were not too revolting. In so far as it depended on her she introduced a little island of orderly activity in the midst of the chaos. It was perhaps just this that the old baron had secretly hoped for and it is known that although he never dismissed the servant, he came to value his daughter-in-law's presence more and more, and to feel the influence of her increasing goodness.

Madame de Chantal did not let her own father in Dijon know how difficult things were at Monthelon. During the Lent of the first year, a time when because of the sermons which were, and still are, a very important feature of the church year in France, she would have liked to go to Dijon, she went for early morning rides to the cathedral at Autun instead. The town is about five miles from the castle, the cathedral of St Lazarus with Gilbertus' impressive tympanum of the Last Judgment over the entrance, its wealth of romanesque carving in the interior, is still much as it was in her day.[1] The cathedral stands on a hill, with old houses and

[1] cf. *Gislebertus: Sculptor of Autun* by Denis Grivot and George Zarnecki, London 1961.

alley-ways clustering right up to the doorway. To the left of the porch a small, delicately carved fountain near which the horses were tethered, remains from the early sixteenth century. Her biographer records that after mass and the sermon Madame de Chantal urged her horse to a quick trot, taking short cuts—'*certaines petites rues secrètes*'—so as to avoid meeting people and to get back in time for the baron's dinner before midday (1, 44). And all this fasting.

The following year she was able to get to the sermon less strenuously: she just walked from her father's home to the Sainte Chapelle, a little way along the streets in Dijon. This fine gothic building was the church attached to the former ducal palace, the centre of religious life in Dijon and one of the famous shrines of medieval France.[1] The preacher was the Bishop of Geneva who had been invited by the magistrates of the town, M. Frémyot among them, to give the Lenten sermons. It was customary for important cities to try and find an outstanding preacher for this season. Dijon had done well in the face of severe competition to secure a young bishop whose name was already well known in court circles, and whom Henri IV had tried, unsuccessfully, to draw to a high ecclesiastical office in Paris. Other considerations apart, the bishop had good reasons for accepting the invitation. The king had given André Frémyot certain ecclesiastical revenues in the Canton of Gex in the bishop's diocese, forgetting that he had already ceded them to Geneva. A lawsuit was pending; the bishop preferred to try personal arbitration with André who was not personally known to him.

André, by this time thirty-one, had at first entered the Dijon parliament after taking a doctorate in law at the University of Paris. But his outlook changed; he studied for the priesthood and took minor orders. At the same time, the benefices which his father could not use were conferred on his son by the hereditary principle which seems anomalous now but was then common enough. The benefice had, as often, been conferred before he had

---

[1] The Sainte Chapelle was destroyed at the Revolution, the municipal theatre now stands on the site of its sanctuary while the ducal palace, which preserves the treasures of the chapel, is now partly town hall and partly museum. See illustration p. 65.

taken major orders; he now found himself Archbishop of Bourges resident with his father at the abbot's lodging of the abbey Saint-Etienne. His ordination to the priesthood was imminent, and by the time it took place at the end of Lent, all dispute had been settled in the rightful owner's favour. The bishop himself assisted as deacon at André's first mass in the Sainte Chapelle on Maundy Thursday, and as the liturgy only allowed of one mass on that day, he received communion at the hands of the newly ordained priest. He had made a lasting friend of a potential enemy.

Madame de Chantal and the children arrived in Dijon just after the beginning of Lent. As soon as the preacher stepped up into the pulpit and began his sermon—it was Friday 5 March, a date she never forgot—she recognized the man she had seen near the wooded hill as she was riding home at Bourbilly along the river. Perhaps she did not at once understand that this former glimpse of him had been a vision and that now the vision was coming true; the fact was that she recognized him. It would in any case not have needed a vision to make her listen attentively to his sermon for it was very good, fully occupying both her head and her heart. He spoke slowly, almost hesitantly, without a trace of showy rhetoric and yet with a memorable insistence all his own that seemed to move the will. His words were simple, his illustrations never far-fetched, his meaning plain. Yet it was obvious that the sermon had been planned by an exceptionally orderly mind where grasp of principle was reflected in every apparently simple statement. At the same time, intelligence did not inhibit feeling but fused with it so as to produce an effect of solution and harmony. While Madame de Chantal at once recognized his supernatural qualities, her quick psychological insight also helped her to realize how a personality of this kind, where thought, emotion and will worked in balanced harmony, could supply for her what she most needed: enlightened and authoritative guidance.

Though the general theme of the sermons is not known, it is certain that the bishop preached from Gospel scenes and texts on matters relevant to the huguenot controversy which was still most acute in Dijon. These sermons would have had special interest for Madame de Chantal as many of her difficulties centred on thoughts against her faith. At the same time, the few brief Latin headings which the bishop noted for his other sermons suggest peaceful, uncontroversial themes of a kind to help her in a different way: 'The woman of Samaria; of the sick man at the pool; you shall seek me; Master, we would have a sign from you.'[1] How did his sermons in fact help her? The bishop himself gives the answer in a letter he wrote later on to André who had asked him for advice on preaching and hoped to glean from him the secret of influence. How, he asks, are preachers to achieve their end?

'Quite simply by speaking with feeling and devotion, candidly and trustfully, by really being in love with the doctrine we are teaching and trying to get people to accept. The great art is to be art-less. The kindling power of our words must not come from outward demonstration but from within, not from the mouth but straight from the heart. Try as hard as you like but in the end only the language of the heart can reach another heart, while the sound of the tongue does not get past your listener's ear.'[2]

The bishop for his part also noticed Madame de Chantal, for she had her prie-dieu put close to the preacher and followed his words with intent absorption. André was proud to reveal her identity when after a day or two the bishop asked who it was that always sat immediately opposite the pulpit in church and listened so intently. He had, in fact, observed her quite closely: she was dressed in a widow's habit and was of rather fair colouring. For he too had thought to recognize her, in the same way as she recognized him. The setting for his vision had been a mountain valley in Savoy: he had first seen her when he was kneeling in prayer in the chapel of his home at Sales and it had been revealed to him that he was one day to found a new religious order. Today, the castle and its chapel have long been destroyed, but on the site, near some great lime trees said to date from the saint's time, a stone cross marks the place where this first vision came to him, while its living monument throughout the world is the Order of the Visitation.

[1] *Saint François de Sales* by Francis Trochu, 2 vols. Lyons and Paris, 1946; Vol. II, p. 104.

[2] *St. Francis de Sales, Selected Letters,* translated with an Introduction by Elisabeth Stopp, London and New York, 1960, p. 22. Referred to henceforward as '*Selected Letters*'.

Chapter 3

THE GATE OF SAINT CLAUDE
1604

————❦————

F rancis de Sales, Bishop of Geneva and resident at Annecy, was at this time in his middle thirties. He was born in 1567 at Sales not far from Annecy in the duchy of Savoy, the eldest son of a distinguished and ancient house. His father destined him for a career at the court of Victor Emmanuel at Turin, the capital of Savoy, and sent him to Paris and Padua to study law. In secret, aware of his father's opposition, he also read theology and took a double doctorate at Padua so as to satisfy his father and at the same time further his own settled desire to enter the church. He had his mother's support and in the end gained his father's grudging consent to what he considered an inglorious way of life. Francis made over to his younger brother his title and rights of succession, and after being appointed provost to the cathedral chapter of Geneva exiled at Annecy, he was ordained and said his first mass on 21 December 1593.

His office to some extent reconciled his father as it was the first step on the way to possible appointment as bishop. But to begin with, Francis was sent as sole missionary priest in charge of the Chablais on the south bank of the lake of Geneva, an area where there were only a handful of catholics left among hostile huguenots. By courageous and steadfast work, by a carefully planned apostolate of writing and preaching—he published weekly broadsheets on controversial points—and by sheer personal holiness he succeeded in the space of four years in bringing the majority of the inhabitants back to the faith. His work in the Chablais brought him to the notice of the Duke of Savoy, ecclesiastical authority

55

right up to the Vatican recognized his quality and it gave his own spirituality the strength which comes of hard experience. He also found himself as a writer. He was nominated coadjutor to the bishop and sent to represent his superior in an *ad limina* visit to Rome. In 1601 he went to Paris on a diplomatic mission concerning the restitution of certain ecclesiastical rights which the King of France was due to make to the Duke of Savoy.

The mission itself was not a success, but as a person Francis gained much from it. He was acclaimed as a preacher when he gave the Lenten sermons at court, and he made many friends, Henri IV not least among them. He found himself in immediate contact with new religious ideas and with the revival of monastic and contemplative life which was just then beginning in Paris as a long-term sequel to the Counter Reformation. Bérulle came his way, Madame Acarie, who was largely instrumental in introducing St Teresa's Carmelites into France, was his penitent. Francis took part in the counsels of religious leaders and was in turn consulted by them in spiritual matters. In a European centre of renewed religious culture, and coming from a hard apprenticeship in remote mountain valleys, he began to find himself as a director and confessor. This in turn served as a remote preparation for his own success in founding a new and entirely original religious order later on. When Francis was on his way home his bishop died at Annecy. After a retreat at the castle of Sales, Francis was consecrated on 8 December 1602 in the nearby village church at Thorens where he had been baptized.

It was just over a year later that he was invited to Dijon as guest preacher and first met Madame de Chantal. He stayed in a house belonging to a friend of the Frémyot family, and in order to get to know the people who listened to his sermons, he used to dine at other houses where guests were invited to meet him.[1] Madame de Chantal was often in his company, trailed, it seems, by a friend her director had assigned as a chaperone while he himself was

[1] This house in the rue de Vannerie is still standing and now forms the entrance to a school called after St Francis de Sales. The record of the expenses paid to his host, M. de Villers, for lodging the bishop and his retinue is in the municipal archives of Dijon, while it is also recorded that the bishop refused all gifts for himself. (*Registre des Délibérations de la Chambre de Ville*, 26 April 1604).

away from Dijon. Apart from the public sermons the preacher also gave informal talks on the spiritual life to a group of ladies who met at the Ursuline Convent. She saw him too at her father's house where she was herself the hostess. It gave them an opportunity of getting to know one another as real people and as members of the same social group; they were able to talk informally and see one another as something other than the dream-like ingredient of a vision.

He watched her closely. Her biographer, apologizing a little for the seeming triviality of the incidents recorded, reports one or two conversational exchanges between them. By this time he had gathered that she was devout and given to the practice of obedience. He teased her with a few tentative questions and watched to see how she would take this. Did she intend to get married again? And if not, why not take down the sign?[1] She understood quite well what he meant, and that evening she put away for good various little adornments permitted to widows of her class. And the attractive lace edging to her widow's peak? Wouldn't the headgear be perfectly neat even without that? She unpicked it all the way round its long pointed edge and appeared at the next dinner without any lace. And finally there were black silk tassels hanging from the cord which fastened her cloak. Wouldn't the cord operate just as well without 'this invention' dangling at the end of it? This time she was even more prompt. She took her scissors out of the purse she wore at her girdle and snipped the tassels off there and then. He was pleased with her reaction. Both of them were quick to see the amusing side of things, and one may take it that this was not done without a smile. It helped to keep her attitude to the lionized preacher in true balance.

It gave her courage, one day when her spiritual anxiety seemed intolerable and no other help was to hand, to ask her brother to arrange an interview for her. It was Wednesday in Holy Week. She had known the bishop for some weeks now without attempting to seek a private interview with him or talk about her difficulties, although, as she says, 'I was dying to do it' (1, 51). As a loyal brother, André guarded the inside of the door against the return

[1] 1, 52. The image used is that of an inn-sign. Cf. *Introduction to the Devout Life* Part 3, ch. 25. 'If you are not prepared to receive guests in your house you must take down the inn-sign.'

of the chaperone whom he had sent on a fool's errand; at the far end of the room Madame de Chantal, simply and with the candour of a child, as Francis himself said, gave an account of what was tormenting her. The week after Easter he agreed to hear her confession, demurring slightly, and saying, so as not to make it too easy for her, that he supposed women were naturally curious and liked to try something new. For she had of course told him about her director, and that she was only consulting him because of the spiritual emergency which had overtaken her during the director's absence. She does not appear to have revealed the full details of this relationship; loyalty prevented her from speaking about anything except the difficulty of the moment. As it was, she suffered great scruples for what she had done, but the wisdom of his counsel, the peace he communicated, helped to reassure her. He for his part felt that here was a person to whom he could give of his best, and he said that he felt her soul intimately contained within his own as he reflected on her problems. Special light seemed to be given to him for guiding her. Not knowing the full extent of her ties, he saw no reason why the director and he should not be able to work together in perfect agreement. She trusted him and followed his advice.

What was the spiritual emergency that overtook her? Her biographer does not state it except in passing; she may even have been told not to stress it unduly. The early letters from the bishop to Madame de Chantal confirm the nature of her main difficulty. She was tempted against the faith. Describing the terrible conflict of divided loyalties which overtook her just before Whitsun and about a month after Francis de Sales had left Dijon, she says that when this inner battle was at its worst, and she could neither sleep nor eat because of it for thirty-six hours, she was suddenly delivered from all other temptation and 'filled with a great light about the things concerning holy faith'. This astonished her, for what concerned faith was 'her greatest suffering and difficulty'. (1, 55) Attention was for the moment wholly focused on the foreground battle. Afterwards the well-known temptations returned. Doubts against the faith remained with her for the rest of her life, but she continually overcame them, in the words used by a witness in the canonization process: 'by her humility, her generous confidence in God, her promptness in despising and repudiating them.'[1] As a result, continues the witness, her faith seemed to shine out most clearly on those mysteries which are generally accounted as the most obscure: the Trinity, the Incarnation, which she called her favourite mystery, the Passion, our Lady's role in the Redemption. Judging by this witness and by the advice given over and again in the bishop's letters, he taught her from the beginning to deal with her abiding temptation by simply turning away from it, that is, recognizing it as something alien that was taking place on a lower level of her personality and really had nothing to do with the realm of faith. Her will to believe remained firm; nothing else mattered.

Again, judging by the early letters, she was preoccupied with the question of her state of life. She was thirty-two and had been nearly three years a widow; some members of her family wanted her to marry again. She had vowed chastity. Had she been wrong? Where did her duty lie? She was beginning to feel strongly drawn to the religious life. Was it possible that in obeying her instinct to stay with her children she was betraying a vocation? Was God asking something more of her that she was too dull or wrong-headed to see? What was the meaning of the ever unsatisfied desire to serve God that tormented her? And how was she best to respond to it?

These were some of the questions which may well have become acute at a time of intensified spiritual activity such as Lent; together with the main difficulty of doubt, these questions formed the substance of her first appeal to the bishop. The help she found in him was in itself the matter for a further conflict now to be resolved: was she free to turn to him for direction or did her vows bind her irretrievably to the other director? Francis de Sales dealt with this problem very discreetly. Here was an outstanding personality, in real difficulty, and not receiving the kind of help he felt well able to give her. He thought it wise to say nothing definite but to allow the situation to develop. All the same, he considered it as well to set a term to it. At dinner one day shortly before he left, he heard her tell someone that she was planning a pilgrimage to Saint Claude, a shrine in the Jura mountains about half way between Dijon and Annecy. He turned to

[1] Mère Favre de Charmette, Canonization Process Vol. 8; Partie Remissionale, Vol. I, folio 171.

her and said that if she would let him know when she intended to go, he would arrange to be there at the same time; his mother had made a vow to go to Saint Claude and he had offered to take her. He also promised to write to her as often as he could and allowed her to write if her director approved.

He and his brother who had accompanied him left Dijon on Monday 26 April, the day after Low Sunday, having spent nearly two months there. His visit had been a great success and he was given a warm farewell. As he left the town, people everywhere knelt for his blessing, Madame de Chantal and her children among them; and at the first halt he gave a messenger a note for her:

'I think that God gave me to you; every hour makes me more sure of it, that is all I can say. Commend me to your guardian angel'.[1]

This does not mean that the question of their future relationship as director and directed had already been discussed in a formal way; he was referring, perhaps, to a last conversation and a scruple on her part for calling in a second opinion. 'Yes,' he wanted to say to her in this note, 'God intended this, it was he who used me to help you. This is right, so be at peace. All is well.' He expanded this later on, referring her to the life of Mother Teresa which he tells her he had been reading one evening to refresh his soul from the labours of the day. She thought it quite right to turn to other spiritual guides for occasional advice while obeying one director only. Besides, what did the name matter, or his exact status in her regard as long as she trusted him and understood that he was ready to help her? The bond between them could not get in the way of any other tie, for it was one of charity and true Christian friendship, what St Paul calls the bond of perfection. 'God gave me to you', he repeats in another letter, 'Look on me as yours in him, and call me what you like, for the name doesn't matter.'[2] Firm foundations had been laid but the situation still needed clarifying. The bishop was content to wait on God and leave her perfectly free to make up her mind.

Four months passed before they met again at Saint Claude.

[1] *Selected Letters*, p. 50; A, XII, 262. A=Annecy edition of the works of St Francis de Sales (see Bibliography).
[2] A, XII, 285.

During this time they had exchanged one or two letters, rather formal on her part, for in spite of her director's grudging consent to the correspondence, she did not feel free to write openly, since he asked to see the letters.[1] After her Whitsun crisis she decided to consult a disinterested third party, the rector of the Jesuit college at Dijon, a friend of her father's who knew her well. What is more, he must have known her first director. As any man of sense was bound to do, he came out firmly on the bishop's side. This was enough for her. If Francis himself approved, she was ready to ask him formally to be her director and in any case to accept his decision without question.

With this intention in mind she set out on her pilgrimage to Saint Claude, a journey of some seventy miles which in the summer heat—she arrived there on 24 August—would take her about two or three days on horseback. She went together with her childhood friends, Marguerite and Rose Bourgeois de Crépy, the first now married to President Brûlart, the second the abbess of a rather easy-going convent at Puys d'Orbe near Dijon. These two had been among the bishop's most devoted listeners during Lent. The letters he wrote to them over the years make an instructive contrast to those addressed to Madame de Chantal. There was no favouritism, though Marguerite was not too sure and was apt to be a little jealous,[2] but the fact remained that he could only give to each according to her spiritual capacity. Compared with that of Madame de Chantal, their capacity was small and the letters inevitably reflect this, though both sisters in their particular state of life were good women. From the beginning one senses in Madame de Chantal a seemingly inexhaustible spiritual capacity to respond, learn, accept, understand and then translate into reality and action.

Francis arrived on the same day, together with his mother and his thirteen-year-old sister Jeanne. Madame de Boisy, his mother, at this time in her early fifties, was devout and retiring by nature. 'She had a generous and noble heart and was at the same time pure, innocent and simple, a true mother to the poor, modest, humble, full of kindness to all', was Madame de Chantal's own

[1] A, XII, 277, where St Francis refers to her first letter, dated 30 May 1604.
[2] Selected Letters, p. 109.

description of her.[1] Her portrait, a painting of good quality still to be seen at the castle of Thorens, shows her as a dark-haired woman of delicate features and a certain child-like candour. She looks still and withdrawn, but without any aloofness. It is a singularly attractive face. She played an important part in her son's life, for she supported his vocation and knew how to mediate tactfully between father and son, not always an easy matter. He in turn was devoted to her, and as he grew older he guided and helped her spiritually, showing by his letters that he had really succeeded in solving the problems posed by this delicate relationship. As soon as Madame de Boisy met Jane she felt strongly drawn to her and their friendship deepened in the years that followed.

When the first greetings were over the bishop took Madame de Chantal aside and asked her to tell him how things stood, which she did 'clearly, simply and honestly, not forgetting anything' (1, 62). He listened, said nothing whatever in reply, and took her back to join the others. Early the next morning he sought her out. He had spent much of the night in prayer and seemed very tired: 'I've been trying all night to work out your problem,' he said. Speaking slowly, and as though picking his words with some difficulty, he told her that he was prepared to undertake her direction. He was now satisfied that this was God's will. The four vows she had made were invalid, and fit only to destroy the peace of her conscience. He had delayed his answer because he wanted to be humanly certain that God and God alone should be the prime mover in this matter. Now he was sure. She listened, she said, as though a voice had spoken to her from heaven. A strong sense of the supernatural came over her.

That same morning she made a general confession to him and he formally undertook her direction while she for her part vowed obedience. It was the feast day of St Louis. They exchanged formal documents, for this was considered a binding contract before God. His short promise was written on the spot, she went out to Notre Dame d'Étang on her return and wrote hers there, choosing the same shrine as before, a happier stage but along the same road.

[1] *Oeuvres*, Vol. 3, p. 98. Article 2 of her Deposition for the Cause of St Francis de Sales.

'All powerful and eternal Lord, I, Jane Frances Frémyot,[1] unworthy as I am to come before your divine presence, but trusting in your goodness and infinite mercy, solemnly vow to your divine Majesty, in the presence of the glorious Virgin Mary and of the triumphant court of heaven, to live in perpetual chastity, and to obey the Bishop of Geneva, excepting the authority of all legitimate superiors. By your immense goodness and loving kindness I very humbly entreat you by the precious blood of Jesus Christ graciously to receive this complete offering of myself; and as you have freely given me grace to want it, so too may you give me all the grace I need to carry it through. Amen. Written at Notre Dame d'Étang, 2 September, 1604.' (1, 65)

He answered:

'I accept, in God's name, responsibility for your spiritual guidance and shall carry it out as carefully and as faithfully as I can, and in so far as my office and my previously contracted duties allow.' (1, 62)

Before they separated he administered a little more spiritual first aid, gave her some idea of how to fit her devotions into her daily life at home, suggested a simple, unconstrained method of prayer. She felt as though she had suddenly been let out of prison, as she said, and was beginning to enter into the peace of a child of God. She had stepped from the Old Testament into the New. The process of readjustment was gradual, a matter of years, but the decisive step had been taken and her face was set in the right direction.

As she rode out to this new life through the massive clock-tower gate of Saint Claude on the morning of 28 August, and thinking of all that had happened, she pondered again on a vivid dream she had had some time ago. She had mentioned it to the bishop, and in a letter he asked her, not out of idle curiosity, as he said, to write out a full account of it.[2] He believed it to have been an authentic spiritual experience. The dream dated from before their actual meeting in Dijon. She dreamt she was in a carriage with a party of people together with whom she was bound on a journey. The carriage went past a church where she saw many people intent on praising God with great joy:

[1] A widow, though still referred to in public by her married name, could return to her maiden name when signing documents. Madame de Chantal always signed her letters in this way.

[2] A, XII, 369.

'I wanted to fling myself out of the carriage to join this happy throng and enter by the great door of the church which stood open and ready to receive me; but I was thrust back and I distinctly heard a voice which said to me: "You must press on and go further; you will never find the peace of a child of God unless you enter by the gate of Saint Claude".' (1, 41)

She had never paid any attention to this saint, a bishop who lived in the Dark Ages and whose shrine was far away in the Jura mountains where she had never been; but from this time on she began to find out more about his cult, which was in fact widespread. Often in times of temptation she invoked him and felt comforted when she remembered the prophetic words addressed to her. His name, standing for the unknown, seemed to hold the promise of a solution, of a new way. This is why a pilgrimage suggested itself to her; her mind was practical and so a concrete approach, an actual road or way towards what she did not know seemed the obvious solution.

Apart from a prophecy so strikingly made true, the dream is also a faithful picture of the spiritual situation in which she found herself. Her first director was trying to form her according to a standard, collective pattern, applied indiscriminately to all the pious women who consulted him. He seems to have been unaware of individual spiritual needs and so it did not occur to him to make any personal distinction except a crude, quantitative one: more capacity, therefore more prayers, more penance, more vows, but still of the same kind. No wonder Madame de Chantal sees herself hurried along in a carriage, a collective vehicle shared with a whole company who are making the same spiritual journey and who, in contrast to herself, seem content with their lot. But she, with every justification, thirsts for something different, and catching sight of the intent happiness of a much freer kind of worship, wants to extricate herself from the common vehicle and fling herself (she uses the vigorous: *s'élancer*) through the wide open door of the church where freedom beckons. But here again, it was the 'great' door and one through which everyone else was streaming; a far better solution, of course, but not as yet the individual one God was holding in store for her alone. The life of the spirit is in the final instance solitary. She was thrust back, not as yet allowed to act, or to escape of her own accord. She was told

Monthelon

The Sainte Chapelle, Dijon (*see p. 52*)

Bibliothèque Publique, Dijon

to go on and pass beyond all the preamble till she reached her own personal way in, by a gate she does not know, in the sign of a saint she does not know, whose shrine—and this is the only thing she does know—lies high up in the mountains, that is, in a solitude:

> *'In order to arrive at what you do not know*
> *you must go by a way you do not know;*
> *in order to arrive at what you are not*
> *you must go through what you are not.'*

> St John of the Cross, Of the Soul's Ascent of
> Mount Carmel. Book I, Chapter 13.

Saint Claude became to her a symbol of the quest.

Through the parable of this dream she was also being taught one of the basic lessons of the spiritual life, that of waiting on God. He would give the signal, but in his own good time. She was to find the difficult point of balance between her own inner readiness to respond, and the impact of divine action coming from without. She had wanted to break out of the carriage in which she was a passive prisoner, but she was now to learn that it was possible to temper personal initiative with patient readiness. In other words she was maturing spiritually, and although her outward circumstances now remained unchanged during the psychologically decisive years of her middle thirties, Saint Claude and all it stood for proved to be the important turning point in her life.

Madame de Chantal was active and vigorous by temperament, reinforced in her independence by having to fend for her children in her widowhood and deal, alone, with an almost intolerable personal situation. She had plenty of common sense by which to conduct her life, she could read spiritual books if she wanted to, though relatively few for the laity were then available; she had a wise father, a brother who was devoted to her, and like-minded friends. Why, it may be asked, did she need a spiritual director, and what exactly *is* a director that finding the right one should have been such a decisive factor in her life?

She felt called to the devout life.

'Ordinarily good people walk in God's ways, but the devout run, and the really devout run swiftly.'[1]

[1] *Selected Letters*, p. 57.

People who are devout in this sense are hardly conscious of being exceptional, for running is their natural way of proceeding; those who walk cannot as a rule see what all the fuss is about. Why run, when all one is asked to do is to move in the right direction?

'Charity is a spiritual fire, and when this fire blazes very brightly it is called devotion; devotion adds nothing to the fire of charity except a more brilliant flame which makes it swift to glow, active and unfailingly obedient not only to God's commandments but also to his counsels and inspirations.'[1]

It is all a difference of degree, not of kind. The swift pace, the brightly blazing fire, these hold dangers unknown to people moving along sedately, and even unsuspected by them. Not that the devout person can give himself or anyone else a clear account of these perils, but he knows perfectly well they are there; he soon realizes that he cannot manage alone, and reaching out to God for help, he instinctively turns to a trained guide who can speak with authority. 'He who heareth you heareth me.' Because he believes this in his characteristically literal way, he is prepared to obey his freely chosen guide as though God himself were speaking. He prays to find him, he may take every human precaution in his choice—indeed, he will have to, as Madame de Chantal discovered to her cost—but once the right guide is found, a sound relationship to him established, he is safe.

'The guidance of souls is of all arts the most excellent,' said Saint Gregory. What is the guide to be like? He must himself be an exceptional man, one in a thousand, or even in ten thousand, according to St Francis de Sales.[2] He must be full of charity, learned and prudent. If one of these three qualities is lacking, there is danger. Unless he is himself on fire with charity he will not begin to understand a soul that is, nor will he have the selflessness to devote himself whole-heartedly to a difficult task. If he is without learning and training, he will lack breadth of vision and fail to see a spiritual situation in its true perspective; neither will he be able to assess it accurately, suggesting right and tried methods of procedure. If he lacks prudence, he will bungle as Madame de Chantal's first director did, and thoroughly confuse a very delicate

[1] *Introduction to the Devout Life*, I, 1.
[2] *Introduction*, I, 4.

66

issue. Even if he passes all the tests, he may not be equally successful with all who come his way. There is a strong element of
personal action and reaction in this relationship; it cannot work
to a mere rule. For a candidate for the devout life has to do many
hard things; perhaps the hardest and one which comes right at the
beginning, is to renounce his own view of himself and submit his
own will in an essentially supernatural relationship. In this way he
can begin to grow spiritually; he has therefore to set out with a
measure of natural trust in his guide, a distinct sympathy on an
ordinary human level.

An imprudent guide will try to force issues while a good director rarely has to get as far as exerting authority. He backs up
divine action on the soul, waiting for this leading, following on
but seldom taking the initiative. He leaves that to the Holy
Spirit. He is not, after all, like a religious superior, forming a
novice to a certain traditional type of life and spirituality. 'I leave
in God's own hands the pruning hook that cuts back useless
shoots,' St Francis said to a penitent.[1] His office is to explain and
counsel, to restrain or encourage, to console often, to admonish
rarely. He is a friend as well as a spiritual educator; and as the
whole human being is involved in the devout life, not just a soul
in the abstract, he will be prepared to offer practical advice as and
when it is needed. The person directed does not abrogate responsibility or lose his essential freedom, but he for his part, as
St Francis insists at the very beginning, must be absolutely open:

'Let your heart be open to him, giving him a sincere and faithful
account of yourself, clearly showing him both the good and the bad
in you without pretence or dissimulation; and in this way the good in
you will be scrutinized and fortified, the bad corrected and remedied;
you will be comforted and strengthened in sorrow, be made steady and
less impetuous in consolation. Trust and revere him in such a way that
reverence does not lessen trust, nor trust reverence. "A faithful friend
is a strong defence: and he that hath found him hath found a treasure.
A faithful friend is the elixir of life and immortality; and they that fear
the Lord shall find him."[2] . . . this friendship should be strong and
sweet, altogether holy, sacred, divine and spiritual . . . Ask God for
this friend, and having found him, bless his divine Majesty, be faithful

[1] *Selected Letters*, p. 276.
[2] Ecclus., VI, 14, 16.

67

and do not look for others, but just go on your way simply, humbly and trustfully, for you will have a very happy journey.'[1]

This then was the kind of relationship that Madame de Chantal entered upon through the gate of Saint Claude. She found in St Francis de Sales a director who fulfilled all the necessary conditions of excellence, and a friend and counsellor with whom she immediately felt in sympathy. Over the next eighteen years until his death in 1622—she outlived him by as many years again —their relationship developed and grew in grace. From 1604 onwards their lives ran side by side; neither can be understood without the other. While he himself had the training, skill and power to help her, the personal holiness to understand her, he was rewarded by finding in her a personality equal in calibre to his own. At the same time he too grew in grace through trying to meet her spiritual needs:

'I ask you to bless God together with me for the effects of the journey to Saint Claude', he wrote, 'I cannot tell you about them, but they are great.'[2]

From Saint Claude she set out on 'a very happy journey', that is, happy in the sense in which St Francis here uses the word, though humanly speaking it was hard. A happy journey is one which gets you there in the end.

[1] *Introduction*, I, 4.
[2] A, XIII, 369.

Chapter 4

SPIRITUAL FORMATION
1604-1606

Soon after her return from Saint Claude, Madame de Chantal went to supervise the wine and corn harvest at Bourbilly. This was the busiest time of the year for her. It had been agreed in consultation with her father and with the bishop that she was from now on to divide her time rather more equally between Monthelon and Dijon, and that after the autumn at Bourbilly, the winter was to be spent for the most part in the city. Monsieur Frémyot was getting old, and finding his thoughts increasingly turned towards death, had asked Francis to write to him from time to time to help him prepare for death, a request which was most tactfully fulfilled by one so much his junior.[1] His daughter's strong faith was a support he felt he needed; and he liked, too, to have her children about the house. Celse-Bénigne was left at Dijon most of the time and entrusted, together with his cousins Bénigne and Jacques de Neufchèzes, to a priest-tutor, *'le bon Monsieur Robert'*, who had also been responsible for André's education. The wholly different atmosphere of her father's house must have been restful in the extreme for Madame de Chantal; yet she also had a strong sense of her obligations towards her father-in-law who, though he could not see it, was in even greater need of her help. Her word of order was contained in one of the early letters from Annecy:

'Try to make yourself more agreeable and humble every day towards both your fathers and work gently towards their salvation.'[2]

[1] *Selected Letters*, pp. 53-56.
[2] *Selected Letters*, p. 69.

69

This programme involved living in two places at once for the next few years, and the continual travelling, especially with young children—the boy was eight, the girls now six, seven and three years old—was bound to be a constant strain. It made her feel her widowhood and consequent homelessness all the more. Visiting Bourbilly, which was at its best in the autumn splendour of its remote forest setting, revived memories which were as yet too close to be without pain. The great spiritual growth of the next few years, with its alternating periods of anguish and joy, doubt and certainty, took its course against a background of inner loneliness, hard work and constant travel. Yet in spite of human shrinking, it was all much more positive, for she was now being consciously guided along a way where every circumstance of her life with its suffering or happiness was seen as part of a great whole: the unity of God's will for her. This meant peace. From now on, although there was much pain in her life, there were no loose ends. After she had passed through the gate of Saint Claude, her director gradually taught her how to gather up all the strands of her inner and outer life and offer them back to God from whom they came. This unifying process can be followed in the letters of the next few months before she saw the bishop again at Whitsun the following year.

Eight letters of his, covering the time between Saint Claude and the Whitsun of 1605, have survived. Among them are some of the most important he ever wrote to her. Of hers there are none. After the bishop's death, his brother and successor sent them to Madame de Chantal to do with as she thought fit. She thought fit to burn them without exception.[1] Fortunately St Francis de Sales was so good a writer and so careful a correspondent that any moderately attentive reader can reconstruct the gist of the lost letters by implication. It is a second best but it will have to do. Besides, a very few of her letters written to him in later years do somehow seem to have survived the holocaust, and they give a clue to the general nature of what has been lost. In her letters Madame de Chantal expressed herself clearly and well. She wrote a large, angular and slanting hand, more legible at this time than it became later on, sparing no effort of the will but making no concessions to what was merely decorative; all was simplicity, candour,

[1] cf. Ch. 10, p. 190-4, for a full discussion of this incident.

whole-heartedness. She had a gift for the accurate and brief description of her spiritual difficulties; the bishop tells her so, in passing, and implies that this helps him considerably in his reply. She also had the habit, possibly by her father's training, of setting out her points systematically and numbering them.

During those first few months her questions centred round a number of distinct topics. Was it quite certain that she had not offended God in abandoning her first director, and was she not burdening her present one unduly? He reassured her, patiently going over the same ground again, and told her plainly that it was a special happiness to him to serve her spiritually. Could he advise her in greater detail what her devotional exercises were to be and how to fit them in to her domestic life? He had mentioned 'liberty of spirit' so often, but she still did not quite understand; what did it mean and how did it work out in practice? She felt that she was being restless and over-eager, vaguely dissatisfied all the time in her spiritual life; what did he think was wrong? Finally, but perhaps most crucial of all: how was she to try and deal with her continual thoughts against the faith?

He gave her a rule of life, cautioning her right at the beginning that she was not to be anxious if she left anything out, putting it down clearly in capital letters that she was to do everything in a spirit of love, not of rigid self-coercion;[1] her fear of disobeying him in any particular point was to be counterbalanced and outweighed by an overall love of obedience and her general readiness to do as she had promised. He told her that she was not immune from the little scruples and fears common to her sex, especially after the experience of the past few years; he wanted to restore in her attitude to the things of God the fearless confidence that he felt was natural to her. It was not like her to fuss in little feminine ways, or be constrained and anxious. He aimed at relaxing her, getting her out into the sunshine to see the wide horizons of a life of true devotion instead of brooding, housebound, over imaginary failings or even very real temptations. He wanted her henceforward to enjoy the liberty of a child that knows it is beloved by the best of all Fathers, 'the complete detachment of a Christian heart following God's known will'.[2] Someone who lives like this,

[1] *Selected Letters*, p. 67, and the whole of this long letter of 14 October 1604.
[2] *Selected Letters*, p. 70.

71

in the sunshine as it were, of God's will, is not attached to consolations, does not cling tenaciously to spiritual exercises if a good reason prevents them, is cheerful and serene, patient when crossed, unruffled when interrupted—at least, as a rule. He will gradually develop the suppleness which will make him see what is and what is not God's will for him in the happenings of everyday life, that is, when charity and real necessity make claims on him which at first appear to go against his own rules or plans. In time he will learn the true balance between the extreme of slavish adherence to rules and a fickle lack of discipline, the only valid alternative to the rigid *either/or* outlook on life which tends to bedevil people of ardent temperament.

The rule which he gave her, together with the advice on how to live it, may seem rather taxing. Three and a half centuries have passed since then, and the relaxation of standards is perhaps nowhere more apparent than in the use of time and the attitude to physical hardship. She was to rise at 5 o'clock but go to bed at 9 or 10, begin the day with an hour's prayer and meditation on the life of Christ; daily mass, holy communion on Sundays and feast days, a daily rosary, half an hour's spiritual reading, a short period of prayer before supper, evening prayers and an examination of conscience, certain essential vocal prayers, such as the Pater, Ave, Credo, Veni Sancte Spiritus, twice a day, and also the litany of our Lady. These prayers were to be said in Latin, the devotional language common throughout the church, and therefore a practical symbol of unity. She was to fast every Friday—and this really meant fasting—and to take the discipline twice a week or whenever the temptations were particularly troublesome. Short little prayers or aspirations were to continue at all times, in the midst of her work and as the hours struck. This was the easiest way to make continual prayer an integral part of her life. She was of course to continue teaching the children, looking after the poor and sick, and he allowed her to spend all her leisure on working with her hands, spinning, weaving, sewing for charitable ends.

Faithfully observed, this programme added up to a considerable total. It was as well that he cautioned her against scrupulosity in its observance. But so transforming was his influence, that in spite of this new rule of life she appeared to be spending less time on her devotions than before. Her servants, who ought to have known, said:

'Madame's first director only made her pray three times a day, and we were all put out by it; but Monsieur de Genève makes her pray all day long, and it doesn't worry anyone.' (1, 73)

This famous comment proves that Madame very soon learnt how to put her director's gracious spirit of moderation and inner freedom into practice; also that it was an attitude which she had had to acquire. By nature she was inclined to rush to extremes, and when pursuing her ideas, she tended to lack consideration for others, notably her servants. She had been brought up to use her servants in the manner of her age, so this is historically explicable, though only to a certain extent. Francis was told at Saint Claude that when she rose early to pray, she called her maid to help her dress and light the fire when it was cold. He stopped this, and pointed out to her that she had been guilty of a certain inhumanity in the name of devotion; for it had come to his ears that the servant, who was devoted to her, was on the *qui vive* more or less all night so as to be ready when the early summons came.

This incident is revealing, for it is one of the few negative traits her biographer has considered worth recording. It cannot have been the only one told by Madame de Chantal against herself, but the rest seems to have been taken as an expression of her humility, and therefore not as objectively true, or else not compatible with the truth of a biography written to edify. This selective policy leads to a certain lack of relief which makes it hard to see a personality in the round. It therefore seems permissible to stress this trait so as to show how, over the years, her director's influence— he combined strength with gentleness to a most unusual degree— gradually cured her of the outward manifestation of a certain inner brittleness. Her immediate response to all the bishop's suggestions (she knelt to read his letters to show she thought of them as coming to her from God) educated her to a state of suppleness which is the prerequisite to progress in the spiritual realm. The negative qualities connected with strength of will and purpose are hard for the person concerned to see, let alone to cure without the help of someone outside.

He also helped her to become conscious in another direction:

73

'There is something in me, you say, that has never been satisfied, but I don't know what it is. I wish I knew what it is so that I could tell you, my dear daughter; perhaps some day when we have plenty of time to talk, I shall find out. Meanwhile, I wonder whether the blockage is caused by too many desires thronging in your mind? I have suffered from this illness. A bird chained to its perch is not conscious of its captivity and does not feel the pull of its chain until it wants to fly; in the same way an unfledged nestling only finds out that it cannot fly when it makes the actual attempt. And the remedy for this, my dear daughter, is not to struggle, not to make eager attempts to fly: your wings have not yet grown and you lack power for too great an effort. Be patient until you get the wings of a dove, and then you can fly. I am very much afraid that you are a little too ardent and headlong, that you pursue too many desires rather too eagerly. You see the beauty of light, the sweetness of resolutions; you feel as though you were very, very nearly there, and seeing goodness so close at hand makes you thirst and long for it inordinately; your longing increases your eagerness, you rush forward to reach the object of your desire—but in vain; for your master keeps you chained to your perch, or else your wings are not yet grown. And meanwhile this constant flutter of your heart exhausts your strength all the time. Of course you must try to fly but do it gently and without struggling and without getting flustered.

'. . . This straining eagerness then is a fault of yours; and this is the undefinable thing that is not satisfied in you, a certain lack of resignation. You do resign yourself, but it is with a *but*; for you want this and that, and you struggle to get it. A simple desire is not contrary to resignation, but a panting heart, fluttering wings, an agitated will, and many restless movements—all these undoubtedly add up to lack of resignation. Courage, my dear sister; if our will belongs to God, we ourselves are surely his. You have all that is necessary, but without feeling it; that is no great loss. Do you know what you ought to do? As your wings have not yet grown, try to find pleasure in not flying.'[1]

This has been quoted at length as it must surely be the best description of Madame de Chantal's state of mind at this time, and from the person who really knew her. He goes on to say that she puts him in mind of Moses who saw the promised land but never set foot in it: 'he had your glass of water at his lips but could not drink'. She herself had then used the comparison of a glass of water dashed from her lips:

'Well now, if you too had to die without drinking of the well of

[1] *Selected Letters*, pp. 78-79.

the woman of Samaria, what of it, as long as your soul is allowed to drink for ever at the source and fountain of life? Do not go chasing eagerly after vain longings, and I would even go as far as to say, do not be eager in avoiding eagerness. Keep quietly on along your way, for it is a good way.'[1]

To her astonishment and relief, he thought her way was a good way in spite of the continual thoughts against faith. He was sorry for her but refused to be perturbed by them. What form did they take? They are never specified in detail; from the beginning there must have been an agreement between them that they should not be dealt with by reasoning and logic, but countered as an assault on her will. 'Suggestions of blasphemy, infidelity and unbelief'[2] is the nearest one ever gets to a description, and these generalized terms probably corresponded to her actual temptations which may well have been vague and indefinable. It is probable, however, that they centred round certain definite fields which would have been familiar to her from her youth upwards as debating points. She could not believe, she wrote and told him, that these temptations came from God. Of course not, he answered; how could she ever have imagined that they did? Perhaps she considered them as a divine affliction, as part of the general dryness and lack of relish in spiritual things? At any rate she thought that the painful barrier she came up against in trying to make resolutions and feel some sort of reaction from them, was the psychological point where her doubts began. God could send

'darkness, helplessness, can keep you tied to your perch, can lead you into dereliction and strip you of all strength, can upset your spiritual digestion and make your inner mouth taste bitter so that the sweetest wine in the world turns to gall'[3]

But thoughts of apostasy, never. God permitted the father of lies to suggest them; that was all.

The general tenor of his more detailed verbal instructions to her on how to deal with dryness, sadness, anxiety of all kinds can be reconstructed from the fourth section of the *Introduction to the Devout Life*. These fifteen chapters are still the classic brief treatise on the subject of temptations, great and small, that are likely to

[1] *Selected Letters*, p. 79.
[2] *Selected Letters*, p. 84.
[3] *Selected Letters*, p. 84.

afflict people who try to lead a devout life. The gist of it all may be summed up in St Francis's own words:

'But even as you protest and refuse to consent, do not look at the temptation itself but look straight at our Lord.'[1]

Madame de Chantal took this advice, and it worked, though not perhaps in the way she may at first have hoped. She was never delivered from these temptations, but she was taught how to live with them and make them serve to increase the faith she could neither see nor know as existing in herself. Her advice in later years to her own nuns in similar difficulties shows that she had thoroughly learnt and practised all she was taught in the early stages of her own spiritual life.

'She always overcame her temptations by her humility, her generous confidence in God, and by her promptness in repudiating them. We felt that her faith showed up most clearly on the most obscure mysteries of the faith: the Trinity, the Incarnation (which she called her favourite mystery), the Passion.'[2]

These then were the main points dealt with in the early correspondence following the meeting at Saint Claude. The process of direction, however, is not just a series of questions put and answers given, difficulties resolved, new resolutions put into effect; it is a dynamic process resulting in a change of attitude, in spiritual growth that only becomes really apparent at the next testing time, and may hardly be perceptible to the person chiefly concerned.

Early the following year (1605) Madame de Chantal felt that letters were not enough and another meeting was essential. In spite of the difficulties of a long journey and the not very encouraging attitude of her director to this project, she asked if she might visit him. In the end he agreed and invited her to stay with his mother at Thorens the week before Whitsun. She arrived at the castle on Saturday, 21 May, having travelled by Saint Claude and Gex where one of the bishop's men met her and brought her to Thorens via Geneva. 'Come joyfully, God is waiting for you. I pray that he may go close beside you for ever,' he wrote in the

[1] *Introduction to the Devout Life,* Bk. 4, Ch. 7.
[2] Canonization Process, Vol. 8; deposition of Mère Favre de Charmette.

little note to be delivered by the guide.[1] On the Saturday he himself rode up into the hills alone to welcome her, and tethering his horse, he sat and waited for some time in a barn by the wayside until she came. He told her later that it had been a time of intense prayer. He had asked her in a letter to prepare herself very carefully for this meeting and promised, for his part, to do the same.[2] She was to think out all she wanted to say, but then renounce her own will and ideas so as to be open to whatever God would put into her mind when the time came. Until then she was to be at peace, to have no anxiety about her preparation but cast all her care on God in absolute confidence, trusting too in his affection. 'Come joyfully in God who is your joy and consolation.'

It was her first visit to the Alps. After the steady climb from the plain of Geneva where the meadows already looked like summer, she entered into a new world of high, rocky mountains, fresh valleys where spring came late and where the fields were still carpeted with narcissi and dark blue columbines. The village of Thorens which they passed at some little distance as she and the bishop rode higher up the valley towards the castle of Sales, lies shaded by mountains throughout the winter season. The castle, a great ancient fortress with rambling buildings and a series of massive towers fortifying the wall, had been built on a plateau high above the river to guard the valley road as it issued out towards the plain. The valley narrows abruptly behind the castle. A sheer rock face and steep cliffs overshadow the road as it mounts towards the forests which lead to the pass high up beyond the head of the valley. From time immemorial this has been a fortified and strategic position, still exploited during the Second World War when the whole region and its pass, the Col-des-Glières, was one of the main centres of the Maquis. The castle stands at the meeting point of two worlds. On the far side, following the course of the river, the valley widens out into rolling, well-farmed country and open fields. The contrast between the two landscapes is impressive and almost disconcerting. The castle of Sales belongs to the austere world of the mountains, but by its wide view towards the south, it shares in the life of the plain. The position of the castle may be taken as in some sort symbolical of

[1] A, XIII, 45.
[2] A, XIII, 40.

the spirituality of the saint who was born there, a spirituality poised between two extremes, gentle and easy in its first aspect, of rock-like strength beneath.

The visitor stayed at Sales for ten days, sharing in the life of Madame de Boisy's large and happy household. The day began with mass at the house chapel, then there was time for work and prayer. After dinner, taken about an hour before midday, a siesta was the rule, and then before the afternoon sun grew cool, the bishop and his guest would walk and talk. Their interviews took place either in the gallery above the courtyard, or else out in the gardens overlooking the plain. The site of this garden is now occupied by an orchard rising gently towards a mound. Family tradition has it, and recent excavations have proved this to be true, that a little pagan temple stood on the hillock and that this is where the bishop and Madame de Chantal used to sit and talk. Keeping always in full view of the house where the main living rooms faced towards the plain, they would walk first through Madame de Boisy's herb garden, then along formally laid-out paths towards the temple which formed a natural goal. There they would sit and rest, looking back towards the house, the mountain escarpments and the forests rising steeply behind. It was an ideal setting for uninterrupted talk. Nor was the talk random. He had advised her to note down her passing thoughts and queries, and in her systematic way she had at once had a small book of blank pages bound in a size to fit her pocket. In this, her *Petit Livret* as she called it, she put down her questions and left a space for his reply, which she filled in later.[1]

[1] Copies of parts of the *Petit Livret* are preserved in the archives at Annecy and have been published in the Works, Vol. 2.

I owe the information about the layout of the gardens at Sales, and the oral traditions connected with Madame de Chantal's visit, to the kindness of the family now inhabiting the castle at Thorens, a few minutes' walk from the site of Sales. A farm now stands on the site of the ancient castle, the only part of which to survive is the saint's birthplace. This was made into a chapel in the seventeenth century. Underneath it are the family burial vaults. A small monument in the form of a cross marks the place of the Sales chapel where St Francis had his vision of the order he was to found. The inscription on it reads: '*Arcis Salesiae hic locus sacelli quo beato Francisco oranti Deus Ordinis Visitationis visionem tribuit*'—'This is the place where the chapel of the House of Sales once stood and where God vouchsafed the vision of the Order of the Visitation to Blessed Francis as he knelt in prayer.'

From the letters which he wrote to her afterwards, one has the impression that she was able, this time, to sort out all her problems at leisure, '*pour une bonne fois*', as she put it. What did they talk about? They went over the same main topics that had already come up over the past year but were now rather differently constellated, as well as enriched by experience, trial and error. She was a person who talked with great absorption and explained her meaning concisely. 'If you want me to talk', she said to her nuns in later years, 'don't just suggest a topic; ask me some definite questions, and then I shall know what to answer.' She herself now had such a clear-headed grasp of her situation that she knew what questions to ask. Nor is it likely that they all remained within the purely personal field. The bishop found in her a ready and intelligent listener to matters of wider spiritual import which he had at heart, more especially, perhaps, the reform of religious houses in which mutual friends were involved; and also the mission to the hugenots close by. In connection with this last point there were her own persistent doubts to discuss. He had instructed her in one letter to leave all further mention of them till they could actually talk. He will have told her of his work in the Chablais and may have shown her copies of his weekly printed leaflets on controversial points.[1] In any case, he helped her to see her difficulties in proportion by widening her knowledge and facing her with the actual facts and effects of heresy; this led her to see the contrast between reality and imagination, between apostasy as such and the unwilled speculations of one whose faith was fundamentally firm.

Her chief aim in coming was to learn how she could give herself more completely to God than she was already doing. In spite of herself, her mind dwelt on the idea of the cloister which seemed the final answer to 'her vehement desire to serve God without any obstacles'. (I, 71) Was he never going to take her out of the world, out of herself? Yes, came his slow and measured reply, one day it would happen, she would come to him and he would do his part, help her to go to God completely detached, divested of self. But not yet, for the time was not ripe, she herself not ready. Meanwhile what could prevent her from giving herself to God still more fully in her ordinary everyday life in the world? Was she

[1] *Controverses*, A, I.

prepared to do this, to hold the world as nothing while playing her full part in it? To want nothing of the world but only to want God, for time and for eternity? Her answer was unconditional and whole-hearted. She would give herself to God's love completely, and, as she said, pray for God to consume her and change her into himself; henceforward the world itself would be her cloister and her enclosure invisible. To make this idea more vivid to her he suggested that our Lady should be her abbess, St Monica, the model of a widow and mother, her novice mistress; these holders of office in Madame de Chantal's invisible cloister play quite a part in the bishop's letters from now on and give her messages with much good advice.

Towards the end of the week the bishop left to go to Annecy for the Whitsun ordinations, while she stayed on to spend the feast with his mother. She left on Whit-Tuesday, taking with her the youngest daughter of the house, Jeanne de Sales, who was to go to school in France at Madame de Puys d'Orbe's convent in Burgundy.

'I want us to call these days the days of our dedication because this is when you gave yourself so irrevocably to God,' he wrote to her before she left. 'I want these days when God made you all his to live forever in your mind . . . and our resolutions, made with such strength and courage, to remain deeply hidden beneath the precious seal with which my hand sealed them' (in holy communion).[1]

Their correspondence takes on a different note after this meeting. Not that all problems suddenly ceased; rather the contrary: her temptations assailed her with increased vigour. But she writes of them against a background of peace and certainty, unfelt by her for the most part, but perceptible to anyone outside from the nature and tone of the answers she receives. There is a sense of steady and settled progress from which there was never, in spite of all suffering, to be any return. Much more is taken for granted between them. She knows what has got to be done, how it is to be done, and her part is simply to do it, to live, to suffer, to grow in grace. At the same time, their personal relationship as director and directed becomes ever more supernaturally effective and therefore closer.

[1] A, XIII, 51.

Thorens

Madame de Chantal in 1607. The Chambéry Portrait
Visitation, Saint Pierre d'Albigny, Savoy

'No, nothing could possibly separate your soul from mine, the link is too strong; death itself cannot break it because it is fashioned from a substance that lasts to all eternity.'[1]

And yet, she is a very human person, so he thinks fit to caution her: all her trust and obedience is to go out to God alone, even if he himself should die; but meanwhile he will listen to her advice, he says, and try to spare himself a little so as not to die just yet.

She went back courageously to face her life at Monthelon and Dijon. She felt now that she belonged to God more completely than ever before, and that by virtue of that very thing that had seemed almost to destroy her life at the time: her widowhood and her vow to remain a widow. It was therefore with real horror that she recoiled from the suggestion made at about this time, and very persuasively put by her own father, that she should marry again. The man in question was in every way acceptable, and it was not from him that she recoiled, nor did her refusal reflect her general feeling about the married state as such. She continued to honour it in her own past and in her friends all around her, but she knew and felt that it was not for her. Her road lay elsewhere. She did not know yet exactly where. For the present, she found her vocation in the acceptance of her lowliness, her solitude in the eyes of the world.

The bishop did not spare her in driving home this lesson:

'It's not really surprising that a poor little widow should feel feeble and wretched. What do you expect? Do you see her as someone far-sighted, strong, constant and self-sufficient? Accept joyfully the fact that your state of mind matches your state of life, and that you are a widow, lowly and abject in every way, except that you don't offend God. The other day I saw a widow in a procession of the Blessed Sacrament, and while the others were carrying large candles of white wax she held a tiny tallow candle which she had probably manufactured herself; and to make things worse, the wind blew it out. This didn't mean that she was either closer or further away from the Blessed Sacrament; she got to the church just as soon as everybody else.'[2]

As was his way, he gave her a concrete picture to think about, a

[1] A, XIII, 52.
[2] *Selected Letters*, p. 93 f.

little parable which helped to shape her attitude at a deeper level, to be detached from her state and survey it dispassionately. As she grappled with the everyday difficulties and humiliations of her life at her father-in-law's house, she could see herself in this image, carrying her small candle as a '*chetifve et pauvrette vefve*',[1] and learn to love her littleness.

A widow had few rights, little social status and no glory. The man whose name she bore and who gave her honour was dead, she had given him the best of her own life. What could she now glory in, except God? 'O blessed glory, o precious crown' writes the bishop, explaining it all to her in letter after letter. Humility, he says, is the recognition of our poverty and nothingness. But that alone is not enough. The right thing is Christian humility, a real love of our poverty and abjection as we look upon our Lord's lowliness, glorying in it because it was also his. The widow's life should follow that of the Master, his name be engraved and inscribed on her heart.[2]

It will strike a modern reader with something of a shock that Madame de Chantal took this metaphorical idea quite literally, perhaps with some unconscious notion that the actual, concrete inscribing of the Holy Name on her own person would hasten the ultimate spiritual reality of belonging to God. Taking a small pointed steel instrument, a knitting needle perhaps, she made it red hot in the fire and branded herself with the name of Jesus in the place above her heart. She did this kneeling in front of a crucifix which now hangs in the Chapter Room at the Annecy Visitation. According to the nuns who prepared her body for burial many years later, she used capital letters about an inch high, well formed and distinct. Though the temper of the time may to some extent explain this action, it remains essentially one in keeping with her particular character. It also at last convinced her family that she was in earnest about her refusal to marry again. For her seemingly extravagant gesture had, as often in her case, a second practical object: the disfiguring scars which formed the letters would now make the wearing of a worldly state dress, with its obligatory decolleté, impossible. The letters might have shown even above the neckline of a dress such as she is wearing in the

[1] A, XIII, 392c.
[2] *Introduction to the Devout Life*, Bk. III, Ch. 23; see also Ch. 40.

Chambéry portrait.[1] She could not make a new social beginning in the very simple high-necked clothes she now wore.

The bishop, hearing of this action, did not approve of it although she had obtained a local confessor's consent. Accepting what was once done, however, he gently directed her thoughts back to the real point of the outer gesture:

'I thought: who will give me the joy of seeing the name of Jesus deep down in your innermost heart as it is branded high over your heart? O how I longed to have the steel of our Saviour's lance in one hand, your heart in the other. Indeed I should have written boldly.'[2]

This image with its baroque symbolism of the heart was always represented in the earliest pictures of St Jane Frances. She is shown holding her own heart on which the name of Jesus is inscribed and this became her emblem and attribute. The incident was also mentioned in her Canonization Bull of 1767. The mystery which attracted her above all others was that of Jesus Incarnate, his humanity, his love, the heart to which she wanted her own to conform so absolutely as to be branded with his name. What she was moved to do in this startling outward way, her director helped her to implement spiritually, conforming her heart ever more nearly to that of Jesus. His name was written large on all she did. St Francis encouraged her in the humble works of mercy, teaching her to fit them into her life as a widow. The chatelaine of Bourbilly had been her own mistress; now she nursed the sick on sufferance and gave to the poor against constant opposition. But the bishop was happy, '*bien ayse*', as he said, about this extra sting, and also about the repugnance which she now admitted to feeling in the physically revolting tasks she imposed on herself; for when a humbly admitted repugnance replaces the youthful exaltation and the heroic glow in well-doing, and yet there is dogged perseverance, then good works really do rise above the natural level, while humility is at the same time safeguarded.[3]

[1] This portrait, facing p. 81, was painted when Madame de Chantal was in her early thirties. She is wearing a sumptuous black velvet dress adorned with vividly coloured, jewelled embroidery. It may have been a picture commissioned by Frémyot in view of a second marriage, a fact which perhaps accounts for the expression on his daughter's face.

[2] A, XIII, 76.

[3] A, XIII, 356.

Her biographer reports her nursing with all the detail of an age accustomed to plain speaking in these matters. Lepers and people with cancerous growths are especially prominent in these accounts, for they most struck the popular imagination and their plight was greatest. But the poor, and tramps of every kind also found their way to Monthelon and were given their full share of attention. It was all methodically organized. First they were fed and washed. They were given a spare set of clean clothes always kept in readiness, then Madame de Chantal would herself wash, boil and thus disinfect the clothes if they were verminous. When garments were just torn and dusty, she would mend them; arrayed in a large white apron, and with white linen sleeve-covers slipped over her own, she would stand at her table beating and brushing the clothes. Her dispensary in the little room above the chapel had neatly arranged shelves with jars of healing oint-ment and medicines which she herself had made up with her skilled knowledge of herbs. '*Propre et bien rangé comme la boutique de Madame de Chantal*' was a proverbial expression in the country-side to designate tidy cleanliness. Day in, day out, in heat and cold, 'for this faithful servant of our Lord was always admirable in her perseverance in whatever she undertook to do' (1, 80), she visited the sick in their homes, made their beds, cleaned and bathed them, cheered them, prayed with them and brought them medicine and food. On Sundays she allowed the children to come with her and carry her baskets, knowing how to turn these expeditions into a much longed-for treat. When death came to a poor house, it was considered the right and privilege of *Madame la Sainte Baronne* to wash the body and lay it out in a shroud.

She persevered in her nursing for all the eight years she spent in the Monthelon district, and this work, done for Christ's sake and taken together with her constant labour in other ways, her prayer and rule of life faithfully kept, her teaching and care of the children, the treatment she received at the hands of the difficult servant, constituted the kind of spiritual training in which holiness can take firm root. No illusions were possible about this life: it was much too hard. Like that of her director who had served a difficult apprenticeship as a missionary in the Chablais, her own spirituality had a hard core of practical strength and common sense. In her later life she was known for the loving but firm way she was able to dispel pious illusions in merely sentimental women.

Corporal works of mercy seem so striking and self-explanatory that they may easily be considered as an end in themselves, especially now that they are called social work, and often divorced from any spiritual dimension. They are concerned with the basic situations—hunger, thirst, cold, homelessness, illness, captivity and death—in which suffering humanity is seen at its most helpless. For some people the sight of this misery tends to become all-absorbing and to obscure the spiritual background; for others spiritual meaning breaks through with an almost unbearable clarity. Madame de Chantal belonged to this last group. Her faith, against which she felt so tempted, was so strong and so literal that she took the words: 'I was hungry and you fed me, I was homeless and you took me in', quite simply at their face value. She served Christ in the vagrant, visited him in hovels, sheltered him in the leper who lay helpless in her little hospital. It needed no effort of the imagination: the spiritual realm was as real to her as the world of actual phenomena. Not more real, for she was exceptionally well balanced. She was not able to ignore matter, and never attempted it, but with a steady realism she fully accepted both matter and form in herself and in others. Her whole life, her particular type of sanctity as it developed over the years under St Francis's influence, are an illustration of this basic tendency. That is why everything she did in the material realm seemed to feed and further what was spiritual in her.

'Share thy bread with the hungry, give the poor and the vagrant a welcome to thy house; meet thou the naked, clothe him; from thy own flesh and blood turn not away. Then, suddenly as the dawn, the welcome light shall break on thee, in a moment thy health shall find a new spring; divine favour shall lead thee on thy journey, brightness of the Lord's presence close thy ranks behind. Then the Lord will listen to thee when thou callest on him; cry out, and he will answer, I am here at thy side.'[1]

This was fulfilled in her always, and even on one occasion, in a way that she could perceive.

One evening in early summer—it was Trinity Sunday—she was walking along a pathway that led through the fields close to

[1] Isaias, LVIII, 7–9; Epistle for the first Friday in Lent. (Knox version).

Monthelon. The castle lies remote from the main road and at some distance from the village; not many travellers pass that way by chance. Her walk took her through the rolling meadowland of the plain where on the one hand, the distant horizon gives a sense of openness and space, while on the other, dark, rocky hills close in upon the town of Autun a few miles away. She was alone. Suddenly, looking up, she saw three men coming towards her, young and well favoured, not beggars and yet obviously in need. They stopped her and asked for alms for the love of God. She had no purse with her, and the only valuable of any kind—she had long ago put off all other jewellery—was a ring she had taken from her husband's finger after his death. She greatly treasured it for his sake, but immediately removing it from her hand, she gave it to the stranger who had addressed her, begging him to share the gift with the others, as this was all she had. They thanked her courteously, told her they were good friends and would not quarrel about the sharing: what was given to one was given to all. As they spoke, she was suddenly seized with a vivid sense of the divine presence, she knelt down there and then on the bare ground and kissed their feet. They did not seek to hinder her, and having said good-bye, walked away, but in what direction she could never afterwards remember. At that moment it seemed to her that she fell in love with the poor for good and all. Walking back to the castle in the evening light she made a vow never to refuse alms asked of her in God's name.

Her biographer leaves it as an open question whether, like Abraham in the valley of Mamre, she had met with heavenly messengers. Such meetings with needy strangers, or with one at first unrecognized pilgrim, often feature in the lives of holy people, in folk-lore, also in dreams.[1] The number here, the relationship between them, implies the Trinity. Whatever the variation of detail, the archetypal situation is always the same: it is a testing, a demand made which can only be fulfilled by an absolute response and complete commitment in a spirit of faith. In the moment of recognition when faith, as it were, becomes vision, the stranger is lost from sight. He has played his part. This meeting, which impressed itself as an authentic spiritual experience

[1] *Psychologie der Legende. Studien zu einer wissenschaftlichen Heiligen-Geschichte,* Heinrich Günter, Freiburg 1949.

on Madame de Chantal, may be taken as setting the seal on the years of her widowhood she spent at Monthelon. The highest value of her life hitherto had been her marriage and her love for her husband. This, by token of the ring, she gave away freely to the needy strangers, to the unknown three who asked her for a gift and before whom she knelt in veneration. In Christ's poor, she pledged herself lovingly to her own poverty as a widow, to her hidden, humble life, to her own spiritual neediness before God, to the unknown, solitary future which was to succeed the known and loved companionship of the past with all its certainties. During these years she learnt to accept her widowhood fully, and she was shown a way by which her great powers of love released could stream forth to embrace the whole of suffering humanity.

That evening at Monthelon the three strangers, Three in One, accepted her offering of what she held most dear, sharing it in the ineffable communication of power, wisdom and love. The God Incarnate with whose name she was signed had led her closer to the final mystery of the Godhead: the Trinity. A few years later on this same feast day of the Holy Trinity, she confirmed her self-offering when she entered on her religious life at Annecy.

Chapter 5

THE YEARS BETWEEN
1607-1609

～◦◉◦～

Madame de Chantal visited Annecy for the first time in 1607, at Whitsun. The year 1606 had seen no meeting between her and the bishop though many letters had passed, sometimes as many as two or three a week on her part, consolidating and confirming all that had been discussed before. It had been an exceptionally busy year for him, with Lenten sermons preached at Chambéry, formerly the capital of Savoy, and with an arduous visitation of his large and scattered mountain diocese. She had spent Lent at Dijon, and after a hot summer at Monthelon there followed a seven weeks' stay at Bourbilly. A dysentery epidemic broke out during the time of the harvest so that she found full scope for her nursing skill. In the end she herself fell seriously ill and only recovered as though by a miracle, getting up from her sick-bed immediately to mount the saddle and try to out-distance the messenger who was taking alarming news of her illness to Dijon. Her habit of long, hard riding is a feature of her life right up to her old age, a proof not only of her physical stamina but of her exceptional will-power. She used the solitude of these rides for prayer. The psalms, she found, expressed her every mood and/or need, she said or chanted them as she rode, using the rhymed version of Philippe Desportes. Most of the psalms she knew by heart, but the little book was always ready to hand in a purse that she had had specially made and attached to the front of her saddle.[1]

---

[1] *Les Psaumes de David mis en vers francois*, by Abbé Philippe Desportes, Antwerp 1603. Her own copy of this book, which went with her on all her travels, is now in the Visitation archives at Annecy.

The ride from Burgundy to Savoy on this occasion was a particularly strenuous one. The bishop had named a day at the end of May. He was to meet her at Thorens and then accompany her and his mother to Annecy. Urgent business delayed her for a couple of days at Monthelon so that she started out late; but in her anxiety to render him absolute obedience and not to keep him waiting, she made up time by staying long hours in the saddle, even continuing her journey throughout one whole night of thunder and torrential rain. She arrived on time. Torn between admiration for her obedience and pity for her literalness, he tried again to explain to her that she should look to his kindly intention and not cling to a rigorous interpretation of his word. It took her some years to learn this lesson; she was not only in love with obedience, but still tended to act compulsively.

Their meeting in 1607 followed the same pattern as before. She gave him a full account of what had been happening in her soul and they also discussed practical difficulties. St Francis had had legal training in Italy and much administrative experience so that he was often able to advise her on complications arising out of her children's estate and inheritance. From the correspondence it appears that she, like most other people of substance at this time in France, was involved in lawsuits. But for the time being he said nothing on the subject of her call to the religious life, the matter which was actually uppermost in both their minds. It had again been the subject of a long letter some months before, and since then had not been mentioned. She tried, according to his advice, to keep herself in an attitude of complete indifference about the future, emptying her heart of all personal desire one way or the other. It seems that she succeeded. In this letter he had again warned her to be careful not to let her fancy roam in this matter:

'Finding yourself absorbed in the hope and idea of entering religion, you are afraid of having offended against obedience. No, I did not tell you not to hope for it and think of it, but only not to linger over such thoughts and dwell on them; because it is quite certain that nothing so much hinders us from reaching perfection in our own state of life as longing for another. Instead of tilling the field in which we have been put, we send our plough and oxen elsewhere, into our neighbour's field, where of course we cannot reap any harvest this year. And all this is sheer waste of time, and when our thoughts and hopes are set in another direction, we cannot possibly set our hearts steadily on the virtues needed in the place in which we find ourselves.'[1]

He was himself certain that one day he would advise her leave everything, '*tout quitter*', but precisely what form her new life would take he did not know. He did not as yet see her in religion, that is, in any of the established orders known to him, the Poor Clares, the Carmelites, the nursing order at Beaune in Burgundy, the Ursulines. He also wanted to be quite certain that her own consent, when the time came, was based on 'great tranquillity and a sense of deep inner agreement'.[2]

After high mass on Whit Monday 4 June, he himself escorted her from the cathedral to his house on the opposite side of the road, and after questioning her again in his slow and deliberate way to see whether she really was 'as wax softened by divine warmth, and disposed to accept any and every form of religious life he might choose to suggest to her' (1, 96) he explained in full detail his plan for the foundation of a new and at this time completely original institute. As she listened—at the beginning of their interview she had knelt to receive his instructions, then he had raised her and they were now walking slowly up and down in his reception room—she felt precisely that inner certainty and peace which he had hoped for and which had been lacking in the case of all other suggestions. Even so, he at once told her that the plan would have to mature slowly and wait for another six or seven years at least. She agreed. There were two great barriers to overcome, and they would in time be overcome, he said, in ways unknown to human surmise: the just claims of her family, notably of her father and father-in-law, even when her children were old enough; and in the second place, the difficulty of founding the institute in his own town of Annecy where he foresaw great opposition. But he was certain that it could only begin here 'in this town of Annecy where God had shown him, as it were a spring of sweet water, small in its beginnings, but serving as the fountain-head of many a great and beautiful river.' (1, 96) '*La Sainte Source*', as the first Visitation has always been called, was in fact founded at Annecy three years later, much sooner than either

[1] *Selected Letters*, p. 123 f.
[2] A, XIII, 208.

of the founders could at that time have imagined, and by ways they could not have foreseen.

Madame de Chantal stayed with Madame de Boisy at Annecy until 25 June, that is, a full three weeks longer. She had the joy of sharing in the Whitsuntide ceremonies in the cathedral, the ordinations on Whit Saturday, the processions of the Blessed Sacrament at Corpus Christi through the town.

'And so come, my very dear daughter, come', he had written to her in May 1607; 'may your guardian angel be close beside you and bring you safely. When you see how small my house is, how simple my way of life and everything else, you will be consoled; but how glad you will be, too, when you hear our beautiful office, for this is my chapter's special excellence.' (A, XIII, 287.)

It was the first time she had seen the bishop in his own official home as the spiritual and temporal head of a large diocese, an aspect very different from the intimate family atmosphere at Thorens.

The visitor who goes to the basilica of the Visitation at Annecy now and sees some great ceremony, for instance the golden jubilee of a direct successor to St Francis de Sales, a bishop[1] in whose honour a cardinal, several archbishops and many other dignitaries have gathered together, has that same impression of a sudden change of focus and emphasis. He may himself have arrived by way of Thorens, still peaceful in its mountain valley, untouched by pomp and circumstance. In the privacy of his own home he may be familiar with the writings of St Francis de Sales, his letters, his ascetical and mystical works, all in the last instance addressed intimately and individually to a single person—and in solitude he can identify himself with that person. But when he watches the ceremonies at the basilica it is suddenly brought home to him: the founder of this institute was a prince of the church, a bishop with all the dignity and power that the episcopal order imparts and implies. Madame de Chantal saw her director as a public figure, and that in a far greater degree than at Dijon three years previously, when he had only been a visitor.

As a diocesan centre, Annecy had always remained an improvisation; the natural focus of this see was Geneva, from which catholics had been expelled during the sixteenth century. The

[1] Bishop Cesbron's golden jubilee, 30 June 1960.

town itself was small and relatively unimportant except for its great fortress which was a ducal residence. There were also one or two ancient churches, the largest of which, St Peter, a plain, dark, early gothic structure, served as cathedral to the exiled bishop. The main entrance is reached from a short flight of steps standing sideways on to a narrow street. Opposite is the bishop's residence, a house that just happened to be there, and not a palace specially built. Immediately beyond the cathedral, behind the high altar, there is a canal, one of many which form a network of waterways between the arcaded streets of the old town, little changed from the saint's time. Behind St Francis's house flows the river, crossed by a series of little bridges. These link the centre with the approaches to the rocky hill from which the fortress guards the inner town. The end of the lake, a long drawn out stretch of transparent, very blue water, lies at a few minutes' distance from the cathedral and outside what was at that time the city precinct. High mountains stretch along the far side of the lake, and the most striking group, the Tournette, a cluster of grey, rugged peaks, dolomitic in their pitted outline, forms the characteristic landmark of the whole region, whether jutting out snow-covered against a winter sky or mirrored in the lake on still summer days. On the near side, behind the town, forests cover the slopes of the Semnoz mountain. It is on this hill, overlooking town and lake, that the new Visitation and its basilica have been built. Far below, by the waterside in a suburb just outside the city gates, lies the Galerie, a small house where the convent was first established in 1610.

Madame de Chantal saw this place of great natural beauty at its best, in early summer. Released from all cares and responsibilities for a while, free to pray, to walk, to talk, be silent, close to people who meant much to her, it must have been a holiday of rare delight. Madame de Boisy and her family introduced her to the ladies of local society who soon found their way to her, some from curiosity, says her biographer, some from a genuine desire to meet a person who already had a reputation for a great but unostentatious piety. As always, and without in the least intending it, she attracted all who came to her. When she returned for good three years later, she did not come to a city of strangers.

Among the people she herself liked best was one of the bishop's younger brothers, Bernard. Returning tired after a procession one day, she wanted to go to her room and rest before dinner. A number of gentlemen who stood aside to let her pass and noticed her fatigue as she began to walk up the stairs, ran forward to assist her; she declined their help, but then, noticing the youthful, eager persistence of Bernard, she smiled. '*Vraiment, je veux bien celui-ci pour mon partage,*' she said. 'He'll do very well for me.' This preference was reported to Bernard's mother who at once used the incident as an opportunity for putting forward an idea that she had probably been turning over in her mind for some time: that the houses of Sales and Chantal should be joined together, and that Bernard should marry Marie-Aymée de Chantal, the elder daughter. The bishop was somewhat taken aback; he felt a little uncomfortable at the suddenness of the whole idea and at having to discuss it with his visitor. Madame de Chantal was also much astonished, but as neither of them wanted to offend St Francis's mother, they were at pains to hide their reaction, and tactfully entered into the plan with her. Madame de Chantal thanked her for the great honour done to her house, but feared that the girl's grand-fathers might not want her to leave France and settle so far from home. She was, as her biographer puts it, humbly non-committal.

After that, events began to move swiftly. She reached home early in July, and in the course of the summer, went to the convent school at Puys d'Orbe to fetch Jeanne de Sales who was to live with her for a while. They went first to the Bourbilly region, staying at her father's house in nearby Thostes, probably in the company of the president's other grand-children. The wine harvest in Burgundy was a time of rejoicing and feasting, not only of hard work, and the children shared in all the excitement. It was also the time of dreaded epidemics, especially of enteric fevers. Primitive hygienic conditions seem to have provided little safeguard against this scourge, even under Madame de Chantal's watchful eye. Jeanne fell ill, and in spite of the most devoted nursing, she died on 7 October 1607.

The death of this girl who had been entrusted to her in a special way by both her mother and her brother, was a terrible blow to Madame de Chantal. She prayed at her bedside, distractedly offering her own life, and then as something even dearer, the life of one of her own children in exchange for this one. At this stage of her life, when her passionate feelings were involved, especially in the too familiar situation of a deathbed, she did not hesitate to bargain with God. The resignation which she showed in later years was very clearly the work of grace acting on a woman of powerful impulse.

'I seem to see you here in front of me, my dear daughter,' wrote the bishop on this occasion, 'with your vigorous heart which loves and wills powerfully. I like it for that, for what is the use of these half dead hearts?'[1]

But though he understood her well enough, he was shocked that she should have bargained. No, he said to her; make a particular practice of wanting and loving God's will more vigorously than anything else in the world. Be willing to let God strike where he thinks fit:

'Lord Jesus, may your will be done upon father, mother, daughter, in everything and in every way, without any qualification, without an if, without a but, without any exception, without any reserves.'

So as to teach her, indirectly and courteously, he gave her a full description of how his mother had taken the news, going to the chapel to pray: not a word of impatience, not a moment's loss of peace, no rebellion. Madame de Chantal needed this lesson, and this is what makes her so human: the long, slow process of sanctification is seen at work in her. It is a comfort that she did not begin perfect and that the bishop's letters are still there to prove it.

After she had prepared Jeanne's body for burial and written to Savoy, a more reasonable idea came to her as she kept watch in the silent house. Remembering her conversation with the girl's mother four months ago, she realized that this was an opportunity for honouring Madame de Boisy's expressed wish. She made a vow to do her utmost to overcome all opposition to the marriage proposal and to give her own elder daughter in exchange for the one who had died. Marie-Aymée was nine years old and the earliest age considered suitable for marriage was eleven. The plan would have to wait but it could be got under way and meanwhile Madame de Boisy could be informed. It was not till then, as she knelt in prayer to confirm her vow, that the full implications of this plan began to dawn on her. In view of her attitude of dis-

[1] *Selected Letters*, p. 142.

interested candour in everything that concerned herself, this sounds true to life. Her daughter's marriage might serve as a bridge for her to leave home as well and begin her new life in Savoy. The two younger girls could come with her, for the kind of institute that was planned would allow of this; Celse-Bénigne was in any case being educated at Dijon and much better in the care of the men of the family. But the reaction of her father and her father-in-law was another matter; she feared not only their opposition, but her own grief on their behalf.

As soon as she could she told her father the first part of her plan. He was sorry to think of losing Marie-Aymée who was his favourite; but he honoured the bishop and his family, and could see that from every worldly point of view the match was to his grand-daughter's advantage. Moreover, like everyone at this time, he had absolute respect for a religious vow, and the one his daugher had made seemed both valid and just to this fair-minded man. He wrote a letter to Annecy. But at Monthelon, where the bishop was not known and loved as a friend, opposition was not so easily overcome, and consent when at last given was grudging. It was not until Francis, an effective peace-maker, had written one of his most persuasive letters that the family tension was somewhat eased.[1] He announced that he would do himself the honour of waiting personally on Monsieur de Chantal, together with his brother Bernard, in the course of the following year.

He wrote to Madame de Chantal telling her that he was praying for the success of the visit, saying mass for the old baron, and that he felt confident in his power to establish good relations with him.[2] Madame de Chantal, for her part, also took an optimistic view of the situation and wrote a note to Madame de Boisy:

Madam, my very good Mother,

And now our grandfathers are considering the matter, for by God's grace, they greatly desire the honour of an alliance with you. Surely then, we can now be very certain, my dear Mother, that all is well with your desire and mine, by God's dear grace? And now all that remains for me is to ask God to make this girl really pleasing to you, beautiful and good, worthy of the great honour of joining your house

[1] A, XIII, 343; 1 December 1607.
[2] A, XIV, 34.

and family. To be the sister of such men—what happiness! I will not try to express all I feel on that score. May God find his glory in this, our children their salvation and peace, you yourself and all who belong to you, much joy and consolation. With all my heart which is and wants to be for ever yours, Madam, my very dear Mother, I send you and them greetings.

Your very humble and most obedient servant,

Monthelon, 16 April, 1608. FRÉMYOT.[1]

The Bishop of Geneva had received a papal commission for arbitrating in a dispute between the clergy of Burgundy and the Archduke of Austria for the use of salt-mines in the Besançon area. He was also put in charge of the reform of the Benedictine Abbey of Puys d'Orbe where his young sister had been a boarder. It was on the occasion of this journey, in the course of which he also visited Dijon again, that he went to Monthelon with his brother Bernard. No details of this visit are known. It seems to have been a success, for as a result the civil marriage contract between Bernard and Marie-Aymée was signed a few months later at Thostes. He reached Monthelon on 24 August 1608, having, according to her desire, dispatched a messenger from a village near Autun to let Madame de Chantal know the exact time of his arrival. He wrote her one of his warm, characteristic notes:

'Here we are at your gates, my very dear daughter . . . and didn't I say it would be somewhere about the time of St Louis' feast day?' (A reminder of Saint Claude four years ago.) 'I bring you a heart full of longing to help yours and to do all the good we possibly can. In about three hours' time, I shall see you, please God.'[2]

After spending the day paying formal ecclesiastical visits in Autun, and seeing the cathedral with its impressive sculpture, the bishop and his party continued on their way to Monthelon towards the evening when the heat in the plain was less intense. When the old baron and Madame de Chantal and her children had greeted their guests, and the ten-year-old Marie-Aymée had been presented to Bernard, the visitors walked up the flight of steps to enter the castle. '*Virtus vulnere virescit*', the motto that Madame de Chantal saw when she first came up those steps seven years earlier,

---

[1] *Oeuvres*, IV, 3. Only two letters survive from before 1611, and this is one of them.

[2] A, XIV, 60.

was there for the bishop to read. As he walked in and out of the house during the next few days which gave him a first personal insight into the conditions in which she had to live, his eyes must often have rested thoughtfully on those words.

The servant who had caused so much of the trouble had not changed. She had promised to use her influence with the old baron to bring about a match with another prospective suitor for Marie-Aymée. Seeing herself foiled, she launched an intensive campaign of calumny against Madame de Chantal. This time the trouble-maker really managed to win over the old man completely. Soon after the civil contract was signed in January of the following year, 1609, he sent off a messenger to Dijon to complain to the president of his daughter's supposed outrages. Frémyot, his suspicions aroused, asked her to explain. She did, and for the first time told him plainly what had been going on at Monthelon and who was responsible. On receiving her letter, he spent a sleepless night blaming himself for his blindness, and her for her brave but misguided reticence. He summoned her and the three girls to Dijon and wanted to insist on a permanent removal; for as yet, he knew nothing of her plans for the future. But she temporized and asked instead for his permission to make another journey to Savoy so as to introduce Marie-Aymée to her future mother-in-law and the de Sales family. Françoise, the second girl, was to accompany them and so was a friend of long standing, Charlotte de Bréchard, who had recently met St Francis at Monthelon and had put herself under his direction. She felt drawn to the religious life, and was to be one of the foundation members of the new institute when the time came. Madame de Chantal was glad of her company.

The bishop was preaching at home in Annecy that year, and so as not to miss the Lenten sermons, the party from Dijon left in early spring. It was a more sedate journey than Madame de Chantal's previous rough rides; they travelled in a carriage because of the children, making slow progress over muddy roads in an exceptionally wet season. '*Ma mere desire que vous facies vostre petit delassement a Sales*', 'My mother would like you to have a little rest at Sales', the bishop had written.[1] So the visitors stayed there first, then together with Madame de Boisy they went on to Annecy

[1] A, XIV, 130.

arriving there during the first week of Lent. Madame de Chantal was welcomed as an old friend, and while there was little formal visiting because of the penitential season, the devout ladies of the country all around managed to renew their acquaintance with her. They also came to have a look at her children, one of whom was soon to join their circle in Savoy by marrying into their bishop's family.

The devotional atmosphere in the town was at that time heightened by the general excitement over the success of the bishop's book, *The Introduction to the Devout Life*, which had just appeared and had become a best-seller overnight. The people of the town and all his many personal friends were proud of him and they did him honour in the way most likely to go straight to his heart: they came in great numbers to the churches to follow the sermons, and showed exceptional fervour in the other exercises of the season. Madame de Chantal and her friend took a full share in everything until the ceremonies worked up to the great climax of Holy Week. On the night of Maundy Thursday the confraternity of the Holy Cross which the two friends joined, visited all the altars of repose in Annecy, that is, the altar where the Blessed Sacrament is reserved till Good Friday. Madame de Chantal put on the white penitential habit of the confraternity. Secretly, as she thought, but observed by Charlotte who later recounted it, she slipped off her shoes and walked barefoot all that night as the torchlight procession of white figures wound its way slowly along ill-paved streets and through icy churches. On Good Friday she knelt at the bishop's feet to renew her vow of chastity and of obedience.

The children were often in the charge of Madame de Boisy who took them straight to her heart. Perhaps with some presentiment —she died in March the following year, and before Marie-Aymée's return—she expressed a wish to keep Bernard's fiancée in Savoy. Although very young marriages were not exceptional at this time, and Madame de Boisy herself had borne her first son, Francis, when she was not yet fifteen, it was considered more prudent to delay the religious ceremony and have it later in Burgundy. Even after that, the families agreed to wait a further time for the young couple actually to set up house together. The marriage was fixed for October and Marie-Aymée was to transfer to Savoy the following spring. It is not known whether Madame de Boisy was in her son's confidence in the matter of the new institute; it seems unlikely: Madame de Chantal had not as yet spoken to her own father about it.

When the Dijon party left for home after Easter, this was the subject uppermost in her mind: how was she to break the news to her father? She stayed with him for the next few weeks, returning to Monthelon at intervals to see to the arrangements she had made there for the poor and to visit the people in the villages. At every journey, it is told, she brought back several large boxes full of papers, documents about the villagers' legal affairs on which she got them free advice from her father. This work of charity brought the two very close together, and while he spent hours patiently dictating instructions to her, the bond that united them seemed to grow stronger all the time. However clear her vocation, its certainty could do nothing to lessen the pain that she herself felt and was about to give. Carefully she watched her opportunity, but no day or hour seemed right. At last, on the feast day of St John the Baptist, 24 June, she made up her mind. Her biographer has left an account of this in her own words; it is a story that Madame de Chantal often told.

In the evening she found herself alone in the house with her father. Children and servants had gone out into the city streets, listening to the midsummer music and looking at the huge bonfires in the squares. It was the special feast of the apprentices, and young people were dancing and singing all over the town. The president was in his study, at work over some documents. Madame de Chantal went up to his door, but even as her hand reached out to open it, her courage failed her. She knelt down, sent up a heart-felt prayer, and then walked into the room, strengthened. Gradually she brought the conversation to the point. She felt the time had come to remove the girls finally from Monthelon because they were beginning to understand too clearly what was going on there. Marie-Aymée was, of course, to go soon in any case. Françoise and Charlotte, said her father, entering into her difficulties, could be sent to the Ursulines for their schooling, and to see if by any chance they had a vocation to the cloister. As to the boy, he was in Dijon already. The word 'cloister' gave her her cue. With a beating heart she told him that

the arrangements he had suggested would leave her free to follow
her own calling to the religious life to which she had felt drawn
now for many years.

The president was a devout man who had himself, at one time,
moved heaven and earth to follow his own vocation to the priesthood, and failed; but his daughter was surely in a different case.
How could she possibly consider leaving her fatherless children,
and himself in his old age? He reproached her, without anger, but
in a way calculated to move her far more deeply. She says that she
suffered martyrdom that day. When she told him that nothing was
as yet decided although Francis de Sales thought it was a right
inspiration and should in conscience be followed, the president
grew calmer. There was hope here. The bishop was a man of God;
but he also had common sense. His final word to his daughter was
that she should decide nothing further till he had himself talked it
all over with her director. They both knew that this could not be till
about three months later, at Marie-Aymée's wedding in October.
The president hoped that he would have made her see reason by
then. She knew, and told him, that 'God would have made his will
clear to them, and that she, for her part, was prepared to put aside
her own feelings and do precisely what the bishop and her father
would tell her to do.' (I, III) Her confidence was boundless, and
in a different way, so was his. They were both the happier for the
complete openness that was now restored between them.

Her brother André was also taken into the secret and returned
a categorical 'no' to the whole proposition. This second interview
with her brother took place at Thostes where the family had
retired during the heat of the late summer. To him she had the
heart to speak far more openly, and as a sister, not a daughter. She
knew that he had been instructed to talk her into reason, so she
gave him a full account of the past few years and of the state of her
conscience in the whole matter. She also explained that to her it
had by this time become all a matter of obedience, that if the
bishop told her to stay in the world after all, she would do it; if he
told her to perch herself on the top of a column in the desert, like
Symeon Stylites, she would not hesitate; but if he told her to help
him found an order, she would do that. She was not looking in the
first instance for any special way of life—those days were over—
but for obedience. André was impressed, took counsel with his

father, and together they decided not to insist any further until the bishop came.

He arrived at Monthelon for the marriage which took place on Tuesday 13 October 1609. He and Bernard were accompanied by their brother Louis to represent the rest of the de Sales family. The ceremony took place in the village church as the house chapel was very small.[1] The marriage was undoubtedly a splendid affair, for Baron de Chantal was used to entertaining on a grand scale. It was an event of importance in local society and in the whole countryside.

It is true, of course, that this marriage was, in a sense, the key-move that opened the way for the next one, but it seems a little hard that in the account of this occasion, Madame de Chantal's problems occupy the forefront of the stage. Both saints, one feels, would have disapproved of this, for the bishop was very fond of Marie-Aymée; his letters are full of charming messages to her. Madame de Chantal on the other hand, liked Bernard not only because he was the bishop's brother, but because he was clearly a lovable person in his own right. The hero and heroine of the day are described in general terms only: she was very good-looking, shapely, tall for her age, good-tempered, at the same time very intelligent and 'much inclined to piety.' Bernard, the youngest of the Sales brothers and his father's favourite, was twenty-five at this time, a gentleman-in-waiting at the court of the Duke of Nemours at Annecy. He was fair-haired and blue-eyed, 'valorous, esteemed on account of his uprightness and piety by his parents and all who knew him.' Judging from the bishop's letters and from the effect he seems to have had on all who met him, he was a person of great charm and even playfulness, a good talker but not handy with the pen: the bishop often had to excuse his dilatoriness in writing. He was devoted to Marie-Aymée and it is quite certain that during the short years of their married life the two were very happy.

After two days of rejoicing and festivity, a council was called

---

[1] The main part of the village church at Monthelon dates from the nineteenth century but the ancient church has been incorporated as a side chapel. This contains an old wooden pulpit from which St Francis preached on the occasion of Marie-Aymée's marriage in 1609. There is also a good modern statue in wood of 'La Bonne Dame', her hands held out in a gesture of giving.

to discuss Madame de Chantal's future. It consisted of Francis de Sales, Frémyot and André. The meeting took a long time, and while they were conferring she went to the chapel to pray, so that when she was called before her judges she was perfectly serene. Her father and André went over the ground again with great thoroughness, cross-questioning her at every turn, as though they were in court session conducting a difficult legal inquiry. Quite apart from the merits of her case, she had been trained in a good school, and her father had to pronounce himself satisfied with all her answers. The bishop said nothing whatever but simply watched and listened, 'while grace worked in their hearts.' (1, 116) He was by this time certain of the case which he had pleaded and only had to look on while events took their course. It was quite in order that she should submit humbly to a formal examination, for father, priest and brother had every natural and spiritual right to exert authority over her as a woman. She gave a full account, not only of the gradual development of her spiritual life and her vocation, but also of the practical side of her affairs, explaining how she had left her finances in perfect order, her husband's estates unencumbered by debt. She proposed, if they agreed to her plans, to make over her fortune to her children forthwith and to give her brother a small capital, the income from which he could pay out to her as a dowry.

When she had finished, her father simply quoted Proverbs: 'This woman has looked well to the paths of her house and has not eaten her bread in idleness.' (Prov. XXXI, 27) The chapter containing these words was one day to be read as the lesson in the mass for his daughter's feast day.—She had won. Or rather, her confidence in God had been justified. When they had agreed on the place where the institute was to be founded—the president was for Dijon, André for Autun or his own see of Bourges, but Annecy was near the future home of the '*petite baronne*',—the bishop at last broke his silence. He gave them an outline of the sort of institute he had in mind. The members were to be recruited not only among the usual postulants but also from among widows, or women not strong enough for a life of physical hardship in stricter orders. They were to divide their time between prayer and work, and also visit the poor and nurse the sick. This meant that they were not, in fact, to be cloistered, an unheard of

innovation at this time. Madame de Chantal would therefore be
free to travel to Burgundy if her children's interests called for it.
This settled all difficulties, and the meeting broke up in the happy
atmosphere of confidence and mutual trust which St Francis
always managed to generate.

The president was charged with breaking the news to Baron de
Chantal who had so far been left out of the deliberations. The old
man, who was well over eighty, took it so badly, bursting into a
passionate grief of affection for his daughter-in-law, that the
president advised her to leave her departure till after his death.
But she said that in the course of time she would win him over,
and somehow she managed it. It was decided that Bernard should
come for Marie-Aymée, her mother, sisters and Charlotte de
Bréchard in the following spring, that is, in 1610, and that this was
to be the final removal from Burgundy.

When St Francis left Monthelon, Madame de Chantal, her
father and brother went with him as far as Beaune, a day's ride
along a hilly road that leads through some of the most magnificent
vineyard country of the Côte d'Or and the whole of Burgundy.
The bishop had been invited to say mass at the Hôtel-Dieu at
Beaune, a hospital nearly two centuries old then and still in use
today, run by the same nursing sisterhood. It is a beautiful example of Flemish gothic architecture, centering in medieval style
around a courtyard, where the long roofs are emblazoned in a
lozenge pattern of green and gold tiles, and pointed turrets rise
up sharply. The main ward is a very large, timbered hall at the
end of which stands a raised platform with a high altar and the
sisters' choir stalls on either hand. Behind the altar Van der
Weyden's great tryptych of the Last Judgement[1] was mounted on
high so as to be seen by all who worked, suffered and were healed
there. The work of mercy in this hospital was carried out with its
last end and final spiritual purpose in full view.

In the centre of the picture Christ sits enthroned among the
blessed above a rainbow which spans heaven and earth. Below
the rainbow throne the tall, white-robed figure of Michael the
Archangel weighs the souls of the dead in balance, and at his feet,

---

[1] 'The Last Judgement' (1443) is one of the finest paintings of the Flemish
school. It has now been moved from the hall to another room which forms
part of the hospital museum.

some figures, small naked human souls, move to Christ's right along the dark fields of purgatory towards the heavenly city. Others, with gestures of despair, move to his left through arid regions down to the burning pit. But neither reward nor punishment are overstressed. What holds the eye, and in due proportion fills the main part of the great canvas, is the majestic figure of Jesus with his Mother and his saints, and the triumph of justice in the angel who carries out God's decrees.

It was against the background of this picture and in this setting that St Francis said mass early the following day, and here he gave Madame de Chantal communion before they said good-bye:

'I left you with our Lord truly present within you, and you yourself were with our Lord's poor.'[1]

After mass they walked slowly round the ward, visiting all the sick in turn while the bishop gave them his blessing.

As the time for parting approached, their thoughts were on the future and on the religious institute they wanted to found. They were about to depart from the traditional forms so perfectly represented at the Hôtel-Dieu. Though their order was not to be enclosed, as had been the rule for contemplatives before, only a small part of time was to be given to active works of mercy: St Francis wanted his sisterhood to live an intensive life of prayer. Like the hall in which they found themselves, the order was to unite within itself prayer, suffering and action, but do this in a way which was novel at the time: the first emphasis was on prayer. As the picture behind the altar found its centre in the person of Jesus, yet contained the whole world in an image, so the new institute was to give neighbourly help to the poor and yet make its main work the contemplative prayer which reaches out to the whole Mystical Body.

The bishop and Madame de Chantal took leave of one another before the gates of the Hôtel-Dieu, to meet again in a few months' time when plans were to be changed into reality.

[1] A, XIV, 77.

Chapter 6

LEAVETAKING
1610

━━━◦◉◦━━━

Afew years before Jane Frances de Chantal's canonization a play appeared whose subject was her leavetaking from Dijon in the spring of 1610.[1] The final scenes of her departure from Burgundy have indeed all the material for a drama in the French classical tradition: a strong conflict for the heroine, torn between natural affection for those she was leaving behind and mystical love for the heavenly bridegroom; an open question of where in fact her obligation lay in this conflict between love and duty, duty and love. The characters were grouped around the heroine and the central problem. On one side were her father and the old baron with their patriarchal and pathetic appeal, her passionate young son, the chorus of the poor from her estates. On the other side was Charlotte de Bréchard as an understanding confidante and Monsieur Robert who was her son's tutor and her own wise counsellor. Dominating the whole stage was the presence of the hidden hero for whose sake she was leaving the world and all things.

The last few months of Madame de Chantal's life at home after her daughter's marriage, set the stage for the final act and already seem to belong to a new life. Letters from Annecy were few, and she herself wrote rarely. It seems as though for the time being all had been said and there remained simply a number of practical tasks to fill the interval of suspense. Towards the end of February

---

[1] *La Retraite du Monde de la bien-heureuse de Chantal. Poème dramatique en 5 Actes.* Anon. Avignon. 1758. The British Museum has a good copy, illustrated with prints.

in 1610, when everything was nearly ready for the journey, one of the sudden deadly fevers that had already taken Jeanne de Sales seized upon Madame de Chantal's youngest daughter. She died within a few hours. Charlotte was the child who had been born just before her father's death in 1601, and the more dear to her mother for that reason. Charlotte de Bréchard was her godmother. It seems that of all the children, this one had the most pronounced bent towards a natural piety. Marie-Aymée had been distinctly drawn to the state of life which was already hers, Françoise, wilful headstrong and out for enjoyment, made no secret of being attracted to life in this world. Celse-Bénigne was anything but devout. He is described as impetuous and difficult to manage, a natural dare-devil, affectionate, spendthrift, talented, spoilt. Charlotte, the youngest, had been a gentle child and a favourite with them all; her death increased the general atmosphere of disintegration which threatened the family unit at this time.

The messenger who took the news to Savoy arrived to find the bishop at Thorens, mourning his mother's sudden death on 1 March. After sending the servant back with a brief note, he found time to write a long letter describing his mother's last days.[1] Though her death was sudden she was well prepared, having gone to Annecy a few days previously at the beginning of Lent to put her spiritual affairs in order. Soon after her return home she had a stroke. Bernard found her and at once sent for his brother who arrived in time to anoint her. Two days later he himself closed her eyes in death.

In the second part of this letter to Burgundy he goes on to discuss the plan of travel arranged between them: she was to arrive in Annecy on Palm Sunday, and he invited her and the children to stay with him.

'Your little room will be ready for you', he wrote 'our simple hospitality, all the little we have to offer, offered from our heart. I mean it will come from my heart which is so very much yours.'

Then he enters into a question which she had put to him about prayer, a subject much on her mind. She was a frequent visitor in the parlour of the newly-founded Carmel at Dijon where she had heard about the prayer of quiet. It appealed to her and intrigued

[1] *Selected Letters*, p. 179 ff.

her but was far from clear. Discreetly, the bishop put his point of view, advising her to listen carefully but not to leave their agreed methods before they met and had time to talk things over. Personal sorrow could not affect his sense of responsibility for her spiritual welfare. All must go on as before. He knew, too, that Madame de Boisy's death would affect her and Marie-Aymée considerably, especially following so closely on their own family loss. He wanted to help her to control and use her own strong reactions to the death of those she loved. In this long excursion on prayer he gently led her mind back to essentials and forward to the work of God that was from now on to fill it completely.

The sudden death of Marie-Aymée's mother-in-law made it clear even to Madame de Chantal's severest critics that she was now needed in Savoy to help establish this very young bride in her new home. Rumour of what was happening had got abroad, for the life of the leading families was common property in those small communities. Many censured her as an unnatural mother and daughter, tongues wagged and some of the gossip was evil. Although she was armed, as she says, with the knowledge that if she pleased the world she could not be Christ's servant, this could not take away the sting she felt in calumny, nor yet her own attacks of doubt whether what she was doing was really justified. She suffered the pain of these last few months with all the intensity of her strong feelings. Her love for her father and for her family seemed to her greater than ever at this time, and continually sharpened her sense of loss. She was spared nothing.

What she was doing was, of course, in a sense unnatural; but then, so is any giving up of home and family ties, and this is essential in following a religious vocation. She was not, as was cast up against her, abandoning her children, to whom in any case she could never offer a settled home of her own now that her husband was dead; unless, of course, she married again. Nor had her father a primary right to hold her, and this he knew and admitted. The enmity of her critics, in her own time and in later centuries, was not really aimed at her, personally, but against what her action stood for: the scandal of an absolute spiritual claim. Her careful provision for everything that concerned her children, the fact that she had the expressed consent of her family authority in the person of her father and her brother, the years of prudent reflection a man like St Francis de Sales had given to the matter before he had accepted it as God's will for her—all these things counted as nothing in the eyes of the world. The world continued to see it as a scandal and took upon itself the right to judge.

Madame de Chantal, together with her friend, her two girls and Bernard de Sales who had come to escort them, left Monthelon on the first Sunday in Lent, that is, almost immediately after the return of the messenger from Savoy. Her biographer describes the scene in detail. The old baron was in tears while she knelt to ask his forgiveness for any displeasure she might have caused him; the poor thronged the approaches to the castle and made such a noise with their lamenting that the Capuchin fathers who had come from Autun to say good-bye, had to try and stop the wailing so that people could hear one another speak. But to pacify them, she herself had to talk to each beggar in turn, asking for prayers and giving a last alms. When she finally got into her carriage in the company of Charlotte and the girls, and with Bernard mounted alongside, the whole crowd of villagers, tramps and poor people followed on behind. They went with her as far as Autun. Meeting there a Franciscan priest she knew, she asked him to go back to the castle and comfort her father-in-law, committing the old man to his care for the future. Baron de Chantal died three years later and this same priest was with him at the end.

At Dijon, she spent the next four weeks of Lent visiting all the people and places dear to her and making the final arrangements together with her father. Frémyot wrote a letter to the bishop and put it into her hand on the last day just as she was leaving.

Monseigneur,

This paper should bear the imprint of my tears rather than my words because the daughter in whom I had set my hope for most of my comfort and peace in my unhappy old age, is going away from me and leaving me as a father without children. However that may be, following your example, Monseigneur, when at your mother's death you made a firm and constant act of trust in God's will, I now resolve to fall in with what God asks of me; and since he claims my daughter for his service in this world so as to bring her to his eternal glory in the next, I am willing to prove that I prefer his pleasure and the peace of her conscience to my own feelings.

She is going away to consecrate herself to God; but let it be on condition that she will not forget her father who has loved her so dearly and tenderly. She is taking her two daughters, one of whom has the happy privilege of joining your own dear family; I hope my daughter will keep the other girl for us. As for her son, I shall watch over him like a good father; and as long as God chooses to keep me here in this valley of tears and grief, I shall try to establish him honourably and in all virtue.

I most humbly beg you, Monseigneur, to continue your good will towards me and to believe that nothing matters more to me, after God's grace and benediction which I implore and sorely need, than to be remembered by you and to remain all my life, Monseigneur,

Your most humble and most affectionate servant,

FREMYOT.[1]

Dijon, 19 March 1610.

On the morning of this day, a Monday, the whole Frémyot family assembled for the last scene of the drama enacted in the entrance hall of the Abbey Lodge which was the president's home. Leavetaking was not, as now, a hurried, self-conscious affair to be got over in decent privacy, but a solemn public ritual. Possibly the ritual absorbed some of the grief; not, however, on this occasion. Looking round the company, Frémyot felt that he could not trust himself and that the sight of his emotion might still further unnerve the rest of the clan. He went back to his study. Meanwhile Madame de Chantal said good-bye to each in turn, her own eyes almost brimming over at the sight of the uncontrolled grief she was causing, but still self-possessed. Finally she came to Celse-Bénigne, her fourteen-year-old son who threw himself on his knees and in a last passionate appeal begged her not to go. His phrases, however, were so flowing and coherent that, to quote the biographer, 'one might have thought it was a set declaration which he had learnt by heart'—'*une harangue étudiée.*' (1, 129) His mother, speaking with some firmness, said what she could to pacify him while all the bystanders 'sobbed out loud to hear this moving interchange between mother and son.' But the boy clung to her, and when she made as if to move to the open street door where her father, who had now appeared, was waiting for her, Celse-Bénigne ran there before her, flung himself down across the threshold and cried out:

[1] A, XIV, 415, Appendix.

'I'm not strong enough to hold you back, but at least it shall be said that you trampled your own child underfoot'—'*au moins sera-t-il dit que vous aurez foulé votre enfant aux pieds!*' (I, 129)

In one way, though not as he primarily intended, Celse-Bénigne certainly succeeded. His action echoed round the town and has echoed down the years wherever the breviary lesson for his mother's feast day is read. It formed the climax of the play mentioned at the beginning of this chapter, it featured in her Canonization Bull, and it has not ceased to be quoted either against the saint, as callousness, or in support of her, as fortitude. It is too often the only thing people know about her. 'Ah yes', they will say, 'that's the woman who stepped over her son's body when she walked into the convent', and with that, dismiss her. It is a scene that certainly needs explaining. A closer examination of its background and of the actual words in the sequence of events reported in the original account, reveals the boy's action and his mother's response to it in a new light.

Biographers of the saint have generally been content to quote this episode verbatim from the original account, and without comment or interpretation. It has, it is true, been suggested in passing in a recent biography of St Francis de Sales, that Celse-Bénigne's action was perhaps prompted by some of the members of the Frémyot family who had a financial interest in stopping Madame de Chantal's project.[1] This is possible, but it seems unlikely that a proud and independent boy should have allowed himself to be used as a mere pawn in someone else's scheme. Moreover, his own misery was real enough even though he personally had little to complain about: a parting from his mother was inevitable in any case at this point of his life. He was of an age to go to court immediately, and was to stay in Paris for the next few years. If the speech he made was a set declamation, why should he not have written it up himself, and thought out the whole coup de théâtre on his own? It would have been in character. Histrionic by inclination, later in life a notorious duellist with a romantic sense of an occasion, he would have needed no prompting to cast his emotions into what he considered a heroic mould.

As to a hero with whom to identify himself, his reading would

[1] Trochu, Vol. 2, p. 362, note.

have provided him with plenty of models. Classical oratory featured largely in the education of the time, the composition of set speeches in Latin, even in Greek, was the kind of exercise his tutor would have given him. This was the age of Shakespeare, Corneille was a slightly younger contemporary and was educated in the same humanistic tradition. Schoolboys read a book like Plutarch's *Lives* as a matter of course; they could also read it in French in Amyot's translation which was in every cultured home and was one of the most popular books of the time. Celse-Bénigne had the run of his grand-father's large library at Dijon; he would have read Plutarch, not only because his tutor considered this morally sound matter, but because it really was full of exciting stories.

There was the story of Pompey, for instance. The soldiers in his father's camp were preparing to desert, and then this youthful hero, little more than a boy at the time:

'. . . going about in the midst of them, besought them with tears; and at last threw himself prostrate before the gates of the camp, and lay there in the passage at their feet, shedding tears, and bidding those that were marching off, if they would go, to trample upon him.'[1]

Pompey succeeded where Celse-Bénigne failed. It was the kind of scene that might well have impressed itself on the imagination of a boy of his temperament and come to mind as a useful piece of emotional blackmail when he was being thwarted.

In other words, he was making a scene, and his mother who knew him, and who blamed herself in later life for spoiling her only son, surely knew what he was about. So, presumably, did her friend, Charlotte de Bréchard, who had lived with the family and to whose dispassionate eye the biographer owes the details of the original account. If this was a deliberately engineered scene on the part of a gifted, theatrical boy, and not, as it is generally represented, a spontaneous outburst of grief, Madame de Chantal's famous action takes on a rather different aspect.

Instead of boxing his ears, which may have been her first fleeting impulse, she was forced to play the boy's game in a piece of showmanship utterly repugnant to her own reserve. She stepped over him because, short of making a second scene of rather a

[1] *The Dryden Plutarch*, Everyman edition, London 1910. 2 vols. Vol. 2, p. 387.

different kind, she could do nothing else. The tears of which the biographer speaks at this point were the result, perhaps, of a rather complex reaction: of sorrow, annoyance and a mother's sheer desperation at the sight of a naughty child. She felt responsible for the character of a boy who could have deliberately chosen to behave in this way at such a moment. After all, everything had long been settled between them in reasonable discussion over the past year. What the boy wanted—and his subsequent career proved it—was not his mother, but his own way at all costs.

Monsieur Robert, the boy's tutor, evidently knew his pupil too. Seeing Madame de Chantal weep, and reluctant to think that her fine composure should have been shattered by this outburst of melodrama, he stepped forward and said:

'Surely, Madam, you will not let a boy's tears shake your steadiness of purpose?'

'Certainly not', she answered with a smile, 'but I *am* a mother, you see!'—'*Nullement*', *lui dit-elle en souriant, 'mais que voulez-vous? Je suis mère!*' (1, 129)

She had regained her composure, else she could not have smiled— at the understanding tutor, at herself. This broke the heightened tension caused by Celse-Bénigne's scene.

He lived to regret what he did that day, and in later years wrote his mother what amounted to an apology for it.[1] But this cannot wipe it out nor do away with the great impression it made on the popular imagination. With all its emotional overtones, this scandalous farewell is still a stumbling block to many. Nor is this surprising. Out of its true context, that is, without regard for the temperament and psychology of the boy who forced it on his mother, her own action can never be seen in true perspective.—It was the daughter of this same Baron Celse-Bénigne de Rabutin-Chantal who, as Madame de Sévigné, put the family gifts to a genuinely artistic use in becoming the greatest raconteuse and letter-writer of her age.

Then Madame de Chantal said the most difficult good-bye of all. She knelt for her father's blessing and he gave it with perfect composure, encouraging her to remain calm for her own sake and

[1] See Ch. 10, p. 200, where there is also an account of Celse-Bénigne's further career.

to help those who were looking on. She was, in fact, never to see him again. The last thing he did for her was to give her strength and free her from the sense of strain left by the tense encounter with her son. Her father's fortitude allowed her to set out in peace, even with joy. The girls were helped into the carriage, she and Charlotte mounted their horses, and with Bernard leading the way, they rode out of Dijon. When they had passed through the city gates and got out into open country, her hand went to her saddle bag and she opened her little book of psalms. With their thoughts turned towards the future, she and Charlotte sang the long-familiar verses which now held new meaning:

I rejoiced in the things that were said to me: we shall go into the house of the Lord. (Ps. 121.)
How lovely are thy tabernacles, O Lord of hosts!
My soul longeth and fainteth for the courts of the Lord.
My heart and my flesh have rejoiced in the living God. (Ps. 83.)

The journey was leisurely. Travelling about twenty-five miles a day, it took them the rest of that week to cover the distance to Annecy, stopping both at Beaune and at Saint Claude. The days followed a regular pattern: when they arrived at an inn for the night, they inquired about the sick and the poor in the village, and went to help with the nursing. In the morning they called again to make the beds of the sick, give alms and ask for prayers before leaving the village. The journey was like a pilgrimage, ending on Palm Sunday when Francis de Sales and a group of some twenty people on horseback came to meet them at a hilly pass on the Geneva road outside Annecy. The whole town, in a festive mood after the procession of the palms that morning, turned out to watch the travellers pass through the streets and welcome them with an outburst of popular enthusiasm. They were received, not after all at the bishop's house, in mourning for Madame de Boisy, but by president Favre, whose house can still be seen in the rue Saint-Claire in the arcaded quarter of the town. After the bishop, Favre was one of the most important people in the town, and his daughter Jacqueline, a girl of eighteen who had met Madame de Chantal on one of her earlier visits, was going to join the new institute.

It was Holy Week and so all other considerations were put

aside for the time being. After Easter Marie-Aymée was taken to
Bernard's seat at Thorens and installed in her new home. This
second castle lies a few minutes' walk from the site of the de
Sales' home and belonged to them, being the patrimony of Francis
himself who had ceded it to his brother Bernard.[1] Marie-Aymée
was not isolated at Thorens. Even during Madame de Boisy's
life time, the neighbouring castle of Sales had been the home of
several of her married sons and one daughter, all of whom the
newcomer had met the year before. They were a united cheerful
family. Bernard had engaged reliable staff—quite a point is made
of this in the letters—and now Madame de Chantal was going to
spend about a month there to see that the household was running
smoothly. It was a peaceful time for all of them, a spring holiday
in the mountains to rest the family after the emotional upheaval
of the past few weeks and help its members to get acclimatized to
their new surroundings. In the course of May Madame de Chantal
and Charlotte went back to Annecy, leaving Françoise with her
sister until her new home with her mother was ready for
her.

It was far from ready when they returned to Annecy, because
the house that had been promised, together with the donor who
had thought she wanted to join them, failed to materialize in the
last minute. This made the bishop's plan of opening the house on
Whit Sunday impossible. Then by the merest chance he heard of
a small house for sale in a suburb near the edge of the lake, a
modest sum was paid on account, his word pledged for the re-
mainder, and by Trinity Sunday, 6 June, the house was ready for
occupation. It happened that this was also the feast day of St
Claude.

The preparations were not elaborate. The ladies saw to everything themselves and were helped by Anne-Jacqueline Coste, a
peasant woman of strong and simple faith whom the bishop had
met years before in Geneva. She had followed him to Annecy and

[1] The older wing of Thorens castle, unchanged from St Francis' day, has
been very well restored by the present owner, Count de Roussy de Sales.
It contains a St Francis de Sales museum with portraits and relics handed
down in the family. The rest of the castle was newly added by the Cavours
with whom the de Sales intermarried in the nineteenth century.—'Thorens'
used to be spelled 'Thorenc' and is still pronounced locally without the
final 's'.

had long been preparing to enter the new congregation as a '*soeur tourière*', or turn-sister. Work began with the chapel for which they used the largest room in the house, a cellar with a floor just below street level, and with three small, iron-grated windows set high in a massive wall. The chapel was immediately to the left of the entrance door from the road. The inner door with its little grating or look-out, the two worn steps down, the holy water stoup in the wall to the right, are unchanged today. The floor was bare earth and granite rock, a part of which still juts out beyond the street wall of the house, and into which a small flight of entrance steps has been hewn. Inside the chapel a simple altar was erected in the centre, the nuns knelt behind it, visitors faced it. A low balustrade and a curtain marked the enclosure. Upstairs there were three rooms along the length of which there ran a gallery, facing south. It was the roomiest place in the house, and it was from this it took its name, '*la Galerie*'.[1] From this balcony one looked down into a small yard with a patch of grass and a pear tree. This back-yard was known as '*la cour des Entretiens*', because the bishop used to give his talks there in fine weather. A covered passage led off at right-angles from the gallery and bridged the street, leading to a well-fenced orchard by the lake side which could thus be reached in privacy. In this garden the fields ran down to the water's edge. The house was isolated and in full view of the lake with mountains all around.

'I have found a hive for my bees', said the bishop, 'or rather, a cage for the doves.' The furnishing of the hive presented no difficulty as it was simple in the extreme: a few chairs, chests and a table or two. Each lady brought a mattress for a trestle bedstead, Madame de Chantal's being the camp-bed used by her husband during his campaigns in the field. The bishop's almoner contributed furnishings for the improvised altar, the hangings round the rock-face walls were coarse, homespun sheets, decorated on the great day with posies of wild flowers gathered from the June meadows in the orchard. The ladies rejoiced in their poverty. The

[1] The name 'Galerie' was not connected, as was formerly supposed, with the covered bridge leading to the orchard.—The present owners of the house are the St Joseph Sisters of the Annecy Congregation who use it as their novitiate. The small, simple chapel, which is open to visitors, has considerable atmosphere.

bishop liked to say that providence had made the Visitation as it had made the universe: out of nothing at all.

On the Saturday night, 5 June, when the Galerie was quite ready, and no further practical tasks were left to absorb her attention, Madame de Chantal was suddenly seized with doubts about the whole project. The devil, says her biographer, was making a last desperate attempt to put a spoke in the wheels. He worked on a state of mind which is in itself not unusual on the eve of a great enterprise long planned.[1] She has left an account in her own words, vividly describing her conflict. (1, 134) Suddenly all the joy she had felt seemed to vanish and she saw the whole enterprise in the bleak light of common sense instead of the glow of a vision from another world. Her courage, a pillar, as she says, which had upheld her so long, fell over and lay shattered in a thousand pieces. The image she chooses seems to express her sense of complete disintegration. Like a nightmare she cannot stop, the pageant proceeds in her imagination. Dragging themselves across the forefront of a stage strewn with the broken masonry of her courage, she saw her old father and her still more pathetic father-in-law. They were lifting up their hands and crying to heaven for vengeance against her. From the other side of the stage came her children, in their own small way doing the same thing. Furthermore, 'a multitude of voices' reproached her, that is, a whole chorus pointed the moral, and what was still more bitter, in words drawn from the scriptures. 'What the world thinks' is often pompously announced in fantasies or dreams by disembodied voices, seeming to come from everywhere and nowhere, their very vagueness condemning their validity. The upshot of what they were all saying was that the church would condemn her as ruthless, and would point to her as having wantonly deceived a good and holy director. His counsel, given, of course, on the basis of her astute powers of deception, was invalid and wrong. The best thing she could now do was to face the music while there was still time, and go back to Dijon there and then. Immediately, her mind began to suggest ways and means of doing this, even now, and of beating a retreat in good order.

This torture lasted about three hours. It was so terrible that she

[1] St Teresa of Avila was in a similar state of panic before her first foundation; cf. *Foundations*, Ch. 3.

was several times on the point of having the bishop called, but as she lay listening to the silence of the night and looked at this idea rationally, she realized that it was impossible. She put her hand to the scars of the letters forming the name of Jesus, and then her mind began to clear a little. Kneeling down, she repeated the prayer: 'O Lord make speed to save me', three times over, and then consigned her parents, her children, herself and all her fears to God's mercy, in time and in eternity. All she asked was to obey and to serve. Slowly, peace returned to her heart, a new and quite different sort of happiness and strength, deeper than she had known before. She fell asleep.

The next day was Trinity Sunday, a day when the church sounds a triumphant note, marking the end of the Easter cycle, and completing the annual re-enacting of the central Christian mysteries in the liturgy.[1] Madame de Chantal and her companions, together with many friends, made their last round of the churches and were then invited to supper at the bishop's house. Between seven and eight o'clock in the evening, he took them to his oratory and there gave Madame de Chantal a summary of the rule and constitutions he had himself composed and written out for the new congregation. Then he blessed them in the name of the Trinity: the all-powerful Father who drew them, the all-wise Son who ruled them, the Holy Ghost whose fire of love burned in their hearts. His face was radiant as he spoke. Bernard de Sales then offered his arm to his mother-in-law, Jean de Sales followed with Jacqueline Favre and Louis de Sales with Charlotte de Bréchard. First they walked to president Favre's house to say good-bye, then they made their way—it is a walk of some ten minutes—towards the shores of the lake and out beyond the town gate to the Galerie. They had hoped to keep the actual time of their departure secret, but everyone in the town was out of doors that fine evening; the children, in particular, had kept sharp watch. As the ladies came out of the house they were greeted with enthusiastic cheers, everyone called out blessings and good

[1] This day and the foundation in general were described by the foundress herself, and manuscript copies of her account later circulated in all the Visitations. There is an early copy in the archives of the Visitation at Angers, a seventeenth-century manuscript of twenty-three pages, from which some of these details have been taken.

wishes, and a procession at once formed behind them; some of their friends had gone on ahead and were already filling the little chapel to capacity. With the help of their escort, Madame de Chantal and the other two just managed to squeeze into their chapel to receive there the last embraces and farewells. Gradually, as this long midsummer day turned into night, the place began to clear; the voices died away across the lake as the crowds drifted back to the town, the door closed behind the last straggler. They were alone.

'This is the place of our delight and rest' said Madame de Chantal. Together they knelt down to pray. Then she read out the rule.

Part II

FULFILMENT

Chapter 7

THE GALERIE AT ANNECY
1610-1615

<hr>

The new venture had begun but it had no name. The bare minimum of a rule was there, but no formal constitution, there was a superior who was herself a novice, a house almost empty of furniture, and no money whatever. It was a situation to appeal to any pioneer. As a founder, St Francis de Sales was never in any hurry. Speaking in his measured, deliberate way, he liked to remind people that he was: '*des champs*', 'from the country', and he made a special point of this in Paris where the sense of gradual, organic development and growth seemed to him particularly lacking. Like the labourers in his own fields at home, he did not allow the over-eager prospect of harvest to distract him from the slow, patient process of preparing the ground. The vision of his order that he had in the chapel at Thorens where the memorial cross now stands, served as a goal to be reached gradually.

His basic aim was like that of every other founder: to give glory to God by helping people to lead a life of perfection in community. Ways and means are secondary. Even his contemporaries, still steeped in the full religious tradition of an earlier age, sometimes lost sight of this basic fact, so it is perhaps not out of place to stress it. He himself never confused the aim with the means, and it is as well to keep the distinction in mind so as to understand his flexible attitude to his order.

St Francis had first-hand knowledge of conventual and monastic life in Counter Reformation Europe. He had visited a variety of institutes in several countries, and had himself been commissioned to reform some of the old-established ones that had got

121

into slack ways. He realized, of course, the need for schools and religious teaching, he valued the work of St Angela Merici and her Ursuline Union, and that of his own contemporaries in Lorraine, St Peter Fourier and Blessed Alix le Clerc who founded the teaching order of the Canonesses Regular of St Augustine. In both town and countryside, nursing was needed and charitable work among the poor. There were also long-established hospital sisterhoods. But these primarily active orders did not stimulate St Francis de Sales as a founder. His interest went out to a way of life which was to be, in the first place, contemplative, and at the same time, to have a small share of active work among the poor outside the convent. This work was not, as in the case of the Sisters of Charity founded later by his friend and disciple, St Vincent de Paul, to be a primary end, but an aid to the life of prayer and contemplation within the convent. This idea, which in the day of secular institutes and visiting sisterhoods seems an ordinary and perfectly acceptable compromise, was in St Francis's own day, original and even revolutionary. Active and contemplative were considered mutually exclusive, not only for spiritual reasons, but for administrative ones: contemplatives were strictly enclosed and never went out. This was the case in St Teresa's reformed Carmels which already had several houses in France and which greatly attracted both St Francis de Sales and Madame de Chantal. St Francis was in touch with them through his former penitent, Madame Acarie of Paris, and through Cardinal Bérulle.

The only institute St Francis had ever known which even remotely resembled his own project was that at Torre di Specchi in Rome, where an informal congregation of Benedictine Oblates, mostly widows, lived together in community. They devoted themselves to prayer in the first instance, but also did good works, living without a formal religious rule and without enclosure. St Frances of Rome, their superior, was canonized in 1608; Francis de Sales took great interest in her cause and spoke of her work to Madame de Chantal.[1] He did not model his own institute on this; the parallels were incidental and based on similarity of circumstance. These Italian Oblates were drawn from among the same classes as those whom St Francis himself directed in Savoy and in France: that is, women of the upper and professional classes, who

[1] Letter of 29 September 1608; A, XIV, 67 f.

were literate, and like Madame de Chantal, had a sense of social responsibility quite apart from their spiritual qualities. But there were differences. The Visitation as St Francis planned it had a further distinction from any other existing congregation, and one most characteristic of the founder.

Among those drawn to the contemplative life, especially to Carmel which was fashionable in France, and to the existing orders, Benedictine, Dominican and Franciscan, which were out of favour in comparison, the bishop found many excellent young candidates not strong enough to lead a life of physical hardship. They were, in the attractive phrase of the time '*de petite complexion*'. There were also older women, generally widows in those days of high male mortality, who had a real vocation but were unable to face the austerity of long fasting, little sleep and hard manual labour. They nevertheless had a genuine desire to leave the world and to give themselves completely to God in the religious life. They did not want the ease and idleness sometimes found in the older convents, but at the same time, they needed something more suited to their physical condition, age, capacity and particular attraction. There was nowhere for them to go. The bishop regretted the waste of such potentially good material for spiritual training and perfection:

'For who would not pity generous souls, ardently longing to leave the noise of the world and live wholly for God, but not robust, strong and young enough to do it? Their aim to pursue sanctity and greater spiritual health is hampered or hindered because they lack physical health.'[1]

He wanted therefore to found a simple and informal congregation where such women could find training in the spiritual life and the mutual support of living in community. The main stress was to fall, of necessity, on the hidden, inner virtues: humility, obedience, poverty, an even-tempered charity, patience. At the same time the programme was also sufficiently difficult and comprehensive to attract the strong and healthy as well as the delicate. Like the host in the parable of the Great Supper, the congregation would gather in all those who, on the face of it, were poor compared with those originally invited, and it would provide them with a wedding garment. But in this case the strong were invited

[1] Preface to the Constitutions of the Visitation, 1619; A, XXV, 51.

too, first of all Madame de Chantal herself. And they came, for they were not slow to discover the hidden and exacting challenge of this outwardly gentle life. For the strong, the avoidance of extremes in itself demands a special kind of disciplined strength.

Inside the convent there was a simple routine of prayer, work, recreation, silence. In worship, the emphasis was on mental prayer of which there was half an hour in the morning and an hour in the evening, on the mass, and on the slow and careful chanting of the Little Office of our Lady. This was substituted for the full Divine Office as being less arduous for the type of woman he had in mind, though the time spent on it was no less. The bishop, himself an excellent Latinist, was exacting in his demands for the correct recital of the office; he and his brother Jean, the cantor at the cathedral which was famous for the excellence of its liturgical services, taught the original community at the Galerie how to say the office correctly. Madame de Chantal who pronounced Latin '*à la bourguignonne*' found the office particularly hard to learn; she laboured over it with the childlike earnestness that is one of her most endearing qualities. The two teachers themselves composed the chant of the office on three notes, an impressive variation which can still be heard in all Visitation convents today. The bishop meant this communal act of worship also to be a joy and a release from the tension of solitude and work. The chanting to be heard now in the basilica at Annecy still holds that same peace which he intended and was himself so well able to impart. The office is muted and gentle, not a brisk to and fro, as is for instance the livelier Dominican way, suited for cities and looking forward to the active apostolate which is to alternate with the contemplative act of worship. If St Dominic's way of singing the office has been likened to the swift succession of waves breaking on the sea shore, the Visitation way might well find its symbol in the calm inland waters of the lake by which it first began.

The bishop also envisaged a modicum of active outside work for his congregation which was not to be enclosed except for the year of the novitiate. This visiting and nursing work, so natural to a woman, was intended to strengthen and feed the life of prayer and worship inside the convent. Two professed sisters were to go out in turn together, for a month at a time, to help the sick and poor; as the community increased, this would mean that each sister had about a month's active work in the course of a year, and then only for two hours a day. This was in fact very little, but enough to suggest the first name he had in mind for his congregation: 'Filles de Sainte Marthe'. He wanted the institute to do its share towards settling the eternal problem of Martha and Mary, a small part of time being given to works of charity, 'and the best part of it to the interior life of contemplation.'[1] But the name did not seem to fit, and Madame de Chantal did not respond to it though she kept this to herself at the time. He suggested 'Oblates of the Holy Virgin' but the word 'oblate' was not known or understood in France, and again the name was dropped. In their letters the founders reverted to 'notre petite congrégation' to describe it. Was this reluctance to label it an expression of their wish to keep it unofficial and unpretentious?

The right name was not discovered till after the foundation, probably when the actual feast of the Visitation suggested a new train of meditation to the bishop. This time Madame de Chantal responded to it at once: 'Visitation Sainte Marie' sounded right to all of them. St Francis found this mystery rich in meaning and full of ideas that shed light on the spirit he wanted in his institute.[2] Mary went with haste into the hill country to visit her cousin who needed her, not so much for practical help, but for moral support and for a strengthening of her faith in the situation in which she found herself. But Mary went there carrying Jesus hidden within her, and she took his sanctifying presence to Elizabeth and to her child. The Visitation was therefore a mystery of worship and adoration, expressed in the insight of Elizabeth's cry of faith, and then immediately offered back to God in the exultation and thanksgiving of the Magnificat. The time these two women spent together was one of prayer in the living presence of God Incarnate, as well as a time of hidden, mutually rendered service. The popular idea that this order owes its name to its visiting activities is therefore based on a two-fold misconception: of a mystery in the gospel whose meaning is not exhausted in an external event, and of the nature and purpose of the order itself, which was not planned along rigid lines. It is quite in keeping with an order

[1] A, XIII, 310.
[2] A, XIV, 349, note; for the meditation, see A, XIV, 323.

founded by Francis de Sales, artist and saint, to have a name which, to this day, both hides and reveals it in the happiest way.

By the late summer of 1610, then, the congregation had a name as well as a provisional rule, developed in the light of experience. The ladies called one another 'Sister' and Madame de Chantal 'Mother', though for the rest of her life she continued to be called and addressed as 'Madame' outside the convent as this remained her correct title as a noblewoman.[1] The dress the ladies wore as postulants was not a habit of special design but just a simple, straight-cut black garment without pleats, gathered in by a belt at the waist. An unstarched white linen 'colerette', or cape, was worn over the shoulders, and the close-cut sleeves had white cuffs. A band covered the forehead, the black veil was shaped to the back of the head like a little hood and was knotted under the chin.[2] The look of it made the bishop hide a smile when he first saw it. 'Really', he said to his brothers when he got home, 'our ladies' headgear hardly improves their appearance!' But the fervour of these first few weeks was so great that nothing else mattered. The tone in which Mère de Chaugy writes of them is throughout idyllic, for this is how the tradition was handed down.

What kind of people were Madame de Chantal's earliest companions? Their stories are not only interesting in themselves, but these women came from different walks of life—the nobility, the cultured middle-classes, the peasantry—and so they give some idea of the social atmosphere of the time. Their lives, together with that of Madame de Chantal herself, help to fill in the cultural background against which the Visitation appeared, in the era when the Renaissance gave place to the century of the *Roi Soleil*.

The early life of Charlotte de Bréchard, the cause for whose canonization was put forward soon after her death, was that of a

[1] The fact that she was always known as 'Madame de Chantal', and therefore, after her canonization, as Ste. Chantal rather than Ste. Jeanne-Françoise, has led to the surely unique adoption of a saint's married surname as a Christian name. 'Chantal', ultimately derived from the name of the region, Cantal, is at present a popular girl's name in France.

[2] These details and some others in this chapter, are taken from Madame de Chantal's own account of the Foundation.

Cinderella and an outcast.[1] If the Sales and Chantal families bear witness to all that was best in the aristocracy of the age, the Bréchards show some of its less edifying aspects. Charlotte was born in 1580 in a castle not far from Bourbilly, the youngest of a large family, unwanted, and after her mother's early death, neglected to a degree that seems incredible. When she was four, she was taken ill, seemed to die and actually awoke at night to find herself lying on a bier ready for burial and with funeral candles lighted all around her. Four years later the plague came to the region. Baron de Bréchard at once fled from the danger zone and left a housekeeper in charge of the younger children. This woman disliked Charlotte, and suspecting that the child had contracted the illness, sent her to a labourer's house in the village where the whole family had already died. The house had been taken over by a couple of young gravediggers, important people at the time of an epidemic, but shunned like the plague itself. Charlotte spent three or four months in this place, verminous and ill, though not of the plague. The workmen did not completely abandon her; in their rough way they were even kind. True, they ate most of the food that was sent over for her from the castle from time to time, but they made attempts every now and again to clean her up, and astonishingly enough, they made her say her prayers.

One day a sick servant was brought in from the castle. She died, the men covered her with a shroud and locked up the house against marauders while they went to dig a grave. When it got dark Charlotte climbed up on to a window sill as far away as possible from the dead woman, and crouched there, looking out into the darkness, terrified and weeping. When the two came back to fetch the body, they felt a little compunction about having left her all alone. They bundled her on to the cart next to the shrouded corpse, then proceeded to the burial by torchlight. When the child at last recovered, she roamed round the countryside looking for wild berries to eat; wolves darted about in the forests and haunted the graveyards. Often she had to run for her

---

[1] The account of Jeanne-Charlotte de Bréchard's life, and also that of Marie-Jacqueline Favre and Anne-Jacqueline Coste, is taken from *La Vie des Premières Religieuses de la Visitation Sainte-Marie*, by Mère de Chaugy. Paris, 2 Vols. 1852, after the MS at Annecy. There is a well documented modern biography of Charlotte de Bréchard by Eduard Éverat. See Bibliography.

life. When the epidemic was over the baron came back and sent for his youngest daughter for whom he now provided a governess. She appears to have been a kind of ogre and even the baron was not quite satisfied. At the age of eleven, Charlotte was put into a convent for her further education. This was a place run along the old unreformed lines; an abbess and three sisters, all of the nobility, lived in comfort and spent their time at house-parties in the neighbouring castles. Charlotte appeared to be an amenable child and was very plain; humiliations had not warped her, for she had somehow learnt the secret of accepting them for God's sake. Gradually she was relegated to the kitchen, set to help the cook and carry the meals to the labourers in the fields. A few years later she was again at home and did the housekeeping, read pious books of which quite a few had survived at the castle although the atmosphere was wholly irreligious. She began to talk about being a nun, a project which met with derision but gave her father an excuse for disinheriting her. Remembering the misery of her own childhood, she began to visit the poor and nurse them.

It was in the course of this work that she first really got to know Madame de Chantal. The two families were in fact distantly related through d'Anlezy, the cousin who accidentally shot de Chantal. Charlotte was asked to be godmother to the child born at Bourbilly just before the baron's death, so it seems probable that she was held in high esteem by the de Chantals who must have felt more for her than pity for an unfortunate neighbour. During the next four years, unsettled ones in Madame de Chantal's life, the friends seem to have met rarely. In 1607 however, Charlotte was invited to stay at Monthelon; a messenger came, together with a letter for her father and an empty carriage to fetch the visitor. The carriage appeared as in a fairy tale at a difficult point of this Cinderella's life.

She felt that she had a vocation but had no idea how to set about pursuing it. Madame de Chantal took the matter in hand and introduced her to the Carmelites at Dijon. They accepted her, but because she was 'de petite complexion', it was soon clear that the life was too hard for her and she had to leave. After that, she seems to have spent most of her time at Monthelon where great store was set on her companionship and her pleasant way with the children. In 1609 she went to Annecy with the family, having met the bishop the previous autumn at Monthelon. He had readily undertaken her direction, he liked and admired her, he considered she had a genuine vocation and it was agreed that she should enter the new institute.

On the evening when the Galerie was opened, he decided that so as to put humility at the very basis of his new foundation, the eighteen-year-old Marie-Jacqueline Favre should be given precedence over her companion who was older by twelve years. Jacqueline was called the second daughter of the Visitation while Charlotte was the third. Her vocation had in fact been discussed after that of Jacqueline who lived in Annecy itself. Charlotte immediately understood and accepted this proposal, knelt down last to receive the bishop's blessing that evening and walked last in the little procession through the streets of the town. Jacqueline was made assistant to Madame de Chantal, that is, second in command, while Charlotte was given the less glamorous and often in their poverty most distressing office of steward or 'soeur économe', and of infirmarian. At the end of the first year however, her gifts for direction were used when she was appointed first novice-mistress after Madame de Chantal. A few years later she was entrusted with one of the earliest and most difficult foundations, that of Moulins. She died in 1637 at Riom four years before her friend. In the mouth of the people she was at once proclaimed a saint, and the reputation she enjoyed throughout her life was second only to that of the foundress herself; in some quarters it was at first even greater. Her holiness seemed less exalted and so she had a more immediate appeal.

Her Riom portrait at the age of forty-one shows her to have been a sensitive woman of considerable intelligence, an impression which is confirmed by her harmonious and balanced handwriting. She looks determined and ardent, her bearing has much natural dignity; if the painter may be believed however, there is a twinkle in her eye and an unmistakable smile about her mouth. This is borne out by tradition. She was vivacious and quick, sometimes even too quick, to see a joke; it is related that in the early days at the Galerie when the office was being rehearsed, Charlotte, the best Latinist, could not help seeing the funny side of all this earnest endeavour, and occasionally broke down in helpless laughter. She was resilient and resourceful, else she could hardly have come out of her terrible childhood unwarped. Romantic dreams of great beauty came to her easily, pointing to a rich life of the imagination. She could write vividly and well. Not only had she a nice turn for occasional verse, often used on commission for Madame de Chantal, but it is to her that the Visitation owes some of its most lively anecdotes connected with the foundation, as well as the majority of the details that have come down about the foundress' life at Monthelon and Bourbilly. It was she who described the farewell scenes at Dijon in 1610. Charlotte was a detached observer of human behaviour.

Her spiritual life was intense, based on suffering and mortification, all hidden by her characteristic smile. There is no doubt that she was raised to a high state of mystical prayer almost from the first at the Galerie. In spite of the treatment she had received from her father, she had the generosity to offer her own life as one of continual suffering if God would, at the last, allow him to be reconciled to his faith. Her prayer was heard. He died in 1617 after a wholehearted repentance; she herself suffered for the rest of her life, both physically and spiritually, but with courage and peace. Her body remained incorrupt after death for many years, and what appear to have been miracles took place at her tomb. In recent years the cause for her canonization has again been put forward. It was dropped in 1714 so that the whole effort could go into the cause of the foundress. It is very possible that the woman who was content to accept third place in the Visitation will also, in time, be its third saint, after St Jane Frances de Chantal and St Margaret Mary Alacoque.

A more complete contrast in vocation than that of Marie-Jacqueline Favre can hardly be imagined. She came from a stable, sheltered background, of a family similar to that of the Frémyots but without aristocratic associations. As her father was the leading magistrate in Savoy, she had every advantage of upbringing and wealth. She was also attractive to look at. As she grew up, her life became a succession of gay social events because she was very popular in the town. No ball was complete without this accomplished young dancer. Marriage, however, did not seem to attract her as she had a passion for independence and freedom. She had been heard to say that she had a natural attraction for the state of widowhood: could she have been certain that her chosen husband would drop down dead a couple of hours after the wedding, she would have made a match of it. Continuing to think along these macabre lines, she made a habit of hurrying to the deathbed of any young and attractive person. The agony of old people did not interest her. But when the moribund person was in the prime of life, it helped her, she said, to envisage her own end. For several days after watching a death struggle, she was filled with thoughts of transience and considerably sobered down. But she was resilient and the impression quickly faded.

The Bishop of Geneva, a great friend of her father's and a frequent visitor at his house, had known her since childhood and had observed her closely. He realized how unusual she was but also how candid and strong; he began to see what was as yet hidden from her. Jacqueline had confidence in him and as he never in any way forced it, he drew her all the more surely as she got older. After reading the *Introduction*, she agreed to try a few minutes' prayer every day and to go to confession every week. But it seemed to make her feel no different and she went on gaily as before. Then one day when she was invited to a ball at Chambéry close by, and the guest of honour, the governor of the province, asked her to lead off the first dance with him, a sudden pang of realization came over her. Faultlessly and with ease she went through the complicated steps of the dance but in her heart she was saying to herself:

'Poor Favre', (for this is how she appears to have addressed herself), 'what will you get out of it, moving around in rhythm like this? What will be your reward? People will just say: this girl is very good at dancing, and that'll be all.'

Suddenly she saw the glitter of the ball room in a different light, the world was changed, death was the end of all things and all was vanity. From this moment the dance seemed to turn into a dance of death, and seeing herself in the position of the young woman in Holbein's sequence who is partnered by a skeleton as she dances, Jacqueline had a vision of human transience. Before the ball was over she had decided to give herself to God.

She told no one, not even the bishop, until one day her father informed her that Louis de Sales, a younger brother, had asked for her hand in marriage. Then she broke the news. It was badly received, except by the bishop who had suspected this all along.

He told his brother that he had a formidable rival. 'The governor of Savoy?' asked Louis, flaring up. 'He's the only one I should call formidable.' But when he was told the truth he took it, as was to be expected, with the fortitude of one of Corneille's heroes:

'Feeling a deep hurt, he quenched the flame of his love and immolated his passion to the divine will which was as dear to him as life itself.'[1]

The president then insisted that his daughter should lead a life in keeping with her new outlook, and not without some regret, she put away her silk dresses. She took to long periods of prayer and began visiting the poor. A young friend of hers, Claude de la Roche, disapproved of the change and said it could not last; and so as to help towards the desired end, she used to trail her from church to church, kneel down at the back and do an exaggerated mime of this new piety, catching Jacqueline's eye when she turned round, and making her laugh. She was playing a dangerous game. By the end of that summer, she was praying in real earnest—within the enclosure of the Galerie.

When Madame de Chantal and Charlotte, whom she had met the previous year, came to stay at her father's house in 1610, Jacqueline's entry was already settled. Louis de Sales formed part of the cortège that walked to the Galerie on Trinity Sunday, but it was his elder brother who walked with Marie-Jacqueline, the second sister of the Visitation. She became an exemplary and fervent nun, a foundress of great capacity and was Madame de Chantal's most beloved and trusted friend. The letters to her 'grande fille', as she and St Francis affectionately called her, have a note of special tenderness. Jacqueline died in 1637 at the comparatively early age of forty-five, in the same year as Charlotte. Her work took her to convents all over France but it was at Chambéry, where she had seemed to dance with death, that death finally came to her.

Jeanne-Charlotte and Marie-Jacqueline may stand for their respective class in society and its early connection with the new institute. Anne-Jacqueline Coste's story represents that of the people and peasant class, the out-sisters, or turn-sisters and 'voiles blancs' who have always been an essential part of the whole.

[1] Mère de Chaugy, op. cit.

In point of time her acquaintance with the founder, then a young provost and missionary priest on the Savoy bank of the lake of Geneva, goes back further than that of the other three. She first saw him when he was conducting an open disputation with some of the Calvinist clergy in Geneva. In her native village in the mountains of Savoy she had been a cattle maid, and in a time of famine had come to Geneva as a servant. Every Sunday, at considerable risk, she used to walk out of the town by secret ways to get to a village church for mass, prohibited under severe penalty in the town itself. Her employer, himself not a catholic, condoned this because she was such an excellent worker. She purposely took a job at one of the great inns of the town, the Écu de France, as she counted on meeting travelling priests there from time to time, and wanted to make herself useful to her fellow-catholics. In this way she did a great deal of good. At one time during a skirmish she even harboured a whole number of Savoyard catholic soldiers in the cellars of the inn and helped them to escape one by one in a disguise which she made for them herself. Her activities at this inn read like a story from penal times in England.

When in 1595 the provost again came to Geneva, on the occasion of his first visit to the Calvinist leader, Théodore de Bèze, he stayed at the Écu de France. He arrived early in the day and before Anne-Jacqueline had broken her fast. She took hold of his bag as soon as he came, conducted him to his room, shut the door, placed a chair for him and asked him to be seated. Astonished but amused, the provost did as he was told. In a few words she told him her story. She was thirty-seven at the time, and not getting any younger; here in this hostile town, she had so little opportunity of getting to church and she seemed to miss this more and more. On the other hand she was able to help catholics in her present position. Was she to stay, or would he advise her to go back to Savoy now? He told her to wait for the time being and see what the future held. After he had heard her confession, he asked her if she would like to receive communion. She had no idea that he could give it to her without first saying mass, and that as a missionary on a special journey such as this—his visit to de Bèze was an official one arranged by the Vatican—he had the privilege of carrying the Blessed Sacrament with him for any emergency. He had the hosts hidden in a silver case worn round his neck. Doors were locked, the candles lit, a small altar prepared on the table, and Anne-Jacqueline went to communion. The provost's interview with de Bèze was not a success; but he had found the first recruit for his future institute.

The servant stayed in Geneva for eight more years during which time she did much good and grew in holiness. Her mistress had died, but not before being converted; and right at the end Anne-Jacqueline had made it possible for a visiting military chaplain to say mass for her mistress in this same cellar, and even to bring her the Viaticum a day or two later. The widower proposed marriage to his servant but she could not imagine herself as a bourgeoise, quite apart from their difference in religion, so she went back to Savoy and found work in Annecy. This was early in 1604, and every Sunday she used to go and listen to the sermon at the cathedral. Now that the provost had become a bishop and a great man, she dared not approach him and just kept humbly in the background, only too happy to be allowed to go to mass, to look into a church as she came back from the market, to listen to the town's many bells which were delightful music to her after the long, silent years in Geneva. One day during the sermon, as the bishop's eyes rested on his listeners, he recognized her, and so as to show her he remembered, his hand went to the silver cross he wore round his neck. As he continued to speak, he made as if to open the cross and looked at Anne-Jacqueline with the ghost of a smile, 'une oeillade douce'. She understood. After the service—it was not in the cathedral but at St Maurice, the spacious, light Dominican church which is still one of the most attractive in the town—as he walked down the central aisle and people pressed forward to kiss his ring, he stopped to speak to Anne-Jacqueline and asked her to call on him the following day. People looked with interest at the servant who had been so greatly honoured and she herself went home feeling it was the happiest day of her life. He undertook her direction from then onwards. Her fervour and humility, her complete absorption in God among her pots and pans, were always a delight to him.

A year or two later, she asked him if he thought she was fit to be a nun. As there was only one convent near the town he wondered if this was the place she had in mind. No, she said; she would like to enter his own convent when it was ready. The bishop looked at her in astonishment because he had not spoken of his plans to anyone except to Madame de Chantal herself. But Anne-Jacqueline could not explain to him how she had got to know about it. In her heart she just knew, and that was all. He neither confirmed nor denied her supposition, but again told her to wait. From that day, however, she took it as certain that there was going to be a convent, and when she first saw Madame de Chantal she knew without being told who her first superior was going to be. During the last Advent before the foundation was made, she asked if she might fast on bread and water and go barefoot all the winter so as to prepare herself in a fitting manner. The bishop answered, and also wrote to Madame de Chantal that he wanted the daughters of his new congregation to have their feet well shod but their hearts stripped bare of their own will in perfect simplicity.[1] This simplicity he had found in Anne-Jacqueline. The following summer, when she was already over fifty but still an untiring worker, she helped to prepare the Galerie for Trinity Sunday. In the early chronicles many delightful stories are told of her and her rough-diamond ways, her childlike candour, the occasional sharp edge to her tongue, her great love of God. When the bishop came to the convent to say good-bye in 1622, before setting out for Lyons on what was to be his last journey of all, Anne-Jacqueline was in tears as she knelt for his blessing. She cried out that they would never meet again. Her heart told her so. But his heart, he said to her with an unforgettable smile, told him that they would see one another again much sooner than she thought. A few months after his death in Lyons, she herself died quite suddenly.

These then were the three women who began the new life at the Galerie together with Madame de Chantal, each personality quite distinct, different in age, experience and background but united in one overriding aim. How did they get on together?

'It is simply not possible' wrote Madame de Chantal at that time, 'to describe the graces and favours which God poured into their souls. When they talked, delight and holy joy and sweetness was in all they said, and such great love united them that I thought it a paradise of happiness to be counted one of them. . . . We were on our own for six weeks, together with our good turn-sister, and we found this life so sweet, that our beloved Sister Marie-Jacqueline Favre used to say, that

[1] *Selected Letters*, p. 170.

if it were not for God's glory and his cause, she wished we could spend
the rest of our lives together just as we were, without ever adding to
our number.'[1]

In spite of this wish, expressed, characteristically enough, by
the youngest of the three, who never lacked ideas, the Galerie
rapidly attracted postulants. They were young girls for the most
part, such as Marie-Jacqueline's teasing friend, Claude de la
Roche, another called Peronne-Marie de Chastel, daughter of a
captain in the Duke of Savoy's army, gay, musical and an avid
reader of poetry and romance. She was one day to be Madame de
Chantal's superior at Annecy and of great personal help to her in
her spiritual trials. Another early postulant was Marie-Aymée de
Blonay, a girl from the Chablais, whom the bishop had known
since she was a child in a large straw-hat. She was superior of the
Lyons Visitation when St Francis died there in 1622. The names
and lives of these sisters are all a hallowed part of the tradition of
the order. By the end of the year 1610 there were over a dozen
sisters at the Galerie and Madame de Chantal had her hands full in
her double role as novice and superior. But the bishop stood by
her, guiding and counselling at every turn, walking over to say
mass for them two or three times a week, giving them conferences
as often as he could manage it and appointing his own confessor,
Michel Favre, to be their chaplain. Marie-Jacqueline was second
in command, Charlotte was responsible for the practical side of
things, the catering, the sacristy, the infirmary, Anne-Jacqueline
Coste laboured willingly everywhere. Each sister took a week's
turn of domestic chores, and Madame de Chantal was particularly
pleased when her 'good week' came round so that she could sweep
and do her share of the cooking. Very few of the postulants, it
must be remembered, had ever handled a broom before. Nor were
they used to unheated rooms, to so much silence, to obedience,
to the exacting routine of constantly changing and interrupted
tasks. The lack of austerity which was soon cast up against the new
community—it was mockingly called the Congregation of the
Descent from the Cross—was only relative.

Then suddenly, Madame de Chantal fell seriously ill. The
bishop sent his own doctor but it seemed hopeless and the illness
could not even be properly diagnosed. She was anointed, the

[1] MS Account of the Foundation.

bishop wrote round urgently asking for prayers, at the same time saying his fiat if God should see fit to take away the person he called the corner stone of his foundation. Perhaps, he said to her, God just wanted us to show our good will in making a beginning. She agreed with her whole heart. Charlotte and those who took their turn at her bedside, were full of admiration for her serenity in spite of great suffering: she had painful swellings all over her body and was worn out by high fever. She had never been able to watch others die without a great inner struggle for resignation; when it came, as she thought, to her own turn, all was peace and acceptance. In fact she recovered, but for several years afterwards she had recurrent illnesses of an unspecified nature. It was thought that the remedies used during her first attack were so strong as to do permanent damage to her constitution. As her own knowledge of medicines was considerable, she had realized that most of what she had been given was unsuited to her needs. But obedience, in this case better for her soul than for her body, had been her first consideration. This trial, she said later, evidently had a specific purpose. Her health had always been good and she had had little personal experience of serious or prolonged illness; but she was superior of a congregation that made a point of not excluding people with poor health. How better could she have learnt to feel with them and have patience with their ailments? Also, she had always been drawn to penance and fasting. Now she could do neither, and she saw what it was like to shrink back from these things because pain and tiredness were penitential enough.

By the early summer she was well enough to enter into the preparations which were being made for their profession ceremony on 6 June 1611. As their vows were to be simple it was to be called oblation rather than profession. The sisters looked forward to the day with fervour:

'When will the happy day dawn?' Madame de Chantal wrote to the bishop, 'The day when I shall again offer myself to my God, beyond recall? In his mercy he has given me an extraordinary and strong sense of this grace of belonging only to him; if it goes on as it is now, it will consume me altogether . . . Alas, the more I make up my mind to be really faithful to my divine Saviour, the more I realize that it is simply not possible to measure up to such great love. Oh how painful I find this barrier of feebleness! But why do I try to put it into words? This is just bringing God's gifts down to my own poor level, and I don't see how I can ever hope to express the love that calls me to live in perfect poverty, humble obedience and a most pure purity.' (4, 4)

The days of preparation witnessed her first and only trespass against this 'humble obedience', a trivial occasion in the eyes of the world but serious enough to distress the bishop who was the least fussy of directors. Money was short, as usual. A present which Jacqueline's father had promised was slow in coming, so his daughter and Charlotte who were trying to decorate the chapel for the great day, asked if they might have money on account to buy new hangings. They wanted to borrow some gold pieces which the bishop had given as a reserve only to be used in case of illness. They agreed that as the money would be replaced immediately the president's gift came, there could be no harm whatever in using it. Madame de Chantal hesitated and then, after all, gave permission; but she soon realized that, strictly speaking, this was disobedience. A note with an unadorned statement of the facts was dispatched to the bishop. When he came the next morning he reproached her gravely and stood waiting in silence as she knelt before him, weeping. On the very eve of their profession he felt that his carefully trained novices had failed to understand the nature of religious obedience with its motives which went straight to the supernatural, and had often, on the face of it, little connection with what merely met the eye. And what had the transgression been for? External show. He had had a bad night. The sight of their remorse, the certainty of a lesson now unforgettably learnt, reassured him. He found it hard, however, to reassure Madame de Chantal who could not easily forgive herself. On another occasion he explained to her that this too might be mere self-regarding.

He turned her attention to a more cheerful subject. There was the question of their habit as professed nuns, especially the matter of the veil. Their dress and headgear should be simple but he did not see why it should be ugly of set purpose. Charlotte, who had designed the offending veil the year before, now stepped forward to be the mannequin. Cotton crepe was suggested for the material but the bishop felt this was too fine a fabric. Then they decided on black muslin, or what is still called 'nun's veiling'. There was no money to buy any, so the travelling dress which Madame de

Chantal had worn when she came from Burgundy the year before was brought out of a trunk. She cut a square piece of material out of the skirt and folded and fashioned it into a veil. Charlotte stood there while it was tried on and draped over her head in various ways. The simplest method seemed the best and the veil was left to hang loosely over the shoulders. Finally the bishop asked for the scissors and himself neatly rounded off the unnecessarily long corners of the cloth at the back. The model was approved by all and it has remained unchanged to this day. This episode, an attractive study in collaboration, was typical for the sensible and realistic way in which the new institute was content to evolve gradually, with everyone co-operating and making the best of whatever material lay to hand.

Monday 6 June, the feast day of St Claude and the anniversary of their entry, was the day chosen for the taking of the habit. The bridal symbolism of the profession ceremony is more marked in some orders than in others but the spirit remains the same everywhere. It is essentially a marriage, a death to the old life, a rebirth to the new. The bishop had himself composed the words and arranged the sequence of events in a simple ceremony: a short address, each sister in turn pronouncing her vows and then receiving her black veil and a silver reliquary cross. Afterwards the solemn symbol of death is followed by that of the resurrection to a new life.

The chapel was after all decorated very simply, with the same white hangings and posies of sweet-scented flowers from the orchard as before. It was like going into a garden, according to the chronicle. Many people crowded in to watch, St Francis wore his episcopal robes and remained seated in his ceremonial chair. Before him in the sanctuary were the novices, sitting on the ground. He took as his text the parable of the seed which falls into the earth and dies so as to bear fruit a hundredfold. Then Madame de Chantal knelt down first and her voice was heard in the formula of profession, beginning with the invocation from the Song of Moses:

'Hear, O ye heavens, the things I speak. Let the earth give ear to the words of my mouth! To you I speak, O Jesus, my Saviour; my heart speaks to you though I am no more than dust and ashes. O my God, I vow to live henceforth in perpetual chastity, obedience and poverty—I offer myself and my life to your divine Majesty and to the Blessed Virgin Mary, your Mother and our Lady—I choose this holy and blessed Mother to protect me, this congregation to direct me ror ever.'

The others followed after her, and when they had been given their veil and silver cross, they lay down prostrate with their face to the ground as though dead, their life hidden with Jesus Christ in God. In the chapel at Bourbilly twenty years before, a white wedding veil had been held over bride and bridegroom while the nuptial blessing was pronounced. Now the bride was covered with a black pall. The bishop sprinkled holy water as on a coffin and read the lesson from the Office of the Dead:

'Man born of a woman, living for a short time, is filled with many miseries . . . Who cometh forth like a flower and is destroyed and fleeth as a shadow, and never continueth in the same state.' (Job XIV, 1, 2.)

The choir intoned the psalm of the dead, the De Profundis. When the miming of death was over and the pall removed, they rose as it were from the darkness of the tomb to the joy of light:

'Rise, thou that sleepest and arise from the dead: and Christ shall enlighten thee.' (Eph. V, 14.)

A flame was kindled as in the Easter vigil and the bishop gave them each a lighted candle and a crucifix, symbolizing the joy of the Resurrection as well as the sorrow of Good Friday:

'My beloved is mine and I am his—O Lord, your word is as a lamp to my feet and a light upon my way. Your light has cast its brightness upon mė and you have given joy to my heart.'

'My beloved daughters', said the bishop at the end, 'go into your dwelling-place, for the Lord has blessed you abundantly.' With that the sisters withdrew to their part of the chapel behind the altar. As an unrehearsed climax Madame de Chantal intoned a verse from one of her well-loved psalms: 'Here, for ever, is my resting place'. Her sisters in the choir and all the people in the outer chapel, the bishop's voice leading the rest, took up the response: 'Here will I dwell, for I have chosen it'. (Ps. 131, 14.)

The bishop intervened to cut short the congratulations of all the visitors who wanted to break through the balustrade to see the sisters. Turning to go, he himself gave the example: 'Now leave them in peace for the rest of the day', he said, 'so that they may taste the joy of God's gift to them.'

'Your life is hidden away now with Christ in God. Christ is your life.' (Col. III, 3, 4.) This was the spirit of the profession ceremony, and though the bishop only added this text later on, Madame de Chantal says that she now made it her meditation night and day. The foundation of the Galerie had attracted a great deal of attention, she herself had not been able to avoid becoming something of a public figure both in France and in Savoy. The new congregation's fervour, its life of poverty and detachment under such a director, did not fail to bring with it some of the more startling outer manifestations of mystical prayer among the sisters. People were beginning to talk. Madame de Chantal felt moved to pray in a special way for the grace of a really hidden life for the congregation and for herself. During her thanksgiving one day after the bishop's mass offered for this intention at the Galerie, she was filled with a great inner certainty that her prayer had been heard and that God would grant the Visitation the grace of a strong interior life, of sharing in the humility of Christ's life of suffering and of being hidden with him on the cross. If they had some part, too, in the glory of his Transfiguration or his miracles this would, as a rule, remain hidden too, to be made manifest in eternity with him. In the eyes of the world their life was to remain 'toute commune', in no way out of the ordinary. The order is not different now: it is rarely in the news and has little outward glamour but its wholly inward spirit remains unchanged.

Madame de Chantal's life from the time of her profession until she died thirty years later, was hardly 'toute commune'. She lived far more in the public eye, but compared with the thirty or so years till she found her way through the gate of Saint Claude, and then again in the years of transition till she entered on her new life through the doors of the Galerie, her real, inner life remained hidden. This is because in its earlier stages her life was personal whereas now it was identified with the development of her order, and therefore more typical. Not that she ceases to be an individual; rather the contrary. But this is not now in the foreground. The emphasis is no longer now on her own story, on her own inner life, a dying life, but on the task to which she was dedicated.

Her relationship with her director is drawn into this change of emphasis quite gradually. Although he continued to be her guide, it was with a difference, because from now on they were working in collaboration at an objective task. In day to day contact, conversations take the place of letters which are now replaced by little notes except when journeys call for something longer. Even then, as the years go on, the letters grow less personal and concern, in the main, the business of the order.

Her own great correspondence with her sisters which, taken as a whole, provides the key to the activity of her later years, is confined to business, spiritual and practical. She and the order are one. In answer to her prayer she is hidden within it, although from the moment she entered, documents relating to her life pile up in great numbers. Indeed, it almost seems as though she were hidden precisely because from that moment all she said, wrote and did has been piously recorded. There is almost too much material, but it all has the same slant: as she was a public figure, every fact recorded was intended, ultimately, to edify. The essential person, in so far as she was not identified with the public role she played within her order, remains elusive. Her life seems to enter a different dimension. Anyone attempting to chronicle her life in the same narrative sequence, and at the same pace as before 1611, is soon caught up in the detail of a mass of names, events, actions, places, while losing sight of Madame de Chantal herself. This is precisely what she intended and what she herself would have wished. Her biographers have had to resign themselves to letting her get away with it because in the last instance the success of her manoeuvre is perhaps inevitable. The second half of her life cannot match the first in outward interest. To begin with, it is true, the story does not seem to change too much. At any rate in the years between her profession and her first foundation in France in 1615, it appears to form a continuum with her earlier life. The following year, 1616, she made a retreat which marks an important transition in her life, confirming what had been going on beneath the surface for some years. Inevitably, as the personal substance fades, the change begins to be reflected in the telling of her story.

Some months before her profession, at the end of January when she was herself seriously ill, her father died at Dijon. The news was withheld from her until the bishop thought she was strong enough to bear it. It was then decided that after her profession, and when the worst of the summer heat was over, she should go to Dijon to see to her children's inheritance. She set out with Jacqueline Favre and her son-in-law Bernard early in September when the bishop was himself on a round of pastoral visits in his diocese. He wrote to her, as he said, with his foot in the stirrup.[1] This was a difficult return for her; but let her be all the more faithful, he urged, in committing her business entirely to God. God does not demand results, only loyal co-operation; this depends on her, success does not.

The last four months of 1611 passed while she moved between Dijon, Monthelon and Bourbilly to see to the estates and visit her father-in-law. Her husband's relatives made a last concerted attack to persuade her that it was her duty to stay at home; it was a shame, they said, to see a baroness tucked away under a couple of yards of shabby black veiling—it should be torn to shreds. The bishop wrote to hearten her against these maligners:

'For most certainly, if you had married again, and followed some gentleman living buried somewhere in the depths of Gascony or Brittany, you would have left everything else utterly and no one would have grumbled. Now that you have been much less radical in your departure and are free to keep an eye on your house and your children, people try to put about the idea that you have failed badly in your duty —and all because your retreat, though not extreme, is for God.'[2]

Her father-in-law was by now sufficiently pathetic in himself to need no special pleading for his cause; her compassion for him was great. Yet she felt that she already belonged to another world and that she had done for him all she possibly could.

Two years later, after his death, she returned once more to Monthelon, this time again with Bernard and with Celse-Bénigne, now seventeen. She was away from Annecy for only six weeks on the second occasion. Between them, she and her sons put the neglected estate in order, for days she sat in the great chamber at the receipt of custom for her children, collecting overdue rents and long-standing debts, completely surrounded by 'papers and

[1] A, XV, 107; and *Selected Letters*, No. 63.
[2] A, XV, 121.

peasants'. Sometimes she rode in a day from Monthelon to Bour-billy, a good forty miles. She interviewed the stewards there, sold part of the furniture and stored the rest, as her son was going to stay at court in Paris for some time to come. The housekeeper at Monthelon who had awaited her coming with terror, was treated with the utmost kindness and good provision was made for her and her children. Madame de Chantal invited her to sit with her and tell her about the baron's last years and his peaceful end assisted by the Franciscan friar who had promised to watch over him. Her magnanimity made a deep impression in the country-side.

On both occasions she found that the farewells were far less poignant than before. Travelling to what had been her home served as a landmark to show her how far she had in actual fact travelled during the past years. She was established in her new life and now Annecy was her home.

One morning on the road back to Savoy after the first of these journeys, they went into a little country church to hear mass. As soon as Madame de Chantal knelt down she was carried out of herself in prayer and noticed neither the priest's entry nor that he was saying mass. When the service was over, Bernard, seeing her continue to kneel there in prayer and not wanting to interrupt her, went on into the village to order a meal at the inn. Presently he came back. Neither of the two had moved, so he had a whispered interchange with Jacqueline: it was getting late and what about dinner? She had not dared to speak to Madame de Chantal, she said; but he, being bolder, went to rouse her. She came to very slowly and looked at them in a bewildered way: did they not want her to stay for mass? When they explained to her that mass was long over, she said nothing but walked with them to the inn. She could not eat. In later years when anyone happened to mention to Bernard that his mother-in-law was not well, he used to say that he would not waste any sympathy on her: it was just our Lord taking away her appetite again, he supposed (a comment un-doubtedly related by Jacqueline).

Madame de Chantal kept silence about this ecstasy until many years later. In 1635 Mère Jacqueline Favre, remembering this journey, asked to be told something about it. Yielding to pressure, she said that she had seen and understood in a vision the joy God

The Lake of Annecy in early spring

The Galerie at Annecy

takes in a pure and perfect soul. Wanting to try and give God this joy she had thought of making a vow about it: when two courses of action, both good but one better than the other, presented themselves, she would try to follow the more perfect course. Before making the vow she had conferred with her director and another priest; they had given her permission. During the bishop's mass at the Galerie on the feast of St John the Evangelist that same year, 1611, she had formally made the vow. The constant generosity and vigilance demanded by this 'voeu du plus parfait' are perhaps not immediately apparent. Saints have been known to make it and then be honourably absolved from it after a loyal effort to keep it. It does not suit every temperament and is not in itself a clue to sanctity, but the very fact that a prudent confessor allows a person to make it at all is most significant. Before Saint Claude, Madame de Chantal had been inclined to scruple and anxiety, to little worries about the spiritual life. A vow such as this throws the doors wide open to scruples in anyone inclined to them; it is for the strong and great-hearted, for one, in fact, who had already travelled a long way past Saint Claude along the road to perfection.

That first year on the way back, riding in hard winter weather, the party managed to reach home on Christmas Eve, Bernard to join his wife at Thorens, Madame de Chantal and Jacqueline to go back to the Galerie where they were eagerly awaited after four months' absence. They were in time for midnight mass, and never, says the biographer, was there such a happy Christmas. On the last day of the year a formal chapter was held, the sisters were appointed to their various new offices, a collection was made of all the little pious objects such as medals, rosaries and holy pictures, even the silver reliquary cross of profession which several of them now already had. The bishop had noticed that women become attached to these things and had decided on radical poverty down to the smallest object. After everything had been pooled, a general redistribution took place. Arrangements were then made for the visiting of the sick to begin, and on the first day of the new year, Madame de Chantal and Jacqueline went out for the first time on their rounds.

Annecy only had one small hospital and the many poverty-stricken invalids for whom there was no provision were a source of concern to the bishop. Madame de Chantal's experience of this kind of work was great, the work itself in harmony with the spirit of service already well developed in the postulants from wealthy families. It was efficiently organized. A doctor whose fees were paid out of charitable gifts to the convent called on the patient of whom Madame de Chantal heard through the ladies of the town acting as her scouts. He made his diagnosis, gave his orders, and then the sisters went to do the nursing, bring clean linen, food, medicines as prescribed. Madame de Chantal herself dispensed the remedies. As milk was often needed for sick children, a cow was bought and put to graze in the orchard by the lake. Madame de Chantal loved to take her turn at the humble and meditative task of minding the cow so that it did not damage the nursling fruit trees or wade too far into the lake. Often she took out her paper, quill and inkhorn to sit there among the trees, writing her letters. And when the sisters walked in silence with lowered veils through the streets of Annecy, everyone rejoiced to see them pass. Many stories, complete with the usual gruesome details, are told of the people they nursed. Their charity went out to all alike, more especially to those whom everyone else had abandoned: a prostitute with a revolting disease who was near to death, a girl from abroad who had crept into a stable when her child was born, old people who were dying alone in some forsaken hovel. The sisters for their part learnt much from the patience and gratitude of the poor.

The visiting consoled them and nourished their life of prayer but it was never one of the principal aims of the institute, being added rather

'as an exercise suitable to the devotion of those who began the congregation and to the kind of town in which they found themselves'

as the bishop put it.[1] It was, in fact, given up within three or four years at the instance of Archbishop Marquemont of Lyons to whom these words of explanation were addressed.

At the end of January in 1615 Madame de Chantal with her assistant and two others went to Lyons to make the first foundation on French soil, having been invited with the consent of the

[1] A, XXV, 338; Réponse de S. François de Sales au Mémoire de Mgr. de Marquemont, Concernant la Congrégation de la Visitation, 2 février, 1616. For the text of this Mémoire, see A, XXV, 322-32.

archbishop. His episcopal carriage drew up one day in Annecy to take them to France in state. No fast, solitary riding this time but a dignified progress lasting seven days, with seven little notes from the bishop to cheer her, one handed to her by Jacqueline every evening when they got to the inn.[1] She stayed in Lyons for nine months while postulants came to join them, and then left Jacqueline as superior in charge. In the course of the summer the Bishop of Geneva came to pay a formal visit to the archbishop and to see the sisters. The courtesy call was returned in the autumn, and by the beginning of the following year, the two prelates were ready to exchange a statement of their views on the new institute. For they differed.

Marquemont had come to the conclusion that a congregation without enclosure, with simple vows and a private constitution as opposed to an officially sanctioned rule, such as that of St Augustine, would not permanently be tolerated in his diocese or in France as a whole. The rapid development in the near future of simple religious congregations, unheard of at this time except in Italy, proved Marquemont wrong. But this does not mean that he was quite wrong in his time and place. In any case, the notable factor in the controversy that now arose, is that St Francis himself conceded these changes. By 1618 the Visitation had been officially erected into a religious order with solemn vows and enclosure. The bishop did not feel, and neither did Madame de Chantal (4, 122) that this changed its essential nature and aim, nor to any notable extent the means by which this aim was to be achieved. On further demands for change, affecting the aim and the means, he remained firm and eventually carried his ideas.

Each man recorded his views. These two expressions of opinion make an interesting study, of vital importance to the future of the Visitation, and therefore to Madame de Chantal. Archbishop Marquemont had every right to determine the external organization of any religious institute in his diocese and moreover in another country, though it is surprising that he did not consider the difficulties beforehand. He felt that the unofficial nature of the whole undertaking might pass in a small town and a little sovereign state, but was a bar to its progress in Lyons, the second city in the kingdom of France. It was, he thought, causing

[1] *Selected Letters*, No. 85.

scandal. So many religious who were supposed to keep enclosure in fact violated it, and came and went as they pleased; people in general, and the parents of prospective postulants in particular, could not be expected to make fine distinctions and see that the going out of the Visitation sisters was actually a part of their spiritual programme as contemplatives. Simple vows which could be rescinded without formality might cause difficulties in connection with the dowries paid out by the parents. A congregation, as distinct from a formally approved order, had little chance of survival in its first fervour, he thought.

Marquemont put the point of view of the world. The tone in which the young archbishop—he was forty-one, new to his office and about ten years junior to the Bishop of Geneva—wrote his statement was brisk, pertinent and sometimes sounded a little like an ultimatum. But in the letter he sent with it, he apologized for a hastily written document and humbly asked for advice, promising to submit to it.[1] He was in a real difficulty. The courteous humility, the sureness of touch with which the bishop replied, shows that he understood his colleague's quandary. It is not only his duty to acquiesce to an ecclesiastical superior, he says, but he will be happy to do it from his heart. At the same time he explains his reasons for constituting his congregation as he did in his own diocese in Savoy, and clearly states the essential points which he cannot change without affecting the fundamental nature of the whole undertaking. Moved by this example, Marquemont for his part made concessions. He had been taught the virtue and art of compromise, and had won his case without the bishop losing his.

As a striking example of how real unity can be achieved by joint deliberation, there remains the letter of petition Francis wrote to Cardinal Bellarmine, the only member of the Sacred College in Rome personally known to him. He asks for the status of the Visitation to be changed to a formally constituted order with the rule of St Augustine. It is at the same time the best summary of the fundamental principles of the Visitation and the most cogent witness to the originality of its spirit.[2] The most important

[1] A, XVII, 405, letter of 20 January 1616, from Mgr Denis-Simon de Marquemont to the Bishop of Geneva.

[2] A, XVII, 238–48, letter of 10 July 1616, to Cardinal Robert Bellarmine at the Sacred College in Rome.

innovation for which he asked the Vatican's approval was the substitution of the Little Office of Our Lady for the full Divine Office, and he finally carried this point. He had definite views about the scandal given by the illiterate and faulty recitation of the office in women's convents in France; the Little Office was within their grasp and could, with some training, be well rendered by the kind of person for whom his congregation was intended.

Madame de Chantal followed the bishop's lead, but not, at first, with his serenity. She too was a person to whom the virtue of compromise did not come easily; by nature, she was inclined to be rigorous. Tempering justice with mercy, more especially where she herself was concerned, was definitely a thing she had to learn. In the early days at Annecy, there was one day an argument with rich but mean parents about a postulant's dowry. Madame de Chantal courteously yet firmly persisted with what she considered a just claim, while the bishop sat by in the parlour and said nothing.

'But I can't give in where I see a just claim, not even if it were to go against myself.'

she said to him afterwards. But he answered:

'My dear Mother, you are just rather than lenient; I don't want you to be so very just. Be more lenient than just.' (1, 395)

She was much struck by this reply and remembered it for the rest of her life. This is one of the small episodes which reveals most clearly what a profound influence he had on her as an educator; he really did change her, often by a few simple words, removing obstacles between her and God of which she had been totally unaware. He was able to reach her at the hidden level where personality changes really do occur, even in middle-age; and this was because she for her part had shown absolute willingness to be directed and helped. In later life she was generally reproached for being more lenient than just.

Meanwhile, she felt strongly about the office.

'May I beg you to write to Monsignor of Lyons' she wrote in a note, 'and in good black ink too ("*de bonne encre*"), for this is so vital to us that it should count as a matter of urgency. My very dear Father will say that I'm still ardent; oh yes, indeed, I'll make no secret of being ardent about this if it will help in any way.' (4, 121)

But to Jacqueline Favre, the superior at Lyons, she wrote stressing the need for unity and obedience, and pointed out that as their chief object all along had been God's service, the name, whether congregation or order, under which they served him was unimportant (4, 122). The ready obedience with which the sisters fell in with the new ideas delighted the bishop, and with justified fatherly pride he made a special point of it in his letter to Cardinal Bellarmine. This was precisely the kind of occasion for which his training had prepared them, when they could show the suppleness of spirit which he had missed in the seemingly trivial affair of the reserve of gold pieces a few years ago.

From a practical point of view as well as from the spiritual, the whole future of the order depended on the spirit in which this first foreign foundation was made. It is very doubtful if the Visitation would have been accepted in other parts of France, as it so soon was, if its establishment in Lyons had not been made possible. It was from every point of view built on a rock and not on sand. The moderation and common sense of the order, the great-hearted nobility of its inspiration and of everything connected with its organization, in short the personality of its founder and his first collaborator—these quickly impressed themselves on all who came into contact with it. Six years later, when the founder died in 1622, there were already a dozen Visitations in France. At Madame de Chantal's death in 1641 there were no less than seventy-two convents and the order had spread further abroad to Italy and Switzerland.

The first house in Lyons, founded in a spirit of humility and just concessiveness, was the beginning of the order's wider influence; it also set the pattern for Madame de Chantal's own approach to the many foundations for which she was personally responsible during the coming years.

Chapter 8

THE LOVE OF GOD

————◇◦☾◦◇————

W hen Madame de Chantal returned home from Lyons in the late autumn of 1615, it was no longer to the Galerie. The community had outgrown the little house, the position of which was in any case not too healthy, and had moved to a larger place in the same suburb close to the town walls. It was then being rebuilt as a formally laid out religious house with an enclosure wall, a church, still standing today and known as the Grande Visitation,[1] and blocks of cells and other buildings designed to serve their correct domestic or ecclesiastical function. The makeshift days were over. The bishop blessed the foundation stone, the reigning House of Savoy contributed generously to the funds, and for years Madame de Chantal battled with the difficulties of an extensive building programme. Picturesque detail was not lacking when they moved from the Galerie: their goods and chattels were carried through the orchard and transported by a barge on the lake, Anne-Jacqueline Coste supervised it all and followed on with the cow, while the sisters walked down the road in procession.

One by one the Visitandines of those early years went out to France to make foundations, others crowded in to take their place and to be in turn trained by Madame de Chantal to carry on the traditions of the *Sainte Source*, while her own burden of work increased from year to year. Her letters of that time make good reading, especially those to Jacqueline Favre at Lyons and to

---

[1] This is now the parish church of the Italian colony in Annecy. A large part of the former convent is occupied by a home for old people while the building that was formerly the *tour* or living quarters of the turn-sisters, is now incorporated into the *Hôtel de Savoie*.

Charlotte de Bréchard, who was superior of the convent at Moulins, founded against incredible odds in 1616. With childlike trust they turned to her for help and she gave it generously, like an untiring mother who knows an answer to every difficulty and can comfort every hurt. Not that she wasted sympathy, but she gave effective counsel and practical help. She was never a demonstrative woman and rarely used two words where one would do, yet somehow the warmth of her affection for them shines through everything she writes, down to the last dry administrative detail. It was a warmth of energy which easily communicates itself where there is love. Her letters are spontaneous, swift and to the point; she always writes at speed, often with the messenger's horse already pawing the ground at the convent gates. She cannot stop to turn fine phrases, so her thoughts flow into her pen as they would come from her lips. Life surges through these pages. They are family letters. And the family was growing.

What was Mère de Chantal's own inner state during those years of increasing activity? Her own letters give little clue, her director's to her had practically ceased now that they lived in the same town. She herself was always reticent about her state of soul, and unlike St Teresa in similar circumstances, she was never ordered under obedience to reveal herself in writing. The clues must be sought elsewhere, to some degree perhaps in the talks which the bishop gave at the convent and most of which were written down verbatim to be published later as *The Spiritual Conferences*. But to a much greater degree the key to her state of soul is to be found in the book which had occupied him for years, almost since he first met her, and which was finally published in 1616: *The Treatise on the Love of God*.

'I am at work on your Ninth Book of the *Love of God*' he wrote to her, 'and today while I was praying in front of my crucifix God showed me your soul and your spiritual state in the image of an excellent musician . . .'[1]

The image took this form in the final version of the book:

'One of the world's most excellent music-makers who played the lute perfectly lost all his sense of hearing and went quite deaf in a short space of time. All the same, he went on singing and he played his lute most sensitively and beautifully because he was so used to it and his

[1] *Selected Letters*, No. 78, p. 216.

deafness had not affected his skill. But the sweetness and beauty of his song and the sound of his lute no longer reached him and so gave him no joy; he only went on singing and playing to give pleasure to the prince whose subject he was. He longed to please him and was deeply grateful to him for having provided for him from his youth upwards. That is why he took incomparable pleasure in giving him joy; and when the prince showed that he liked his singing, he was quite carried away by happiness.

'But sometimes, to test his dear musician's love, the prince would command him to sing, then straight away go out hunting and leave the singer all alone in his room. Yet the player so longed to fall in with his master's wishes that he went on singing as carefully as if the prince had been there all the time. True, it gave him no sort of pleasure; being deaf he missed the beauty of the melody, and the prince being absent, and therefore beyond the reach of his sweet song, there was no pleasure to be had from seeing his joy.'[1]

In her own hand Madame de Chantal copied out—the pages are preserved at the Visitation in Venice—the passages which most struck her in the original manuscript of the *Treatise*, lent to her by the bishop as he was writing it and reading it aloud at the convent. Among these passages was the earliest and perhaps the most impressive version of an image he had mentioned to her long ago in a letter, and which was now made a painful reality in her:

'My dear Philothea', (this was the name used in the first version instead of 'Théotime'), 'suppose we think of it like this: a sculptor has made a statue and he puts it in a niche in some room or passage. Now if this statue could talk and we were to say:

'"Why are you here in this niche?"—"Because this is where my master decided to put me", it would say. "Why don't you move?" "Because he wants me to stay put", would be the answer. "But what exactly are you doing here?" "Nothing at all; my master didn't put me here to do anything special but just to be here." "But what's the use of that to you?" "I'm not here to please myself but to do my master's will, and if he's pleased, that's all I want." "But don't you see him?" "No, I don't, but he sees me, just here, where he put me." "But wouldn't you like to move so as to get closer to him and serve him in some other way?" "Certainly not, unless he wanted me to." "Really? So all you want to do is just to be a statue in that niche?" "Yes, that's

_____
[1] A, V, 137; *Treatise on the Love of God*, Bk. 9, ch. 9.

all, unless my master changes his mind; but as long as he wants me to be a statue and nothing else, that's all I want too."

'Oh, my dear Philothea! What a good way of staying in God's presence—at his own good pleasure and of our own free will!'[1]

In yet another parable concerned with the same subject, a surgeon plies the steel. While he was away from home his daughter, it seems, fell ill of a fever. She realized that she could do nothing to help herself, and that it was therefore no use worrying: she would leave it all to her father who knew best. With that she fell asleep. Meanwhile the doctor returned,

'. . . and he thought the best thing to do was to bleed her, so he laid out what was needed and went and stood close to her so that she woke up. He asked how she felt now that she had had some sleep, and if she agreed to be bled so as to help her get well. "My dear father," she answered, "I'm all yours, and I have no idea what I ought to want for my own cure; it's for you to want for me and to do whatever you think best. For my part, I'm quite content just to love you and to honour whatever you decide, as in fact I do." So then her arm was bandaged and her father himself struck the vein with his lancet; but as he struck and the blood spurted out, she never once looked at her wounded arm nor at the flowing blood, but like a trusting daughter, she kept her eyes fixed on her father's face. "My father loves me and I'm all his", was all she said, repeating the words very softly once or twice. And when it was all over, she said no special thankyou, but just the same words of childlike love and trust again and again.'[2]

Blood-letting was not then the streamlined, painless procedure familiar to blood-donors at a modern hospital. This adds to the force of the image.

After the first blissful year or two at the Galerie and the ecstatic prayer of the kind she experienced in the wayside church on her return from Burgundy in 1612, Madame de Chantal entered upon a state of aridity and desolation that lasted almost without intermission for the rest of her life. The music-maker of the parable

[1] A, V, 401–2, First MS version of the *Treatise*, from Madame de Chantal's notes. These notes are bound in with a copy of the *Life and Works of St Catherine of Genoa*, given to her by the bishop and inscribed in his own hand with the opening verses of Ps. 121: 'Laetatus sum in his quae dicta sunt mihi: in domum domini ibimus', one of the psalms she loved best.

[2] A, V, 156 f.; *Treatise*, Bk. 9, ch. 13.

might still have found a little comfort in harmonies unheard by the outer ear; the statue has been abandoned to loneliness and immobility but seems at peace; so does the surgeon's daughter who can at least see her father as he bends over her to hurt her for her good. But Madame de Chantal's peaceful acceptance of her state of inner darkness lay deeper than all conscious perception: it was a stark act of faith, constantly renewed. She lived on her bare will, in what her director called 'the fine point of the soul', tempted against faith and hope. Outwardly serene, she was able to pass on confidence and peace to all who came to her for help while she herself suffered spiritually for the rest of her life. She had offered herself as a sacrifice and God took her at her word.

It is the *Treatise* which, rightly read, gives the most reliable portrait of her inner state during the years of her religious life till her director died. It also provides a key to her remaining years, spent in the service of her order, and in a sense it may be taken as an analogy to her whole life: it traces the development of the human soul in love with God and its progress towards divine union. St Francis had intended, sometime, to write an account of her spiritual life as he knew it and it was for this reason that he sidelined and annotated her letters. He did not live to write the account, the letters themselves are lost to posterity, but the *Treatise* remains. The portrait of the soul he knew best of all is indirect, but it is there. No mere account can make up for the powerful, cumulative effect of a personal reading of this book; but it is not an easy work to grasp as a whole. A few words about it might help towards the end now in view: a better understanding of Madame de Chantal at this time.

Not every treatise on the mystical life is as clearly arranged as, for instance, *The Ascent of Mount Carmel*, a book, by the way, not published until three years after the *Treatise*, though written more than thirty years earlier. St John of the Cross provided a key poem for his book and an emblematic picture of the soul's journey up the mountain towards God at the summit. *The Interior Castle* of St Teresa which St Francis de Sales certainly knew, has a dominant image of a crystal globe in the shape of a castle with seven mansions leading ever closer to its brilliant centre. There is no striking symbol, no single guiding thread to lead the reader through the *Treatise*. The key to it lies ultimately in the author's own soul and in that of the person closest to him. It was a portrait painted from life. The reader addressed was Théotime, a man's name with a feminine look about it, as he himself pointed out; that is, he was writing for—or about—anyone, whether man or woman, whether in the cloister or in the world, who wanted to love God perfectly and had already tried to live according to the counsel given to Philothea in the *Introduction to the Devout Life*.

After a first reading of this long work, one might be inclined to say that the dozen Books of the *Treatise* do not constitute a unity. True, there are repetitions and prolixities, for it was the work of an excessively busy man who could only snatch odd moments for writing, and that over a period of many years. But structurally it forms an organic, living whole whose originality lies precisely in the way it links up theory and practice, the mystical and the ascetical, prayer and life in one great synthesis. The theme of the *Treatise* is the development of the mystical life, that is, the love of God unfolding, flowering and bearing fruit in the human soul. Books Five to Nine, the central and most revealing part of the *Treatise*, describe the culminating experience of the mystical life, the opening Books (One to Four) show its origins and the laws that govern it, the final Books (Ten to Twelve) go right back to first principles and to the unselfed soul's humble practice of virtues in the light of common day yet remaining. If this simple analysis is used as a guide, the main line of St Francis' work will stand out clearly from the wealth of detail, and there will be no difficulty in understanding the *Treatise* as a whole or grasping its inner coherence. The structure is threefold: a central climax develops naturally out of an opening statement and leads up to a rather unexpected ending. When the three parts are not considered just as the three stages of an argued exposition, but as reflecting the living reality of an individual spiritual struggle, the *Treatise* at once springs to life.

As President Frémyot's daughter, Jane's will was turned from the beginning towards God. She learnt to love him as a child and then began to know him more closely: her love grew in proportion to her attempt to follow Christ's example in every detail of her life at Bourbilly and in her charity to the poor. Learning to use the sorrow and trials of her widowhood, she

passed through the gate of Saint Claude under the guidance of a
director who showed her her own individual way to greater love
of God in her state of life. During the early years at the Galerie her
spirit reached close union with God, a union still further strengthened by the increasing detachment forced upon her when she
lost those she most loved. Nearly twenty years of life remained to
her after St Francis died. Transformed by divine love, she
dedicated her life to the humble service of her order, in the valleys,
as it were, working as she herself once said, like those sturdy
peasant women who are hired at harvest time because they are
strong; and when they get old, they just sit and spin, and talk
about the father of the household, long dead, and of what he said,
and how he wanted things done (1, 452).

In the *Treatise* a gradual mystical development of this kind is
analysed in universal terms. How does the human heart come to
love God? What part does the will play in this? What moral and
philosophical laws govern the relationship between the soul and
God? These are the questions that St Francis discusses in the four
opening Books. Unaided, nature only has 'an imperfect little
love'. But God wants his creature's love and so he gives man the
instinct and the power to love him, yet leaving his will free to
assent or to refuse. Nourished by faith and hope, the will is controlled by love and at the same time rules by love's power in the
inner sanctuary of the heart. This means that the whole personality with all its faculties is gradually drawn towards God, the
Three in One, in a relationship of loving oneness. For love tends
towards union. Union may be lost, not only by actual sin but by
indifference and by standing still. Perseverance and hope make the
heart press on towards an ever closer union.

The five central Books of the *Treatise* form the part best known
and understood by the contemplatives, Madame de Chantal first
among them, for whose instruction and spiritual formation they
were written. How is this love nourished and increased, and in
what way does it reach fruition here on earth? How does it affect
the person caught up in it, and what are its psychologically
observable results? In what way should the loving will now
respond to God's call? The answers to some of these questions lie
beyond what is expressible in logical and descriptive terms.
Having pushed his explanation as far as he is able to do by means

of concise statement, illustration and comparisons drawn from the world about him, St Francis now instinctively turns to parables to make his meaning clear on a deeper level. In a series of symbolical vignettes like the ones already quoted—the Deaf Music-Maker, the Surgeon's Daughter, the Statue—he gives concrete expression to states of soul which the kind of person for whom he was writing found more accessible on a symbolical plane than in logical definitions. Madame de Chantal and her companions could respond intuitively to such teaching. St Francis usually conveys the gist of the parable by a simple, easily memorable dialogue of question and answer, so that the soul can the more readily identify itself with the fiction and feel personally addressed and involved. Parables act as a focal point round which confused ideas and feelings may crystallize and become conscious, thus being made available to the understanding and ultimately to the whole personality. In time, they will help to shape and transform conscious attitudes.

St Francis was a teacher mapping out the little explored territory of the mystical life, and in Madame de Chantal and her sisters he found the kind of pupils who stimulate the teacher so as to call out his best powers. They were sensitive, intelligent women, often well read, but they made no claim to theological learning; they had entered the convent with the aim of loving God more, a task that was to continue for the rest of their lives. Although they needed no complex theological training for this, grace had to have intellectual matter to work in and on, in their minds as well as in their mortified lives. That is why the bishop wrote a textbook for them, a grammar of divine love, but one which was dead without the reality of their own freely offered love. He put it together empirically as he went along, drawing on the greatest teachers of the past: the Church Fathers, St Thomas, the learned ignorance of St Teresa. His pupils, for their part, learnt as they lived their hidden life, at the same time acquiring the clear concepts which their teacher knew would ultimately help to strengthen their will. This would be important for their spiritual progress as well as for their psychological health.

In this central section of the *Treatise* then, Théotime is instructed in prayer. The ground for unitive prayer is prepared by meditating on God in his mysteries, as Philothea did, then rejoicing in him and praising him until, in time, words turn into silence, emotions into stillness in the prayer of quiet. The soul having faithfully acted is now more largely acted upon, drawn out of itself in contemplation till it stands beyond itself in the true and quite simple meaning of the word 'ecstasy'. Man's will has learnt to conform to God's will in what he commands, counsels or inspires, and is now completely subject to him, dead to self. The human personality remains limited of course, but the secret place of the soul, its fine point and inner fortress, has been built up and integrated with the rest of the personality so that the whole human being is now joined to infinite love. The union goes on developing, and though this may never be felt, it can deepen in quality without, however, changing in kind. This is as far as union can go here on earth, or at least, as far as it can be apprehended and described.

Book Nine, devoted to the unitive state, is the climax of the whole work. Madame de Chantal copied out most of it in her own hand and she had passages from it read to her on her deathbed. She said that anyone wanting to have a faithful portrait of her director's soul should read the final chapters of this Book.[1] But at the same time the author himself knew even as he wrote that the portrait was one of her. He told her so. And did he not always refer to her soul and his as being one, *'notre âme'*, *'notre coeur'* ?

The unexpected ascetical conclusion to this mystical treatise has a profound significance and is characteristic for St Francis's whole approach to spirituality. In the last three Books, Ten to Twelve, he returns to better known and mapped-out territory. He explains how unitive love, having simplified all the powers of the soul and subjected them to one overriding purpose, can only show itself here on earth in the humble practice of elementary virtues. True ecstasy lies in the will and finds expression in what he calls the 'ecstasy of daily work and living'. From Mount Tabor, Théotime returns to the valleys which he might by now have come to regard as only Philothea's domain. Christian morals are once more scrutinized, but now this is done with the knowledge of mature love. Foreshadowing the work yet to come after his own death when Madame de Chantal continued in exile on earth, he shows her the practical way in which she can offer herself as a

[1] Deposition for the Canonization of Francis de Sales, *Oeuvres*, 3.

living sacrifice to love, and how she can do it humbly, without running any risk of illusion. The end of the *Treatise* seems to take the soul back to where it started out at the opening of the *Introduction to the Devout Life*. The loving will, it appears, was trained only to be broken down in the paradox of mystical death, and then it is quietly set to work again as from the beginning. But with a difference.

Just before the *Treatise* was printed at Lyons and published in the summer of 1616, Madame de Chantal made a Whitsun retreat which marks an important transition in her life, though there was no marked outward change. She was forty-four at this time, entering on middle age and making ready for the great effort of the foundations which was to occupy the remaining years. The experience of this retreat, akin to the process described in the great central Books of the *Treatise*, was a further stage on the road towards her spiritual maturity.

The subject she herself proposed for her meditation was detachment, the refrain for her prayer, suggested by the bishop, was the verse from Job used in the Office of the Dead:

'Naked came I out of my mother's womb, and naked shall I return thither. The Lord gave and the Lord hath taken away. Blessed be the name of the Lord.' (Job I, 14.)

As the bishop was ill and therefore himself making an enforced but most welcome retreat, daily notes passed between the convent and the bishop's house. By some chance her letters escaped the general holocaust so that the correspondence of those few days forms the only brief series of sequent question-and-answer letters that has been preserved.[1] She also made some notes about the questions she wanted to put.

'Ask him', the first note reads, 'to specify those things in particular which he thinks will touch you most closely, so that you can at last make a perfect and unconditional surrender and say: I live, now not I, but Jesus Christ lives in me. Ask him not to spare you, not to allow you to withhold anything, great or small.' (2, 39)

Detachment was hardly a new subject of meditation for her; she remembered that when he proposed it to her on some earlier occasion, she had said to him with that curious illusion of finality

[1] *Oeuvres*, I, 109–18; and A, XVII, 212 ff. and Appendix I.

St Francis de Sales in 1622. The Thurnfeld Portrait
Visitation, Bad Hall, Austria

qu'il en mort. Pensés si j'auray rayson de —
15 jours pour consoler sa pauure vefue, et
toute cette fascherie et pour rasseurer un
peu mon coeur qui est certes grandement
esmeu. Or sus il est neantmoins de tout mon
coeur a Dieu. Je me tais et ne treuue point ma
bouche car vous saues fait. J'adore les decret
de sa prouidence et embrasse la croix quil
luy plait nous presenter. Ouy pere eternel
car. La semblable m'ayt bon deuant vous. Ie le
va vos priere et de tous nos amis general ma
Le 28 may 1617. Vre treshumble confrere
Fran. E. de Geneve

Je salue bien vostre monsieur
le marquis d'... son ... frere.

St Francis de Sales writes to Monsieur de Blonay on 28 May 1617 about the death of his brother, Bernard de Sales (pp. 176) that comes so easily: 'What else can be left? I just don't know.' Some time, he had replied, he would make it clear to her, and then he would detach her from everything on earth. It was not to be done in a day, and in a sense it would go on all her life, but there were mileposts on the road. During this retreat she began to understand what he had been talking about.

'How deeply the steel has cut into my flesh!' she wrote. 'How gladly one can leave every other thing, but to strip off the skin, the flesh and bone right down to the marrow, which, as I see it, is what we have done—this is a great thing, and hard, impossible even, except to God's grace. To him be the glory of it, and for ever.' (1, 116)

To express almost inexpressible pain of soul, she chose an image from the sensory life of the body, speaking of what she had often seen in her nursing work. She felt the spiritual process as a physical hurt, as an operation. What measure for her further healing had the surgeon-father now prescribed for his daughter?

Madame de Chantal was very dependent on her director. Her particular situation in life made this dependence inevitable, and her director had understood how to use it wisely as a part of her spiritual training. A gradual weaning process was only a further part of training—for it was in Pauline terms of nurse and child that St Francis put it to her. To a large extent, her dependence resulted also from the nature of the common task they had undertaken together, for during the first year and more, when she was herself a novice, he acted as the unofficial novice-master. For twelve years now, though rather differently before she entered religion, she had looked towards him for guidance in every important event, and since she had come to Annecy she had sought daily help and consolation from him in the same way as her own nuns looked to her. After she had discussed the affairs of the convent, she talked of her own spiritual needs, and his inexhaustible charity not only allowed this but welcomed it. And yet he was waiting for a sign from her that she was ready for greater detachment. There is a stage when dependence which was once right can become an obstacle. But it was not his way to impose any new measure before God has made his own leading clear in the person directed. He waited till the time was ripe, then acted incisively and with her full co-operation.

One day after a conversation of this kind, when he had been

unable to comfort her in some difficulty though he had done his best, he rose silently and left her; and she, not knowing where to turn, did the only right thing and went to the chapel. In prayer before the Blessed Sacrament she humbly admitted the truth:

'I learnt what I had never till then really understood, that one must not expect one's whole comfort from creatures but from God, and that the real way of healing lies in giving oneself up completely and without reserve to the divine mercy. Monseigneur wrote me a note the next day to ask what sort of a night I had had, for he knew that when I was in such a state, I got no sleep, and he was so full of charity that this grieved him; but I wrote and said that our Lord had healed my heart before I left the chapel.'[1]

During this retreat it was made clear to her that she was to have no nurse in the spiritual life from now on; she seemed to see herself quite alone at last, helpless and weak before God:

'The Lord in his goodness wants, I suppose, to put his hand right into every place in my heart, to take everything away and strip it bare. May his most holy will be done', she wrote. (1, 116)

'Our Lord loves you, my dear Mother,' was the reply, 'he wants you to be all his; let no other arm now carry you, his providence alone be your rest. Do not look elsewhere, let your spirit dwell in him alone . . . not in friendship, nor in the union God gave us, nor in your children, your own heart, your own soul or anything else whatever, for you have given all to God. And now, whatever you have to do, do it not because you want to do it, but only because God wills it.'[2]

After her death, these were among the words found written in her Book of Rules that she always carried in her pocket.

The letters and retreat notes of 1616 are only a rather unsatisfactory shorthand, a mere hint at the impressive spiritual experience which lay beneath. The retreat really was a kind of death, prefiguring the final detachment from him which was demanded of her six years later. In the meanwhile, both his work and hers, if nothing else, called for an increasing division of their ways, never in spirit, except in the way he had shown her, but in external ways. In 1618 she went to make a foundation at Grenoble close by in France, and later in the year she left Annecy for Bourges, Paris and a number of other important foundations in the north

---

[1] From the Deposition of a contemporary, quoted in a footnote, Mère de Chaugy. (1, 165)

[2] A, XVII, 218.

of France which kept her on the road for more than four years. She only returned to Annecy early in 1623, and after the bishop's death. But in the meanwhile, death also visited her own family and his, destroying the link of human relationship on another level and leaving nothing to show it had ever existed.

Bernard de Sales, then a colonel in the duke's army, died in Turin in May 1617, not in battle, but during a fever epidemic in camp. Marie-Aymée who had lost a child early that year, was again pregnant and was staying at the convent in Annecy in her younger sister's quarters, having found Thorens too solitary without her husband. In so far as the bishop could be said to have a favourite among his many brothers and sisters, it was Bernard, the youngest. When the news reached him he undertook to break it to Marie-Aymée herself. He told her after he had heard her confession at the convent the following morning, and before saying mass during which she received communion. She bore her grief with a resignation that astonished even those who thought they knew her well but had not realized how far this girl of not quite nineteen had progressed in her inner life. The next few months proved it to them unmistakably. She asked to be allowed to stay near her mother for the time being and some friends in the town were going to look after her when the child was due. But suddenly, early in September 1617, the child was born before term in the small hours of the morning, before Marie-Aymée could be moved. Madame de Chantal herself saw to everything and baptized the child which died almost at once. When evening came the bishop was called; it was clear that Marie-Aymée had not long to live. She died at midnight. Her dying wish was to be formally received into the Visitation, so after St Francis had anointed her, he put the novice's white veil and then the black one beside her on the bed; she pronounced her vows and he professed her while the nuns, her mother and her sister Françoise knelt round her in prayer. At this profession ceremony death was not a mimed symbol but a reality beyond recall. The bishop himself wrote an account of her last hours in the Book of Vows of the Annecy Visitation in which the first entry was her mother's name.[1]

[1] This book, *Le Livre des Voeux*, which the sisters sign on the day of their profession, is still in use at the Annecy Visitation.

'My greatest possible comfort in this sorrow' she wrote a day or two later to the bishop, 'is to have known and felt the love you brought out in her, launching her in this love like a single precious drop of water in a boundless ocean.' (4, 223)

From the time of her marriage he had been Marie-Aymée's director and it was under his guidance that this unassuming, charming and apparently quite ordinary girl had reached holiness. The letter which her mother wrote to Jacqueline Favre and Charlotte de Bréchard who both knew the girl well, reveals her grief more clearly. Describing what had happened she says:

'This will give you some small idea of what I feel and of the pain which makes my spirit turn more avidly than ever towards heaven and cry out with all my strength: Lord, what would you have me do? My soul lies open before you and wants to live only in you, look only to you for ever. Work your most holy will most perfectly in me . . . Ask for prayers and for a communion that from now on I may no longer live for myself, but that only my Saviour may live in me. I know you will pray for her.' (4, 219)

She felt that it was yet a further stage along the road of her detachment. She had not deserved such happiness, she said, as she and her now nineteen-year-old daughter had felt increasingly in their companionship and deepened understanding of one another; perhaps the continued joy of it would not have been expedient for either of them, so God had sent another death, his hand had reached yet another secret place in her heart.

Tragic losses, even in great number, cannot in themselves and as though by magic create detachment, though they may contribute to it. Even Job had to work out his complete self-abandonment gradually and wait while his inner resignation caught up fully with the outer catastrophes and his unreserved acceptance of them. But even for Job a moment of testing came when outer event and inner attitude were fused together in such a way that the integrated whole of himself could respond to God. In Madame de Chantal's case this final test was yet to come, and with it the completion of a transforming change which was, in its turn, no more than another new beginning.

Chapter 9

FOUNDATIONS
1618-1622

————◦◦◦————

The following spring, 1618, Francis de Sales went for the second year in succession to preach the Lenten sermons at Grenoble. This flourishing alpine town, an influential ecclesiastical centre and the seat of a university, was the first important French city south of Savoy, and comparable with Lyons to the west. A glance at the map will show that Lyons and Moulins, the already existing French foundations, prepared the way for the expansion of the order in central France and towards the north and west in the direction of the all-important capital, Paris. Paris then became the centre for the convents to the west along the river Loire towards Brittany—Orleans, Angers, Nantes —and north along the Seine towards Normandy—Rouen. Grenoble, on the other hand, and also Lyons which lies on the Rhône and at the meeting place of great cross roads, opened up the way to the south and to Provence. Madame de Chantal's own Dijon paved the way for the foundations in the east of France and right over to the independent kingdom of Lorraine where houses were opened at Pont-à-Mousson and Nancy. Its appearance across the Alps in Turin and in what is now Italy, is explained by the fact that this city was the capital of Savoy itself.

Foundations play a great part in Madame de Chantal's life from 1618 onwards, and to the reader not well up in French geography, their never-ending succession described in the biography may well become just a series of names. The whole movement of the astonishingly rapid spread of the new order can, however, be seen as a coherent geographical pattern radiating from the bishop's town at Annecy to places which in turn become the focal point of a new sphere of influence in their own region: Lyons, Moulins, Grenoble, Paris, Dijon. This makes the situation less confusing and Madame de Chantal's movements during the coming years less apparently haphazard.

During the previous Lent when St Francis preached at Grenoble, there had already been an insistent demand for a Visitation from a group of his penitents who were ready to provide the money, and from the ecclesiastical authorities, who welcomed the project. But the founder wanted to be quite sure of his ground so he counselled delay till the following year. In the meanwhile four postulants from the town came to be trained at Annecy. Towards the end of his second Lent in Grenoble, the bishop sent for Madame de Chantal who arrived on the eve of Palm Sunday 1618, with Peronne-Marie de Chastel[1] as superior designate, some professed nuns and the Grenoble novices.

By this time a certain ritual of leavetaking had been established. On the day of departure the sisters chosen to go knelt in the chapter-room, and before the whole community they promised on oath to observe the rules, constitutions and customs of the order in their new home. The promise was then written in the chapter book and signed, each sister was embraced in turn by all the others. A practical little travelling veil, foiling curious glances without obstructing vision, was fixed to their headdress; then the sisters mounted their horses which stood ready for them outside the enclosure door in the courtyard. Monsieur Michel, the bishop's almoner, or some other trusted priest was always one of the party. Sometimes benefactors sent a carriage. St Teresa's covered wagon, slowly drawn by oxen across the sunbaked plains and plateaus of Spain, had given place to the recently invented suspended carriage, an engineering achievement of the late sixteenth century and far more comfortable than one with a fixed body-work. It was, moreover, horse-drawn, and the great highways of France were among the finest in Europe. Whenever possible, especially in the summer heat, the sisters travelled by water, in boats or barges along the riverways: the Rhône, the Loire, the Seine.

---

[1] For an account of this interesting sister, and some idea of her personality, see *Peronne Marie*. By a Religious of the Visitation, London, 1912; and *Selected Letters,* p. 302, and Letter 83.

In the course of the journey the rule was observed as far as possible, mass was heard, time set aside for prayer and the office. The sisters generally lodged with friends of the order. On the way to Grenoble for instance, they stayed at Chambéry with Jacqueline Favre's father who was president of the local parliament. On longer journeys later on, when their way took them through unfamiliar country, they found shelter at country inns as Teresa of Avila did. These hostelries seem to have been more pleasant places than the Spanish variety half a century earlier. On rare occasions, for instance in Provence, where there were hostile huguenots, the sisters were dependent on the charity of humble cottagers.

On arrival at the town of their destination the sisters went to the main church, removed their travelling veils and intoned the psalm: *Laudate Dominum omnes gentes*. In procession they then walked to their new house, that is, if one had been found. If not, as was the case in Grenoble, they were received by friends, Madame de Mions this time, who was devoted to Francis de Sales.[1] Then there was the house-hunting, sometimes with local support but often against opposition. This came from the citizens' fear that a new convent would mean an increased call on charity and less help for the already existing communities not enjoying the appeal of novelty.

The foundation at Grenoble, where the way had been so carefully prepared by Francis de Sales, went more smoothly than most. The local bishop was kindly disposed towards the new institute; he himself received the sisters at the town gates to take them to their temporary home, and the following day he said mass for them and distributed the palms. Immediately after Easter Madame de Chantal went house-hunting, and after six weeks she managed to establish the community in a secluded, hilly place with a wide view of the river valley and the chain of snow-covered Alps beyond. Then she left for home. Her own letters and those of St Francis to the new superior, show how untiringly the founders helped her in every difficulty during the hard, initial stages. Francis had left Grenoble earlier, and going right up into the mountains, had made a retreat at the Grande Chartreuse where the solitude and silence held a life-long attraction for him.

[1] *Selected Letters*, p. 257, and A, XVIII, 197, for one of St Francis's most characteristic letters.

With three houses in France the Visitation had begun to acquire considerable status, and this was officially confirmed when, on Madame de Chantal's return, the brief arrived from Pope Paul V, declaring the simple congregation to be raised to an order with the rule of St Augustine, with enclosure and solemn vows. At the same time Francis de Sales was given apostolic authority to establish foundations without further formalities and this smoothed the way for all local bishops in the future. This change meant too that the rule and constitutions could now be printed instead of being available only in handwritten copies. Furthermore, the concession to which the founder attached such great importance, that of the Little Office instead of full Divine Office, was granted.[1]

On Sunday 16 October of that same year 1618, the bishop went to the lakeside convent (the new building was nearly complete by this time) with his brother Jean, the Grand Vicar, a small retinue and two lay witnesses; for these he chose, not local dignitaries, but characteristically enough, just two of his servants. Then he read a translation of the pope's brief to the community, explained the technicalities to them and said that against his own initial ideas, God had worked his will with the congregation. This was better, he thought, not only because it was God's will, but because in this way the chrysalis had been transformed so quickly into a queen bee. He solemnly blessed the doors, then the keys, to signify the beginning of strict enclosure. This ceremony completed the small beginnings made at the Galerie in 1610, eight years previously, and it officially ushered in an expansion which was already well under way.

The following day Madame de Chantal left with four sisters to make a foundation at Bourges and then go on to the most important one of all, Paris. She was not to return home till over four years later, and although she travelled constantly for the rest of her life, this was her longest single absence from Annecy and home. Perhaps it was also the hardest.

At about the same time that autumn Francis too left Annecy

---

[1] For the full text of this document, see A, XVIII, 423. See also A, XXV, 505, for the entry which St Francis made in the episcopal register at Annecy. Madame de Chantal wrote a letter about this to her brother André, 16 October 1618 (4, 280).

for Paris in the suite of Cardinal Maurice of Savoy, and did not manage to get home till about a year later. The cardinal was entrusted with the negotiation of a marriage between the heir apparent of Savoy, Prince Victor Amadeus of Piedmont, and Christine, the younger sister of Louis XIII. While the bishop on his diplomatic mission travelled slowly on board the ducal barges down the river Loire, Madame de Chantal rode first to Lyons and then to Moulins to visit Jacqueline Favre and Charlotte de Bréchard, neither of whom she had seen for some years. She arrived at Bourges on 22 October and stayed there for the next six months.

Her brother, Archbishop André Frémyot, who was a year her junior, was now forty-five years old, an emotional, affectionate man possessed of strong family feeling, devoted to the children of both his sisters. One nephew, Jacques de Neufchèzes, had taken orders and was attached to André's retinue. When André agreed to his sister leaving France in 1610, he had put in a plea for the new institute to be founded in Bourges and not abroad, in Annecy. The plea had failed but it was agreed that Bourges should be among the first foundations, and he had not ceased to work towards this end. He felt that as head of the family he still had authority over his sister and he was quite prepared to assert it. Since her entry into religion he had seen very little of her and had perhaps not realized how different she now was, that is, how completely identified with the order she served, and how the order itself had developed. This only became clear to him over the next few months, and even then he still tried to close his mind to it. His sister, he felt, still belonged to him and to her family. The truth, as he gradually realized, was that the parts had been reversed, and that it was he who looked towards her for guidance in his spiritual as well as his temporal affairs. The tact with which she fulfilled this role for many years, and the straightforward way in which he afterwards submitted to the change, show the true mettle of this brother-sister relationship. He allowed his family feeling to flow into the order, and it was he who was put in charge of the official inquiries for Francis de Sales' canonization process at Annecy in 1628. He practically financed it out of his own pocket and worked in close collaboration with his sister at every turn.

In the meanwhile, he was determined that once the Visitation had been established in his town, Madame de Chantal should stay there for good as superior. He made no secret of this, she made no secret of her intention to obey her own bishop's next order, whatever it might be. The battle of wills between the two Frémyots is amusing to watch.

In spite of the great preparations made for her coming and the initial enthusiasm of the town's welcome, the foundation proved the most difficult she had yet made. Of the many rich postulants who were supposed to be eagerly awaiting her, only one came forward in the end, though there were many less well-endowed girls whom she gladly accepted. The townspeople already had other convents to support and considered this one, perhaps rightly, as rather a family affair for which their wealthy archbishop should himself be financially responsible. At all events, André was not well served by the officials he had entrusted with the material and monetary arrangements. Often the nuns went hungry, without bread even. Madame de Chantal would not allow complaints to be made to her brother, with the double object of avoiding ill feeling and exercising poverty. To Jacqueline Favre she wrote:

'No other beginning of ours has been so completely dependent on providence; this is what makes us happy.' (4, 288)

A good omen, she thought, for the first house opened after the official recognition of the order, especially as their poverty was so inglorious: everyone thought they were rich. There was also some difficulty about the superior designate.

Anne-Marie Rosset was dear to Madame de Chantal both for her loving good will and for her association with some of the most important days of her life. She came from Saint Claude in the Jura mountains; it was in her parents' house that Francis de Sales had lodged when he took his mother on pilgrimage in the summer of 1604 and had his decisive meeting with Madame de Chantal. Anne-Marie was then a child of eleven, but so great was the impression the bishop made on her, that when the Galerie was opened she was one of the first postulants to offer herself. She had the gift of mystical prayer, and in writing on ecstasy and rapture in the *Treatise*, it was her he mainly had in mind. Not that the founders laid much stress on astonishing mystical phenomena; rather the contrary. But Anne-Marie was at the same time exceptionally obedient and humble. Although she seemed made for a hidden life, the bishop thought it just possible that she had the makings of a good superior—St Teresa's raptures had, after all, not robbed her of practical prowess—and he wanted to see whether the grace of office would bring out ability for leadership. It did not. When he passed through Bourges on his way home from Paris a few months later he advised that she should be relieved of her office and wrote to Madame de Chantal:

'Everyone admires her virtue, but few like her manner of conducting affairs. Don't let this dismay us, my dear Mother; not every soul has the grace to combine action with the passive way and switch from one to the other without inner prejudice.' (4, 343, note.)

Madame de Chantal herself had the grace to combine the two. Visions and raptures, though not absent from her life, were hardly characteristic of her, but she undoubtedly had the power to pass from the absorption of passive prayer to businesslike action. According to the bishop's testimony, she did this without prejudicing either, but never, as long as she lived, without suffering. In later years she wrote to St Vincent de Paul:

'*Mon esprit haït grandement l'action*', 'My spirit greatly loathes action, and because I force myself to action as occasion demands, body and mind both feel crushed all the time.' (6, 114)

She had to proceed to some very resolute action so as to be allowed to leave Bourges when Francis summoned her to Paris. Her brother was determined not to let her go. She tried to reason with him, making what the biographer calls '*plusieurs aimables remontrances*', but the situation seems to have been a deadlock. She fixed a day for her departure. Early in the morning André arrived at the convent parlour and announced that he had given instructions forbidding anyone in the town to let her have horses or transport of any kind.

'Very well then, Monseigneur', she said; 'if there are no horses we shall walk. Obedience has sturdy legs.' (1, 195)

He knew that she meant it, even though Paris was seventy miles away. With all his show of authority, and right to the end—he died at the age of sixty-eight, the same year as his sister—André never seemed quite grown up in relation to her. She treated him with all the respect due to his position in the hierarchy, but with a cheerful, motherly firmness all the same. He always had the grace to know when he was beaten and then gave in with the eager candour of a boy determined to play fair. On that occasion his own carriage drew up in front of the convent within a short time, he saw her into it and gave orders that she and the five sisters who had come from Moulins for the new foundation should be taken in comfortable stages as far as Paris. She arrived there on the Saturday after Easter, 7 April 1619.

Francis de Sales had prepared the way in Paris. This most important of all foundations was, he considered, like a nurseryman's plot of ground, '*la pépinière pour la France*', where trees for the forests all over the country should be carefully cultivated. In his letters he had warned Madame de Chantal that the way was not likely to be smooth. The reason for the attacks that had already begun was envy, and fear that this new order would steal vocations and so prejudice the chances of older establishments:

'They are afraid you will steal away the vogue other convents now enjoy, and that once people have seen this Madame de Chantal, no one else will stand a chance.' (1, 198)

Powerful friends came forward, it is true. Good works and religious foundations were as fashionable in the Paris of Louis XIII as brilliant pageants at court and sumptuous clothes; but one of the stories put about against the Visitation was that the Baronne de Chantal and her nuns had immense financial resources, and ought to dispense charity rather than expect it from others. The first year in Paris was therefore one of extreme but never apparent poverty. Madame de Chantal did, of course, arrive in her brother's splendid episcopal carriage and attended by his liveried servants—maybe she would really rather have walked after all—but no one knew that she only had nineteen silver pieces in her pocket and that this small sum was in fact all she had to provide for her community. She was happy. Just before she reached Paris she wrote to Charlotte:

'I have not been given any details, but it seems that all is going to be littleness and poverty. I am just to come and see for myself and am told that I shall find a situation which will give me a chance of using all my courage for God.' (4, 315)

In the same letter she quotes what the bishop had written to her:

'We are taking a long chance in this matter, and more than that even. But God wants it done and it is better to have his holy providence as our sole support rather than guide ourselves by human wisdom and prudence.'[1]

It was the kind of situation both founders enjoyed. They did not, of set purpose, fly in the face of common sense and prudence; but once they had carefully considered a project and made a reasonable decision—namely that a foundation could be made in the capital and was to be made now—they faced every subsequent difficulty with a fortitude unknown to those who rely only on natural courage. They were not given to exchanging what a later age may regard as mere pious platitudes. Their words corresponded to a spiritual reality.

It was three weeks before Cardinal de Retz authorized the foundation. During this time the sisters stayed in a house in the faubourg St Marceau while obstacles of every kind were put in their way. They were told to put down a vast sum of caution money, 45,000 silver pieces, in aid of other convents and so buy the privilege of establishing themselves; they were instructed to make themselves useful by taking charge of a penitentiary for fallen women which needed reorganizing. A suitable house was to be found first of all, and as everyone knew, the housing shortage in Paris was acute. The ecclesiastic in charge of the negotiations laid these conditions before Madame de Chantal in the form of an ultimatum: accept, or else leave Paris. But he was dealing with a person who had much experience of dilemmas and of pleading a just cause effectively. She had won over her father and brother on the day of decision at Monthelon. Now she had behind her the legally constituted order and its rule to which she could appeal and with which no one could tamper. In Paris, as at Monthelon, her director smoothed the initial stages and then let her put her own case before the authorities. On the last day of April,

'coming back from court one day, Cardinal de Retz took pen and paper and himself wrote out an order for our reception. And this was considered little short of miraculous.'[2]

---

[1] A, XVIII, 365, letter of March 1619.—Some of the details in this chapter have been taken from the account which Madame de Chantal herself wrote of the Paris foundation. An early handwritten copy of this—her own MS was burnt during the French Revolution—is preserved in the archives of the First Paris Visitation.

[2] From the MS account.

The following day, 1 May 1619, Francis de Sales came to say mass at the small house which had been found for the community in the faubourg Saint Michel. After the sermon he formally established the first Paris Visitation.

As he himself was shortly to leave Paris, he installed as ecclesiastical superior a younger friend, Monsieur Vincent. This was considered a surprising choice, for there seemed little to qualify him for the task of directing an enclosed contemplative community. But Francis had known him since his former visit to Paris as long ago as 1602, and when he renewed contact with him, he felt that the promise he had sensed in him then had been fulfilled. Monsieur Vincent had been tutor and confessor to the family of Cardinal de Retz's brother, the superintendent of the French galleys or slave ships. After his pioneer work among the slaves, and an absence of some years in a country parish, he had been summoned back to Paris to organize works of charity among the poor. Long after the death of St Francis de Sales, when he was deeply involved in his own foundations, the Mission Priests and the Daughters of Charity, St Vincent de Paul remained loyal to the charge his friend had conferred on him in 1619. He watched over the spiritual welfare of the Visitation and became Madame de Chantal's director. He made a deposition for her canonization process and also deposed for Francis de Sales, but no written record of the friendship between the two most popular saints of seventeenth-century France has survived. The relationship of each to the other, their mutual trust, implies that all three recognized sanctity in one another.

While the spiritual side of things was assured at the new Visitation, the material conditions remained as poor and abject as even Madame de Chantal could wish. It soon appeared that the house they had at last managed to find, and had in their innocence rented, had been empty for a good reason: it was wedged between two houses that were gambling dens and worse. The noise and shouting never stopped. Nor was this suburb near the Porte Saint Michel salubrious in other ways. It lay close to the left bank of the Seine which was the only public sewer of the city. Unused to town life, most of the sisters fell ill with the approach of the summer heat, and Madame de Chantal was left alone with two young novices to see to everything: the nursing, cooking, answer-

ing the bell at the turn, receiving visits in the parlour from prospective postulants or curious ladies. With it all, she led the singing in choir and so vigorously sustained the tone of the other two
frail voices, that visitors on the other side of the grille imagined
there were a good many sisters in the choir. Emergencies always
brought out her great reserve of strength, making her look
towards the future with hope and undaunted confidence. Before
the end of May, when there were only six of them at the convent,
she wrote to Jacqueline Favre at Lyons for no less than a hundred
copies of the newly printed rule:

'We shall pay for them, of course, but you must give us a little
time.' (4, 323)

'*Croyez que je ne suis pas sans occupation*' (4, 321) was the most
she ever said about this situation in her letters. There are close on
two hundred letters left of those she wrote during her four years
away from Annecy. They are a disappointment if one is looking
for local colour or news of her own state of mind. She had no time
or inclination to write any but business letters and was in any
case, as may be seen from the last quotation, an artist in under-
statement. The general impression left after reading these letters
is one of speed, with intense concentration on the question or
need put forward by her correspondent: a superior counselled or
consoled in a difficulty, a diffident novice encouraged, a meddle-
some ecclesiastic satisfied, a self-willed benefactress handled with
honesty and tact. The more personal note, except in the few letters
to Francis de Sales, was almost entirely lacking. There is nothing
that is not strictly relevant to the business on hand. She was
overworked, it is true, but even apart from the lack of time, her
mind moved naturally in a realm of essentials.

For three months the sisters had to stay in the unfortunate
house near the Porte Saint Michel. Almost as soon as they had
moved to a slightly better place and were beginning to receive
postulants, the plague broke out in Paris. Everyone who mattered
fled to the country. The city was deserted, grass grew tall in the
streets, no one called at the convent to help. In tears now,
Madame de Chantal went to the chapel to say an Our Father at
what was supposed to be dinner time. She begged for her daughters' daily bread, and this was sometimes forthcoming, more

often not. When their hunger was for once stilled, she immediately stopped the emergency *Pater*, saying that it was a delight to have only what was strictly necessary and be without provision, for this made them depend on God alone. When the plague ceased, the winter cold began. They had not enough fuel or blankets to keep warm either by day or by night, and the roof leaked so badly that the sisters who slept in the attics on bundles of faggots for want of mattresses, often woke up in the morning to find themselves covered with snow.

The interesting point about this story is that the sisters did, in fact, sleep. In other words, no one ever lost heart, presumably because the superior knew just how to exploit poverty as an element of spiritual training.

'God knows', St Francis wrote to her 'that we have not come to Paris to show ourselves off, but rather to show God's goodness to many souls who honestly want to serve him; so he will help us.'[1]

The Visitation had come to train people for God's service. Their first lesson, they found, was to be poor, cold and hungry in the middle of one of the richest and most luxurious cities in the world, a place of grim contrasts where they experienced in their own bodies the hardship that St Vincent's Sisters of Charity were soon to alleviate.

St Francis had left Paris in the course of that summer while she stayed on there for another two years. Very gradually the situation improved. In the following summer, 1620, the entry of one of the bishop's penitents belonging to an influential family made the community solvent for the time being and brought about an improvement in the attitude people took to it. The whispering campaign ceased, a new and more suitable house was bought.[2] This was part of a well-known town house in the rue Saint

[1] A, XVIII, 359.
[2] The wealthy postulant was Mademoiselle Lhuillier de Frouville, cf. *Selected Letters*, No. 119; and p. 303. This house, most of which is still standing, was an annex of the Hôtel Zamet. Contemporary architect's plans in the archives of the Paris Visitation show the exact lay-out of the building after it was adapted to monastic use and a church had been added by Commander Sillery in 1636. This church, a miniature copy of the Rotonda in Rome, is a distinguished piece of seventeenth-century architecture. After the Revolution, when the order was dispossessed, Napoleon gave the church to

Antoine close to the Bastille, which marked the confines of the Paris of that day. The rue Saint Antoine, on the right bank of the Seine at some little distance from the river and running almost parallel with it, was a wide, spacious street in a favoured residential quarter. The road with its many ancient hôtels is still in good preservation today and is one of the most attractive parts of old Paris. It was about a mile away from the Louvre, the island of the Cité with the towers of Notre Dame was close by, also fashionable river-side mansions with gardens and fields to make the air fresh and country-like. The river, coming from the country, was as yet unpolluted by city garbage. Beyond the fortress of the Bastille, close to the faubourg Saint Antoine which is still the street of the furniture trade in Paris, there were forests. The new home of the Visitation combined the advantages of town and country life.

When the bishop was consulted about the purchase he agreed that it was perhaps too fine a place, but that for lack of one that was good enough, they would just have to make do with one that was too good. The Visitation became *à la mode*. The parlour, with its stream of visitors from the court, now took the place of poverty as a penance in Madame de Chantal's daily life. This penance she kept mainly to herself, shielding the young sisters in her care from the impact of the fashionable world; they might perhaps have felt its sting less keenly than she did. She was an exacting and just superior who commanded respect as immediately as she inspired love. The fervour of the house suffered no decline with its improved material condition.

The three or four months at Paris in 1619 before St Francis had left the town were so crowded with business that he and Madame de Chantal had little or no time to talk as they did at Annecy. In July when they had been together in Paris for three months she wrote to Jacqueline Favre:

'Monseigneur is well. We see him from time to time; but it is impossible to talk to him. Our poor sisters have not yet had this consolation, nor have I. May God's holy will be done in all things.' (4, 330)

---

the protestant community in Paris who use it as their *temple*. It is still known as 'Sainte Marie' and though now in poor repair, is open to visitors.

The few letters that came to her from the bishop's house at Annecy in the Paris years were almost entirely filled with Visitation affairs. The same sure warmth in the greeting at the end, an occasional reflection on some spiritual point that had struck him, but very rarely a personal note or any direct reference to her own state of mind. Other and younger people now in need, Angélique Arnauld of Port Royal, for instance, who was trying to reform her convent and herself, were getting the kind of letters Madame de Chantal had once received. He judged that she now needed little personal direction; he was there for all, but with ever less time and energy to spare. She understood, and although one side of her rejoiced in the opportunity for sacrifice this provided, it was still painful and a strong emotional need remained.

'You have no news for me, you say? Oh haven't you even a few words to draw from your heart? For it's such a long time since you told me anything about it. Dear Jesus, what a comfort it will be when we can talk again heart to heart one day! May our divine Saviour grant me this grace, and in the meantime make you more purely and simply all his.' (4, 569) August 1621.

She felt she needed to review the state of her soul with his help, and hoped that neither he nor she would die before this could be done, else scruples and fear might overwhelm her again. Was her need perhaps not one purely concerned with the state of her conscience? Another time she admits this. She had remained human, though perhaps different from the days when she asked the bishop to pray that she should die before he did.

'I have already told our Lord quite peacefully that I don't want to think about anything whatever concerning myself . . . Not that there has been anything important since I last saw you, and I don't know if all this isn't just a temptation; you can best judge, for there is nothing new, except for what concerns my office as superior; I think there are frequent faults because I act imprudently and without enough charity, zeal and care to set a good example; however, I only confess the actual faults I am aware of, and only include those in my general purpose of amendment. True, none of this worries me, but I hope to have a good look at it one day together with you, and to stay at peace in the meanwhile.' (4, 569)

On another occasion she tells him about her prayer and how absolutely simple it has now become; nothing is left that she can feel as prayer or discern as a conscious act of her mind. Her spirit does not go through the process of uniting itself with God but simply stays united all the time, pressing home ever more deeply her longing to remain at one with him: may he do with her, with all creatures and all things whatever he wills. This is her only prayer, the Our Father her only petition for all her own needs and those recommended to her. Her soul just flows on in this union and ever further into it. This seems to her enough. Nevertheless, fears often beset her: will this really do? Then she forces herself to make acts of union and adoration. Can this simple, wordless kneeling before God really be enough, when even that goes on unfelt, unknown, and utterly remote in the fine point of the soul?

'I am not asking for a long answer; in a dozen words you can say it all, just to reassure me, so that it stops frightening me and weighing on my mind. My only Father, I don't know how I come to be writing all this; I never intended it when I put pen to paper, but now I'm glad it has been written. I ought to add this. Union in the spirit does not prevent all the rest of me from sometimes feeling drawn towards the thought of you; and this is the only inclination or affection I in fact do feel. All the same, I do not dwell on it in any way, nor does it disturb me, thank God, because the point of my spirit is united to his will.'

She repeats the lesson learnt in 1616, then candidly goes on:

'When I allow my heart to feel the incomparable joy of kneeling at your feet again as you give me your blessing, and I see this happening in my mind's eye, then I am suddenly overcome with sadness and the tears start, for I know I shall weep when, by God's mercy, I see you again. But I quickly turn away from the thought and don't allow myself to dwell on it. It is impossible for me to long for a meeting of set purpose; I leave everything that concerns me entirely to God and to you.' (4, 551) June 1621.

She was prepared to stay in Paris as long as he thought fit. For the time being he does not seem to have given her even the brief reassurance she asked for, and he left the decision about her return home to her; she was to stay in Paris as long as she considered it useful:

'Naturally speaking, the idea of your staying away longer is distasteful to me, but don't let this influence you. Stay quite freely if you judge it necessary, for I like treating myself roughly when the natural man in me wants to follow his inclinations.' (A, XX, 128)

She did not manage to leave Paris till the following February (1622), and by that time, after three years in the capital, the Parisians felt that they had a proprietary right over her. Not only the people at court and in the town objected to her departure; the new superior whom she had been so carefully training in detachment wrote a special appeal to Annecy, signed by the whole community of thirty-four sisters: could Mère de Chantal stay a little longer?

'Oh if only God had arranged things so that we need never part company' St Francis replied, 'how delightful that would be! But just think how this would work out in practice: our mountains would spoil Paris and would block up the Seine, and Paris would starve our valleys if it were here in our mountain land. One day, or rather, in eternity which is our goal, we shall always be present to one another; that is, if we live in this place of passage according to God's will.'[1]

Madame de Chantal herself found it hard to leave the convent which had been established with such difficulty and was now so flourishing. It was very much her creation. She had spent longer in Paris and was more intimately associated with it than with any convent except Annecy. It held a special place for her always. In her farewell talk to the sisters at the last chapter meeting, she did not, at first, try to hide her emotion.[2] Her most urgent advice to them was to remain small and humble in their own eyes and to remember that as an order they were the last comers and were to behave as such. The fashionable vogue of the Paris Visitation which continued to increase throughout the *Grand Siècle* grieved her; it went counter to all she had prayed for.

'The moment you lose your love of being despised and mortified,' she said, 'you will lose your own special spirit as an order and you will make void the designs God has had for you from all eternity: that is, to be very lowly, very small and very abject in your own opinion and in everyone else's . . . Not that we should go out of our way to look for occasions of being despised; we must just accept them cheerfully and even rejoice in them when they happen to us. And be obedient in all things, my dear daughters, to God, your superiors, your rule, and whatever providence ordains. And even as children remember their

---

[1] MS account of the Foundation.
[2] 2, 157: 'Derniers adieux de la Sainte à une communauté', Paris, 1622; and also 2, 475, her final words of advice written in the Paris Book of Vows.

parents' last words, bear in mind what I now say to you. No, all is well! I am not dying . . .'

Stifled sobs interrupted her at this point and she hastened to reassure the weeping sisters. Quickly, she who was so expert in untearful leavetaking, brought the atmosphere back to normal as she continued her talk, leaving them cheerful almost in spite of themselves.

Escorted by the almoner sent from Annecy, she set out on her journey on a very cold day in February 1622. Her instructions were to make a foundation in her own home town, Dijon, and to visit several convents on the way. At Bourges she was going to see her brother and take with her Anne-Marie Rosset, allowed to retire to obscurity again and live her life of mystical grace undisturbed by any further attempt at leadership.

The welcome Madame de Chantal got in Dijon when she arrived there at the beginning of May was tumultuous and astonished those members of the city council who had voted against yet another convent in the town. Everyone turned out to meet her, even the shops shut for the occasion, a notable tribute from this intensely commercialized city. The cheering was so tumultuous that the sisters inside the carriage no longer heard the thunder of the wheels on the cobbled pavement. It seemed, said the sisters, as if the people were carrying her along in their enthusiasm, together with the carriage. The crowd surged so close all round her that it took the carriage an hour to cover a journey of a few minutes. In the evening when the sisters had settled in a small temporary home, a large crowd of country-people from the villages round about Dijon, who had heard of the return of the baroness, their '*bonne dame*', came in to see her. This gave her more joy than everything else, for they were her own people whom she recognized after years of absence. She let them all come right into the small courtyard of the house, and she and the sisters, their faces unveiled, moved among them and spoke to them. Before they left, the people insisted on kneeling for her blessing, and quite simply, she gave it.

This welcome in her home town on the part of the '*menu peuple*', the little people, was the first of the spontaneous, popular ovations that she was to receive from now on wherever she went. She had never lacked a welcome from the clergy and her friends when she arrived in a city, but this was something different. It was an instinctive recognition of what she had become during the past years. Her town took stock of her, and her stay of six months there was a good time for her too to take stock of the past. There is, however, no record of her personal reaction, her thoughts and feelings during this peaceful interval which came immediately before the next great crisis in her life. Her letters were as impersonal as usual and give no clue to what was going on in her; whatever letters she may have written to Francis de Sales are not, unlike the few from Paris, among those which escaped destruction. Her biographer is entirely concerned with external events connected with the founding of the new house.

But the Dijon welcome and the whole journey from Paris in 1622 speak for themselves. At the age of fifty Madame de Chantal had become a public personality, widely known in France as well as Savoy. This was the first confirmation on a nation-wide scale of her new status, of what had been happening since she had left Burgundy. When she stopped anywhere on her way from Paris, at Mabuisson, the convent affiliated to Port Royal, or at the Carmel at Pontoise, where like St Francis, she had come to pray at the grave of Madame Acarie, she was immediately sought out by religious and lay people alike for spiritual advice. They realized that she had the gift of reading hearts, that she was altogether exceptional in a way they could not quite explain. Those closest to her were also aware of some new quality in her which was coming to fulfilment.

Even her daughter realized this and paid tribute to it in her own way. Françoise, now twenty-three, had married a wealthy and influential man many years her senior. As the Countess de Toulonjon, she was chatelaine of a castle close to her own old home in Burgundy. Her various changes of heart, her light-headed behaviour, had given her mother much anxiety in Paris and called for a number of serious letters. Madame de Chantal visited her on her way from Paris. As Françoise went out to meet her mother's carriage, she felt impelled to do what she had presumably never done before, else the biographer would not have thought it worth the telling: she knelt down and began to move towards her mother on her knees. While Madame de Chantal was at her daughter's castle, waiting to meet the nuns who had been sent from Annecy for the Dijon foundation, people came from Autun and Monthelon to visit and consult her. They came for spiritual food as years before they had come to Monthelon for bread. Françoise herself began to realize, perhaps for the first time quite clearly, what kind of a person her mother was. She had taken her too much for granted, and the grief of losing her first two children—she was now carrying a third—had opened her eyes to many things in her mother's life which she had probably never considered or understood before. After this, her loyalty to her did not falter again.

Madame de Chantal's first grandchild that survived was born within a few weeks of this visit to the castle. As soon as she was well enough to travel, Françoise took the child, a girl, to Dijon to show her at the Visitation and have her blessed. The sisters were now installed in a good house in the Place Saint Jean, a spacious square just within the city walls, at some distance from the crowded city centre where Jane Frances had herself been brought up. Jacqueline Favre was appointed the first superior of Dijon, so for a little while during this peaceful interval Madame de Chantal had the happiness of being with one of her earliest and perhaps the most beloved of all her companions. She had not lived in the same house with her since the Lyons foundation seven years previously.

'How very much I look forward to your coming!' she wrote, 'I can't really put it into words. What joy to be with my very dear daughter again for a while! It will do me a world of good. But what about all the timid people who say one shouldn't express one's fondness? I'm not of their way of thinking, and don't you be either, my dear child; our hearts couldn't stand it.' (5, 19)

Chapter 10

A DEATH
1622

━━━━━━◦◉◦◦━━━━━━

After Jacqueline had taken over as superior Madame de Chantal left Dijon towards the end of October 1622 for Lyons. There she had a hurried meeting with Francis de Sales who was on his way south to Avignon with the court of Savoy. Her further instructions were to visit two other newly founded convents, to make her own annual retreat and return to Lyons early in December. The bishop was then going to return to the town, Lyons being the place chosen for a meeting between two royal couples: the Duke of Savoy with his wife Christine, and Louis XIII, her brother, with Anne of Austria, his queen. The king was making a triumphal return along the river Rhône towards Paris after taking a personal share in the final stages of the religious civil wars in the south where the huguenots were finally defeated.

The two royal couples with their retinue entered the city on 8 December. This feast day was also the anniversary of Francis de Sales' consecration as a bishop at Thorens twenty years previously. He excused himself from court duties and went to preach at the Visitation. Refusing the offer of a more suitable lodging at the governor's house—Monsignor Marquemont's palace was occupied by the king himself—he had chosen to put up in the gardener's cottage attached to the Visitation. This meant he was close enough to say mass there and to give the sisters what little spare time he had.

On a day when he had managed to free himself for a stretch of some hours he walked over to the parlour to ask for Madame de Chantal. It was three years and more since they had last had time to talk at any length. Many problems connected with the convents, especially that of their individual autonomy and relationship to the local bishop, had to be discussed between them; he was against the idea of establishing a Mother General but wanted the order to remain under the government of the pope and the diocesan bishop of each house. Formal centralization remained repugnant to him. There were also points connected with the constitutions and the ceremonial. She had all this in mind and had prepared a sheaf of notes. At the same time there was something else: this was the moment she had not allowed herself to hope for but had never been able to put out of her heart completely.

'Now which of us is to begin?' asked the bishop as he sat down in front of the convent grille which divided them.

'May I please, Father?' she at once replied. 'My heart badly needs looking over by you.'

'How is this, my dear Mother? Still an eager desire? Still a personal choice?' he asked gently but very insistently. 'I thought by this time you would be quite angelic.'

He knew her so well; he could not have expected her to succeed altogether in being as detached as the angels. But he wanted her to be perfect; so she just had to go on trying, and he had to go on helping her even to his own cost. She expected his help in one way, he gave it in another, knowing what she now needed: a last lesson in detachment and humility that only he could give.

'We shall talk about ourselves at Annecy; now we'll get down to the business of our congregation.' (1, 211)

Without a word Madame de Chantal at once folded up the single sheet on which she had made notes for a personal consultation, put it away and took from her pocket the papers concerning the institute. For the next four hours, in close conference on either side of the grille which separated them, they worked together with a will. At the end he asked her to leave Lyons at once, before Christmas, to visit the convents at Grenoble and Belley, and then go to Chambéry where a foundation had been planned but not yet made. From there she was to return to Annecy and see him again. She knelt for his blessing, and very early the following morning she left the town.

It was too cold for her to go on horseback so she travelled in a litter while the chaplain, Monsieur Favre, rode alongside. Her small conveyance was something like a large sedan-chair suspended on a pair of long poles between which a horse was harnessed front and back. As she got older, this more comfortable and secluded mode of travel was the one she came to prefer. The interval of solitude, and the privacy behind the lowered leather blinds when she passed through a town, was good for prayer and thought. Suddenly, as her mind went back to the previous day, a great sadness and heartache seized her that she had not been allowed to say one personal word. But as soon as she found herself dwelling on her pent-up feelings unrelieved, she made an act of resignation to God's will and her hand went out to her Book of Psalms: 'The Lord is my light and my deliverance: whom have I to fear? . . . For my father and mother have left me but the Lord takes me into his care.' (Ps. 26) This last verse she repeated several times over.

'And so her heart was healed, for this was her usual remedy for interior suffering: abandoning herself to God and reading some verses from the scriptures.' (1, 212)

She spent Christmas at Grenoble which is at a distance of some sixty miles from Lyons. When she was at prayer on the feast of the Holy Innocents, she heard a voice say to her distinctly: '*Il n'est plus*', 'he lives no longer'. In her mind the phrase at once completed itself as she referred it in a mystical sense to her director: 'No, he lives not now, not he, but Christ lives in him.' (Gal. II, 20.) It did occur to her to wonder whether the words could have meant his actual death, but she refused to envisage such a thought. The chaplain received the news the following day by a messenger who also brought a letter for Madame de Chantal from the bishop's brother and successor, Jean de Sales. Anxious to spare her until the next stage of her journey was behind her— they were about to set off for Belley—he decided to wait until they reached this convent and she had spent the Epiphany in peace and joy. This was a feast she loved specially.

A conspiracy of silence was arranged at the convent where the news was already known. When she had rested and Michel Favre at last handed her the letter with a brief word or two about God's will, her heart began to beat wildly, as she writes in a letter to Jacqueline Favre, 'and I took immediate refuge in the thought of God and of his will. In that short space of time the full meaning of the words I had heard at Grenoble flashed upon me, and this was quickly confirmed when I read the letter. I threw myself on my knees, adoring the divine providence, embracing as best as I could God's most holy will and with it my incomparable grief. I wept a great deal all the rest of that day and the whole night until after holy communion; but my tears were gentle and peaceful, for I was at rest in God's will and in the knowledge of my Blessed Father's glory.'

From now on she only spoke of St Francis de Sales as '*notre Bienheureux Père*', and this is what her daughters call him to this day.

All she wanted now was that she and the congregation should continue to live according to his spirit and his precepts. This became the ruling purpose of her life. Her letters at this time show the energy and generosity with which she harnessed her own sorrow to the comfort and encouragement of all the others who had lost him. To the superior at Moulins she wrote:

'I bow my head and bend my heart beneath God's most holy will, kissing and loving the hand that dealt this great and heavy blow, adoring and honouring his most holy will with all my feeble powers. The only thing left to me in this life is a burning desire to see our monasteries continue in the perfect and most loving observance of our Blessed Father's legacy to us. You too must share in this and get all our dear sisters to see it, but do it gently and lovingly.' (5, 93)

Then without any further transition she plunges into the business part of the letter, answering the questions the superior had put to her. As she proceeds to the accomplishment of her duty, her grief is translated into action. This is the pattern of the rest of her life.

The first letter she wrote on the day she heard the news was one of condolence to Jean de Sales, assuring him at the same time of her obedience and loyalty. She had enough imagination to see what it must feel like to step into a saint's shoes, especially when the saint had been a beloved elder brother. The terms of the will were that if Francis de Sales, Bishop and Prince of Geneva, could not be buried in his rightful cathedral in that city, he wished his last resting place to be at the Visitation in Annecy. The body was embalmed and robed in a gilt chasuble and mitre, his staff placed in his hand. The cortège slowly made its way across France to Savoy.[1]

He lay in state in the cathedral at Annecy, the coffin, by a spontaneous gesture of joy and triumph, draped in a pall of white satin instead of mournful black. Thirteen white candles surrounded it, by his own wish bearing shields with the name of Jesus instead of his own arms as a nobleman. The same device was on the hatchment of the coffin. His brother sang the Requiem and his friend, the Provincial of the Capuchin Fathers, preached the funeral oration. It was 29 January, the day which is now his feast day in the universal church calendar. The following day Barnabite priests carried the coffin through the streets of the town to the Visitation church by the lake, and put it near the high altar. Madame de Chantal and her sisters, each holding a lighted candle, were waiting behind the convent grille, and until the tomb in the crypt was ready, the coffin was left there, close to the choir.

After this, Madame de Chantal's letters, to the Visitations in France, to her brother, Archbishop André, assumed again their resolute, practical tone, and she herself reverted to what she called her *'façon ordinaire'*, her 'usual manner' (5, 123). She does not allow herself to dwell now with a backward look on the loss of the person who was her 'only treasure and only joy in this world', for

'too grasping is the heart not satisfied by God alone, too mean the heart contented by anything less.' (5, 99)

She had used words of this kind before, and sincerely, but now they corresponded to a deeper reality within her. She was at peace.

Never had there been any lack of active resignation in her attitude, but her correspondence from now on shows that there is a definite change in her, as though all her energy, some of which had still, in a sense, been held captive by something within herself not yet completely renounced, were now released. For years she had been aware of some obstacle within herself which without her conscious realization of this fact, had found a focus in the person of her guide in the spiritual life. She had tried to face it, but again

---

[1] St Francis's testament, the chasuble and mitre in which he lay in state, and also his staff, are now in the museum of relics at the castle of Thorens. The small red silk cushion on which his head rested in the coffin on the journey home is preserved at the Visitation, also at Thorens.

and again it had proved to be beyond her conscious reach. It was as though with all her fifty years, some part of her personality had never been quite available to herself, but projected outside, first on to her own father and his authority, to some extent on her husband and finally on her spiritual father. In her director she saw a freedom from attachment which she knew had so far eluded her. She saw this as sanctity; but in itself this freedom was perhaps just a stage on the way to sanctity, that is, integrated wholeness, and maturity of character on a natural level. At some time or other in a saint's life, sometimes not until towards the end, the natural and the supernatural are fused together, though before that, the two do not necessarily keep pace; emotional development, strongly influenced as it is by circumstances and temperament, sometimes lags behind precocious spiritual insight and achievement. 'One day you will come to me' he had said many years ago, 'and I will detach you from everything.' Over and over again: when she entered the Galerie, during her 1616 retreat, at the last interview in Lyons, she thought she had understood, and that the understanding was final, the process of detachment somehow complete. Perhaps she had not yet quite realized that the sense of finality she was looking for existed only in the unknowing of faith. It needed another death, his death in her, to help her towards the complete integration of her personality and towards the altogether exceptional spiritual maturity he had always envisaged for her.

'We will talk about ourselves at Annecy.' This was his last promise to her. When she came away after long hours of prayer beside his tomb, it was clear to the sisters from the expression on her face that he had kept his word.

Shortly after the death of Francis de Sales, the Franciscan, Louis de la Rivière, began to write a life of him.[1] He consulted the Visitation at Annecy about certain points connected with the origins of the order. Madame de Chantal replied briefly and simply to all his questions, and having occasion in one of her letters to mention some personal details in support of a point, namely that St Francis had had plans for his order several years earlier than

[1] *La Vie de L'Illustrissime François de Sales de très heureuse et glorieuse mémoire*. Paris 1624.

the actual chain of events which led to its establishment in 1610, she added:

'I had not intended to tell you all this but it flowed into my pen, and I think it good for your Reverence to know these facts so that you can stress the point that divine providence guided the plan for this congregation in a special way. At the same time, I hope, my dear Father, that you will not actually mention all these details, nor any others in which I play a part. I beg you of your kindness to do me this favour; because the truth is that I am unworthy of any mention in this saint's life, and the possibility of this has long been a matter of apprehension to me.' (5, 305)

Confidence, and the lack of self-consciousness that comes of simplicity were part of her nature. None of her letters contain fine phrases or subterfuge; at the same time she had in all matters, excepting it seems, herself, clear powers of judgement and she was incapable of affecting shyness. It would appear, then, that she honestly considered it possible for the life of St Francis to be written, and the origins of the order to be described without even a mention of her name. This is remarkable. It goes some way towards explaining one of the more disconcerting things she did after her director's death: burning all her letters when his brother and executor sent them back to the convent.

'After doing so many things for our benefit, our revered Mother ended this year (1623) by doing something we regret and shall always continue to regret', writes the biographer. 'Monseigneur of Geneva had had time to go through his brother's papers and had found among them a very great number of letters from our revered Mother. Knowing that they contained the most secret things of her soul, and having the greatest possible reverence for her, he sent her back all her letters. These she proceeded to burn, nor were our sisters able to prevent her. The late Monsieur Michel Favre, with whom we talked of this matter, and who was our Blessed Father's confessor, almoner and confidential secretary, told us for a fact that the holy prelate had taken the trouble to sort out those of her letters which were to be used for her "Life", and that with his own holy hand he had side-lined a great many of them, making little marks and comments in the margin. He had hoped that when he had laid down the burden of office and was at leisure, he could fulfil his wish of writing a personal account of what he himself knew of her holy soul. God has cheated us of all these treasures.' (1, 221)

A witness to this holocaust remembered that Madame de Chantal could not help exclaiming as she watched the letters burn: '*Ah! les belles choses qui brûlent!*' Not that she meant to imply, of course, that she had written many fine letters. As she stood looking into the fire that December day, she was looking back at the past eighteen years and at all that had happened since she had written the first of those letters from Dijon to Annecy. Her letters had been answered, their object achieved. Now that they had done their part, the fire could consume them, just as she herself could merge completely with the order to which she had been led by the process of spiritual formation signified by the letters.

For this holocaust was at the same time a sacrifice offered up as a final act of detachment. Not *his* letters were to be burnt; she knew they belonged to the world and to posterity. Accidentally, through them, she was quite willing to reveal the most intimate secrets of her spirit; only *her* letters were to disappear, she saw them in the way she saw herself, as a means to an end. She was to decrease, the saint to increase. She looked upon St John the Baptist as one of her patrons and he was perhaps the one most kindred to her in spirit. Burning her letters was therefore a logical act but one that might easily be misunderstood by ordinary standards.

It is not recorded whether she glanced at the letters first; actually to read them would have been out of character for her. Time was too precious. It seems certain that whatever she made of the comments in the margin and of the neatly sorted bundles, she knew nothing of his project of writing about her. For telling her a plan of this kind would have been out of character for him, and quite alien to his method. Indeed, his training had been so successful that, in a sense, the responsibility for God cheating posterity of all these treasures may be laid at his door. He had trained her in humility with the result that what was patent to him even then—that a 'Life' of her would one day be written—would have been impossible for her even to imagine.

Obedience to the expressed wish of her director was a matter of course to Madame de Chantal. Had he left any instructions that the letters were docketed with this intention and were to be kept, it would never have occurred to her to go against his wishes, whatever her own opinion. As there were no directives she felt free to follow her own conscience in this matter. It was not an impulsive action done on the spur of the moment but something more like a sacrificial gesture in retrospect and standing for what was already an accomplished fact: a fire of sacrifice kindled. Cardinal Bérulle, the founder of the Paris Oratory, met Madame de Chantal in Dijon long before she entered religion, and made a famous prophecy about her:

'This heart is an altar where the fire of love never goes out; and it will burn so fiercely that not only the offerings of sacrifice but the altar itself will be consumed.' (1, 355)

When she was young she had branded herself with fire as one set apart for God, and perhaps that gesture had been an impulsive one; the sacrificial fire of the letters was a deliberate act.

But possibly there was another aspect to the question. An *advocatus diaboli*, whose business it is during the inquiries leading up to a canonization process to weigh every action in the balance, might have put a different interpretation on this event. She, after all, made no statement about it, so that any interpretation rests on probability and on analogous quotations from her own writings. Was it her business, the devil's advocate might ask, to judge whether or not she was 'unworthy to be mentioned in a saint's life', and to proceed to such drastic action on the grounds of this unworthiness? Might this not have been a hidden pride? She had wilfully destroyed evidence about this saint's skill in dealing with souls, and this might well have added to his accidental glory. This lack of regard for historical evidence, the advocate might continue, characteristic as it was for her age, could also be seen as a kind of *suppressio veritatis*. Any private person, of course, has a right to his privacy: but here was someone closely connected with a public personality and herself on the best way to becoming one. Such questions make it obvious that she must have had other compelling motives, quite apart from the overriding one of her humility.

She was well aware, and the ovation at Dijon must have put it beyond doubt even for her, that she had become a public figure in France as well as in Savoy. She was no longer the obscure widow who had written about her personal problems to a director to whom she had been united in a close bond of friendship. In the eyes of the world, she and Francis de Sales were identified with

the order which they had since then founded, an order still in its
initial stages. She had realized, especially in Paris, how vulnerable
the order was to attack and how many enemies it had, through
envy, malice and sheer love of intrigue. Francis de Sales had been
invested with the ecclesiastical power of his bishopric and already
had a general reputation for sanctity in his life-time; but even
through him, as she had discovered, the order could be attacked.
How much more, then, through her, a woman, anything but a
saint in her own estimation, and not even invested with the rank
of a Mother General.

If she had kept her letters, even if they were not published
during her life-time, they would sooner or later have become
public property. Then they might well have been used as an
instrument of attack on the order with which she was so intimately
associated. By the very nature of the problem, she herself was at
that time the only person who had enough inside knowledge of
the situation to survey it with all its implications. She thought
herself useless now, and she had, in fact, through no fault in her
own temperament, been a scrupulous and anxious person when
she had first met the bishop. All this she had freely described.
Although the change in her since then was largely hidden from
her, she had no illusions about her failings at that early stage. All
her life she had had temptations against the faith, a delicate subject
and one apt to give scandal if ventilated indiscreetly. In earlier
times she had written explicitly about these doubts, describing
them in detail, as she did her other problems. Her difficulties
concerned subjects raised by argument and controversy in places
such as Dijon and Poitiers, where Calvinism was in the air. In
time, enemies would seize upon her temptations and use them to
discredit the order.

The same use would inevitably be made of a subject still more
liable to misunderstanding: the friendship between her and St
Francis. It was expressed in his letters, and presumably also in
hers, in terms which out of the context of their unique setting,
were likely to cause astonishment in the worldly mind. Insight
into the true character of each saint, perhaps more especially into
that of St Francis who guided and controlled the relationship, is
the only way to understand the unusually close bond that united
them in their love of God. If, then, she burnt her letters, she had

several sound reasons besides the overriding one of her humility, expressed in her letter to St Francis' first biographer.

Fostering the founder's memory in the most practical way possible now became her great responsibility: she organized the collection and editing of his written and spoken word, and she herself made all the initial arrangements for the preliminary inquiries towards his canonization. Her brother André was put in charge of the first official commission which met at Annecy. The saint's living monument, however, was the order he had founded, and the last nineteen years of her life—she died in 1641 at the age of sixty-nine—were completely given over to building up and strengthening the structure of the Visitation. There was no standing still in her own spiritual development, rather the contrary; but to a large extent, it receded into the background after her director's death and after the act which marked the end of an epoch for her: the burning of her letters. She had now finished with herself, becoming one with her work, dedicated more completely even than before to the divine will, 'adoring it in silence.' (5, 87)

During the coming years she worked and travelled incessantly for her order, but as far as she herself was concerned, everything she did was increasingly cloaked in a kind of anonymity. She could pursue each separate task, each journey, follow up each personal contact with an even greater faithfulness, just because it had ceased to exist in its own right for her, and presented itself purely as the will of God in whom she was absorbed. The best way to understand these last two decades of her life is to see them in the light of one of the parables from the *Treatise* which at earlier stages of her life had already proved a faithful portrait.

'What happens to starlight when the sun comes up over our horizon here on earth? It is not destroyed, of course, but the royal light of the sun draws and consumes the lesser light so that the two are made one in a happy union. And what happens to our will when we yield it up completely to the divine pleasure? It is not destroyed altogether but it sinks so deeply into God's will and is so utterly merged with it as to vanish from sight, and no longer to want anything of its own apart from God.

'And now turn your mind to our glorious king, St Louis . . . watch him boarding his ship and setting sail for distant lands; then see his dear wife and queen going on board together with his majesty.

'Now if we had questioned this dear lady and asked: "Where are you going?" she would of course have answered: "Wherever the king goes." And if we had continued: "But do you actually know where the king is going?" she would have said: "He did tell me in a general way, but I'm not in the least anxious to find out exactly where he is going: I just want to go with him." If we had then countered: "So you have no plan of your own in making this journey?", "No" would have been the reply, "No plan at all, except that I want to be with my lord and husband." "But I understand he is going to Egypt and from there to Palestine, stopping at Damietta and at Acre and several other places. Isn't that where you intend to go?" "No, my sole intention is to be close to my king. The places are of no importance except in so far as he will be there. I shall visit them without wanting to go to them—the king's presence is all I want. It is the king who goes on the journey and has decided on it; for my own part, I don't go, I just follow. It is not the journey I want but only to be near the king. Where we make a halt and how we travel, and all that happens on the way—all this is a matter of complete indifference to me." '[1]

Outwardly Madame de Chantal's life did not change after St Francis' death, except that she was perhaps busier than ever before in the daily round of conventual life: prayer, work, correspondence, the parlour. Nor had Mère de Chantal ceased to be Madame la Baronne, the mother of a difficult son and a lively daughter for whom she had continued to do her utmost in every way open to her. She did not consider herself exempt from the duty of arranging good marriages for her children, an important aim for any family of standing, though not too easy to pursue from behind the bars of an enclosed convent. She had some help from her brother André but ultimately the responsibility was hers. It was she who had arranged the match for Françoise with the Burgundian Count de Toulonjon; and because of the girl's volatile temperament, this had not been easy.

In her letters she enters into the very last detail of all the arrangements, including the type and quantity of dresses and of jewellery for the trousseau; the bride's demands were rather exorbitant. Françoise received much good advice from her mother and it is quite apparent that she needed it all. She was an attractive strong-willed, worldly person, fond of show but not of hard work

---

[1] *Treatise on the Love of God*, Bk. 9, ch. 13; A, V, 150.

and responsibility, though well capable of both. A Frémyot at heart she had, outwardly, some of the dash of the Rabutin-Chantal side of the family. Marie-Aymée seems to have been beautiful and good, a model child, yet with enough of her father's charm to leaven the more solid Frémyot qualities; Celse-Bénigne was wayward but at the same time all brilliance, gaiety and wit. Françoise comes somewhere half way, rather plain in appearance, less gifted than the other two, but still with a very definite personality and intelligence of her own.

As the youngest—she was eleven when she left Burgundy—she was the one on whom her mother's changed condition of life reacted least favourably. The older ones had their own sphere: her sister was married, her brother at court. She lived with a mother who was no longer exclusively her mother, and in a home that was not a home in the ordinary sense. Young companions came to join her at the convent, the first of the Visitation boarders of the '*petit habit*' (called after the uniform or modified habit they wore). The education of a small number of girls who perhaps felt inclined to the religious life but were too young to enter, was to be a feature of the convents and one that helped to spread the Visitation influence in French families. This boarding school existence might in any case have been Françoise's lot before her marriage, and it had its charms, judging by the accounts of it. But though the child's mother was there with her, she knew that she was no longer entitled to this mother's whole or chief attention, however conscientious the care she received. As a result she was inclined to be a problem to herself and to others, unsettled, tending to rush to extremes in her need to attract notice.

At first she wanted to follow her mother into the cloister and lead a life of penance. One day she was caught in the convent garden laying about herself with nettles. Then she veered round and took to dressing up giddily when her mother was away from Annecy.[1] Francis de Sales met her on one occasion just as she was going out, all curls and ribbons, and wearing a dress with a fashionably low-cut neckline. His look of mild astonishment, a few pins he quickly conjured up from about his person to restore

[1] *Les deux Filles de Sainte Chantal*, Comtesse A. de Menthon, Paris 1875, p. 227. The information about Françoise is taken from a MS life of her in the Annecy archives.

the modesty of the offending décolleté, an affectionate word or two of reproof, were enough to restore her sense of decorum. All she needed was a little attention. When the time came to choose a suitor she proved difficult, changing her mind over and over again at the last minute, and finding no one good enough till the Count de Toulonjon proposed to her. He was a man old enough to be her father and very wealthy. In time she settled down. Motherhood and, in due course, early widowhood, brought out the finer side of her character and increased her devotion to her own mother. She lived to a great age and saw the celebrations in honour of Francis de Sales' canonization at Annecy in 1662.[1] When she died she was buried at the Autun Visitation, close to her own home and to Monthelon.

Celse-Bénigne was a much greater problem to his mother than Françoise. The boy who had made such a dramatic scene when she left Dijon grew up true to type, that is, to the brilliant but rather unstable streak in the Rabutin-Chantal family. As a baron in his own right and carrying arms, he had not followed a regular course of studies in Paris but gone to court at the early age of fifteen. His charm won him great popularity at the Louvre, and his way of life seems from the first to have been reckless and daring. He was particularly given to gambling and to duelling, he craved for the thrill that only danger could give, was prodigal of his money and quixotic in the defence of his friends. What added to his attractiveness was an irrepressible sense of fun and a gift for personal mimicry, all part of the '*Rabutinage*' inherited by his daughter who coined this word to describe all her father stood for. Madame de Sévigné did with her pen, and in the privacy of a family correspondence, what her father had recklessly acted out in a brief and brilliant court career. '*Chantal se moque de tout le monde*', they said of him, and though no one could bear him malice for long, the king's favour which he enjoyed, brought him envy. From the first to the last, from the contrived scene at Dijon, to his

---

[1] Françoise represented her mother at the canonization and saw the beautiful piece of embroidery Madame de Chantal had made for an occasion which she herself had hoped to witness on earth. It was the bishop's cope which he wore during the procession round Annecy: 'All was palms, hearts and flames' runs a contemporary description of this baroque masterpiece of fine needlework.

heroic and spectacular death in battle, he remained an accomplished showman. He was a man who could have stepped straight out of any Dumas novel.

Would he have turned out a different sort of person had his mother stayed in the world? Probably not. It was a father's example and influence he most needed. Lacking the solid bourgeois virtues and the common sense of the Frémyots, he had all the panache of his paternal lineage without his father's real distinction of character. His resemblance to his father and at the same time the tantalizing difference, made him the delight and despair of his mother. He was also the spoilt favourite of his uncle, Archbishop Frémyot, but the affection of Celse-Bénigne's only close male relative did little to make up for paternal discipline. Francis de Sales who was fond of him, did his best to help, and tried, without success, to establish him at the court of the Duke of Nemours in Annecy where his brother Bernard had served. Celse-Bénigne often came to Annecy to stay at the bishop's house and visit his mother and sisters. Gently the bishop teased her in the early days when she thought herself very detached. In a note announcing her son's arrival, he said how sorry he was not to be able to witness the welcome of 'a mother insensible to everything connected with natural love', for he imagined that she would be 'terribly mortified'.

'Ah, no, my dear daughter, don't be so cruel! Let the poor lad see how happy you are to have him with you; we mustn't let it appear outwardly all of a sudden that our natural passions have died within us.'[1]

When her son visited her in 1618 she had learnt better than to imagine that 'all natural passion had died within her mother's heart.' (4, 302) He caused her constant anxiety, and from that time onwards she asked for prayers for him in her letters. He was then twenty-two, and although he now seemed settled in his unsatisfactory ways, she never gave up hope of being able to influence him for the good. He treated these attempts with reserve and a non-committal courtesy. When he arrived at Annecy with some friends that year, he seems to have been in a rather fractious mood with authority. At the same time he was everyone's darling, and specially attractive to Françoise who 'would not let him out of her sight.' (4, 239) In a note sent back from the convent to the

[1] *Selected Letters*, p. 209 and A, XVI, 37, June 1613.

palace after the messenger had brought word from the bishop, Madame de Chantal said:

'I could not wait any longer, my very dear Father, without hearing from you. It will be no use talking seriously to this boy now, but I hope that with God's help his mood will change for the better and that before he goes, he will open out to you and give you an opportunity of speaking to him more openly for his good. Yesterday I was only able to talk to him when the others were about, today I shall have to put my finger on the sore places. My very dear Father, please say mass for this intention so that God may help him and touch his heart; I shall not be able to help letting you know how things go. I should be very happy if you could also have a little private talk with his friends. I hope that God will help you, my very dear Father; I ought to add for your information that this boy has a way of being reticent with people in authority; all the same, I feel sure he will become more tractable before he goes. May God be our help and our only love, my very dear Father.' (4, 237) Illustration on page facing 225.

Whatever the success of this particular maternal manoeuvre may have been, it had no lasting effect. The following year when both Madame de Chantal and Francis de Sales were in Paris, he got into more serious trouble than ever before. The nature of his escapade is unknown, but whatever it was, it made the talk of the town at a time when she was trying to found a convent against strong opposition and could least afford to be in the public eye. Not that this was her chief concern. This time she really feared for her son's salvation:

'I am most distressed to hear about your affliction', St Francis wrote to her. 'My very dear Mother, mortal life is full of such happenings, and the pangs of childbirth often last a good deal longer than midwives realize. And what better chance is there of making great acts of our heart's union with God's will than when our own love is mortified, and we learn to love our own abjection, indeed, our crucifixion? Come now, God will be right at the centre of your heart and will give you strength; and I hope he will lead this son of yours safely into port, and that in spite of all, you will have the inner consolation of knowing it one day.'[1]

This hope was fulfilled, but not until right at the end.

The only way to steady him, Madame de Chantal felt, was a good and happy marriage. She explored many possibilities but it

[1] A, XVIII, 332, January 1619.

was not until four years later that the right solution was found. It was the Visitation, one might almost say, that in the end made the match. The de Coulanges family, only recently elevated in rank, lived in the aristocratic quarter of Saint Antoine where the Paris Visitation had finally been established. The de Coulanges frequented this new convent where virtue and religion seemed closely allied to nobility of race and heart, and they knew Archbishop Frémyot who had left Bourges and settled close to the Visitation. Marie de Coulanges, the bride, was a gentle, pretty girl, judging by her portrait; she came of a united and happy family and had a large dowry. She was, moreover, really in love with Celse-Bénigne. He for his part contributed to the match an illustrious ancestry going back to the twelfth century, an ancient castle in Burgundy with much land kept free of debt by his mother's constant vigilance. But his most important asset, perhaps, in the eyes of the girl's family was actually his mother and her growing reputation for sanctity. They had a real cult for her, and they found her as attractive for her goodness, as the rest of Paris found her son irresistible for his valour and charm.

The marriage took place in Paris on 14 May 1623 when Celse-Bénigne was twenty-seven years old. His uncle André was the celebrant. Madame de Chantal would not come from Annecy for the wedding though she wrote warmly to the de Coulanges. She did not consider it part of her duty and thought it would set a bad example for an enclosed nun to do this. Francis de Sales, had he still been alive, might have found a good reason for sending her to Paris under obedience on some Visitation matter, for he always helped her to be less hard on herself than she was inclined to be, especially when her motherly feelings were in conflict. But now she had to make her own decisions. Celse-Bénigne understood, and after his marriage he wrote her what amounted to a handsome apology for the scene at Dijon:

'God's ways with us fill me with admiration. If you had stayed in the world as we wanted you to, if you had taken every imaginable step to advance our interests and done everything possible suggested to you by your motherly love and your unsurpassed prudence, you could never have settled me more happily than you have in fact done. For in my marriage God has given me every sort of advantage that anyone of my condition, age and temperament could wish for.' (1, 241)

He was certainly steadier, but his reform was by no means complete. A year later, on Easter Sunday when he was at mass in the great Jesuit church in the rue Saint Antoine, and kneeling with his wife and her family, a friend's servant approached to whisper something in his ear. Chantal at once rose and left the church, going out into the street as he was, in fine clothes and velvet slippers, to act as second in a duel. It was at the Porte Saint Antoine close to the Bastille. Now duelling was strictly forbidden by the church and by the king, both on moral and practical grounds; for the church it was an offence against the fifth commandment, and King Louis XIII found it cost him too many of his bravest fighting men. These duel-crazed young nobles were rushing through life, as Madame de Chantal put it in a letter, 'looking for hell at the point of the sword.' (5, 312)

On this occasion the duellists were caught, they managed to escape their captors but were condemned to death by hanging, the greatest ignominy for a nobleman who was entitled to execution by the sword. They themselves were safe in hiding—Chantal in Burgundy with his sister Françoise—but their effigies were meanwhile hanged in a public square in Paris. This meant complete and final disgrace. Yet somehow he did manage to return to town after a time and live there unscathed, but his career was virtually at an end. He had no profession except that of arms and he felt disinclined to hide himself away in the solitude of his lands at Bourbilly. His daughter Marie, the future Madame de Sévigné, was born early in 1626, but domestic joys could not make up for the excitement of life at the Louvre.

All that remained to him was to try to prove to the king and also to Richelieu, who had a strong personal dislike of him, that he could still be the crown's loyal servant. When volunteers were called for in the fighting in the west of France where the huguenots were making a last stand in the civil skirmishing, Chantal took arms and set out immediately. English allies of the huguenots were trying to take the Isle de Ré in Atlantic waters to form a landing base for reinforcements for the west coast. The island was held by a garrison which was besieged by a strong English force under the Duke of Buckingham. This is where Celse-Bénigne went and where he was killed in battle, his heroism contributing largely to the final success of the French troops. The story of his end is best told in the words on the memorial tablet put up to him more than two hundred years after his death when his body was exhumed and buried again in the church of Saint Martin on the island:

'Here lies Celse-Bénigne de Rabutin, Knight and Baron de Chantal, son of Christophe de Rabutin Chantal and of Jeanne Frémyot, foundress of the Order of the Visitation, canonized on 16 July 1767. He was related to the family of St Bernard and was the father of Madame de Sévigné. He was born in 1596, killed on 22 July 1627 on the beachhead of Sablonceaux, while opposing the landing of English forces and leading the squadron of Gentlemen Volunteers whom he commanded under the Marquis de Toiras. After a battle lasting six hours, in the course of which he received twenty-seven wounds and had three horses killed under him, he was overthrown in the thick of the fray. He leaves a name dear to religion, to his country and to letters. May he rest in peace.'[1]

On the morning of this battle he had made his peace with God, attended mass and received communion. In the last letter his mother had written to him (July 1627), she had once more put it to him that he should live with a care for his soul, and as he would have wished to live when he came to die:

'I want this to be your chief care and desire, my very dear son; all the rest is but as smoke that fades and vanishes before our eyes; but grace makes us happy in this world and wins for us the bliss of a glorious immortality, the sovereign good which even reason should make us strive for all the time, despising all the rest. And please do write to Monseigneur your uncle as often as you can . . .' (6, 66) was the final motherly admonition.

André Frémyot was in the Visitation parlour in Annecy on the feast of the Assumption, the day when the news of this death was brought. He and his sister were there together, at work on the depositions for the cause of Francis de Sales. All she could at first understand was that her son had died in a state of grace, not in one of his unhappy duels, but actually defending his faith and at peace with God. Her natural sorrow was held in balance by relief. It was otherwise with André who reacted in what he considered a more human way; he therefore allowed himself a plain comment:

[1] Quoted by Comte de Franqueville, *Histoire de Bourbilly*, Paris 1907.

'My dear sister' he said, 'your resignation terrifies me ("*m'épouvante*");
only you, with your virtue, could be capable of it. For my part, such
heights are as yet beyond me.' (1, 244)

He wept loudly and relieved his feelings by telling the ecclesiastical dignitaries assembled in the parlour little stories of his
nephew's kindness and good nature. His sister listened in silence
at first and then interspersed an occasional word, trying to bring
the conversation back to a less emotional level. She, the mother,
had to be the comforter, and although it was evident that she felt
all the pain of this loss, she remained composed. Her biographer
makes a point of describing in detail everything connected with
any death, how the news was broken and how received. Hagio-
graphically speaking, this was considered a touchstone by which
increase in submission to God's will could be measured. And
certainly, as her life goes on, there is a marked change in the way
she takes the death of those she loved. The woman whose
composure in the parlour at Annecy frightened her brother was
still the same passionate person who had run out into the woods
at Bourbilly in her grief of many years ago. But her will was no
longer her own; it was held by God's will and at one with it:

'What happens to starlight when the sun comes up? The royal light
of the sun draws and consumes the lesser light till the two are made one
in a happy union.' (A, V, 150)

Her son's death was to her in the first instance a manifestation
of God's will. This did not lessen the pain; her letters prove that
to the end she felt every blow as keenly, and with almost childlike
wonder returned to this paradox: why do we feel the pain so
terribly when we know that it is sent by a loving God?[1] What
terrified André was her outward composure which showed him
the distance she had travelled while he still lagged behind. He was
filled with awe at the literalness of her faith and her closeness to
God.

Madame de Chantal wrote to her son's widow, finding just the
right words to comfort her. Marie survived her husband by only
a few years, leaving her daughter, the last of the Chantal line and
sole inheritor of Bourbilly, to be brought up by the de Coulanges
family and the Visitation in Paris. Whenever possible, she saw her

[1] Letter to André when Celse-Bénigne's wife died in 1633; 7, 239.

grand-daughter, wrote to her and watched over her at all important occasions of her life. The future Madame de Sévigné, who was fifteen years old when her grand-mother died, remembered her well and always spoke of her with veneration as someone beloved but too great to be known intimately. Madame de Chantal realized that she could really do very little for the girl she called '*la pauvre petite pouponne*.'

Except to Francis de Sales, she never came out of her reserve in writing to others about her children. In her letters she asks for prayers for them, briefly reporting their doings to the few who knew them well: Charlotte de Bréchard, Jacqueline Favre. Even to such close friends, the most she ever said was that she had yet again had occasion to discover '*un coeur fort maternel*' within herself when she was distressed about them.

The night before she entered the Galerie, she had had a nightmare vision in which her children rose up to cry vengeance on her for the step she was about to take. The dream faded with the morning, the latent fear that prompted it probably remained with her always. Whenever Celse-Bénigne or Françoise proved really difficult, she must have felt inclined to see this as her own doing and her personal responsibility. In so far as certainty in such a matter was humanly possible, her conscience was clear: God had authorized the step she had taken and had blessed her life as a foundress with another kind of fruitfulness. And in the end all was well, also with her children.

Chapter 11

SERVING THE VISITATION
After 1622

<figure>—————⋙◦☉◦⋘—————</figure>

Madame de Chantal's last discussions with the bishop in Lyons had centred on the organization of the order. He wanted each house to be autonomous though united in spirit and custom with every other, looking for directives towards the *Sainte Source* but in no sense governed by Annecy. The sisters were to remain what they had been in his time: '*filles du clergé*', that is subject to the Holy See through the bishop of their diocese. This was a measure of protection for the order, both against dangers from within by slackening of initial fervour, and from without by the abuse of ecclesiastical power. His intention was to counteract these dangers by spreading authority among the bishops within the tried framework of diocesan administration. At the same time he trusted to the constitutions, the rule and the customs of the order to preserve the integrity of each individual member and so of its general spirit.

For Madame de Chantal, however, this was no easy legacy: she had to organize and continue to form a rapidly growing institute without having the actual powers of a commander. She succeeded in this delicate role, not only as a result of her inborn personal ascendancy, but because she invariably approached questions of policy and ruling with humility and tact. She looked upon herself as the eldest in the family group 'who had had more chance of working alongside the father of the family and talking to him', (1, 224) the order's '*chambrière de peine*', or maid of all work (5, 197) whose part it was to advise and suggest. Very rarely did she find that she had to put her will across against opposition. Preventing faults rather than correcting them, winning loyal co-operation by affection—this was her method, as it had been her director's.

From the purely practical point of view, one of the first conditions for success was to build up a clearly formulated body of instructions for the sisters as a supplement to the rule and the constitutions, already printed in the founder's life-time. By 1624 Madame de Chantal was ready to call the first general chapter of superiors at Annecy to discuss the '*Book of Custom*' which she had herself drawn up from joint notes and oral instructions. During the octave of Whitsun, a version was agreed and approved by the new bishop and the assembled superiors who had travelled to Annecy from every part of France. When all was ready and the revised *Coûtumier* itself neatly copied out, Madame de Chantal led a little procession of sisters to St Francis' tomb near the chapel grille, placed the book close beside it and invited all to join in prayer. If the founder's intention had been misunderstood in any particular they prayed that God would make it plain to them.

This episode in the chapel sets the scene for all that Madame de Chantal did during the remaining years of her life and for the spirit in which she worked. The church has given her the title of foundress but she herself shrank from this appellation and always refused it, because she knew that she was not by nature, like Teresa of Avila for instance, a pioneer and an innovator. This role belonged to St Francis while hers was an essentially feminine one: she followed where he led, she nurtured the institute and brought it up, conserving what his original genius had designed. Leadership and responsibility in a new venture were thrust upon her; she had no inclination for either and often said so, not just in humility but realistically accepting this as part of her natural make-up which she knew to be conservative and traditional. She had to work against the grain to be a leader, and the fact that she did it with great competence never altered her attitude to it. After her husband's death she had been a faithful steward of his estates; the same thing happened when the head of the Visitation family died, leaving her to administer his legacy.

The amount of sheer hard work this involved can best be judged by considering the growth of the order over the next two decades. Between the year of the founder's death and 1633, when

Madame de Chantal was sixty-one years old, forty-eight more Visitations had been founded, making fifty-nine in all. By the time she herself died at the age of sixty-nine in 1641, there were eighty houses and the order had spread beyond Savoy and France to Switzerland, Italy and Poland. She was not, of course, personally responsible for all these foundations but she made the most important of them in person, for instance that at Pont-à-Mousson in 1626, then an influential university centre in the kingdom of Lorraine. In 1638 she went to Turin, the capital of Savoy and the seat of the Piedmontese court. Her tours of general visits were an almost constant feature of her later life, only interrupted by the years from 1628 to 1632 when a great outbreak of the plague came via Germany from the Near East and Hungary, in the wake of the Thirty Years War. This prevented travel, laid waste the towns and countryside of France, and brought Madame de Chantal an interval of comparative rest. The longest tour, lasting nearly two years, was in the mid-thirties; it took her to the north and west of France, and from there right down to the extreme south in Provence. In the end she died, as St Francis did, while on the road.

Thousands of letters, mostly directed to the Visitation superiors and dealing with day to day administrative or spiritual problems, and also her many conferences and instructions, bear witness to the great task of organization and training which filled this last part of her life. These years belong, in the main, to the history of her order with which she was now one. Her biographer devotes the last third of the 'Life' to them, but the impression left on the reader who knows none of the names and few of the places, is one of confusion, even weariness: one foundation reads much like another, and Madame de Chantal herself seems to disappear increasingly behind the mask of the fêted foundress.

Her letters, which rarely give news of the place where she happens to be staying, but simply answer questions and give instructions, do little to fill out the personal background or even to differentiate to any great degree one journey from another. The pattern set by earlier foundations, for instance those at Bourges, Paris and Dijon, was scarcely changed, except that the special kind of welcome first given to her at Dijon now became the general rule. Her fame grew and spread all over France as she got older and as her order became a recognized and increasingly valued feature of French religious and civic life.

Almost from the beginning the order seems to have enjoyed—to an extent which often disturbed the founders—the patronage of the great; especially that of the courts in the various countries in which it was established: France, Lorraine, Piedmont, that is, northern Italy. Why was this? Not because the founders themselves belonged to this social group, but rather because the particular spirit of the founder, the novelty and independence of his whole idea, attracted the same type of person as the very first member of the order. It at once roused the interest of people who were sufficiently devout to understand what a life of prayer and a contemplative vocation meant, who had a spirit of adventure and were willing to encourage a new idea, who could read and had the time to do it; in short, the people who were in contact with the forces which were stirring all over France in an unprecedented religious revival. This in turn was a manifestation of the Counter Reformation spirit all over Europe. Religion was à la mode, good preaching in high fashion among the great and in wealthy cities, the habit of being able to account reasonably for the faith of one's birth or choice was important in a time of sharp religious controversy. A well informed faith led to a more intense spiritual life and so to an appreciation of all that the hidden life within the Visitation meant.

In the same way as the attractive common sense and literary skill of St Francis de Sales had put the devout life within the reach of all such people, that is, of people in the world, his Visitation continued the same apostolate on another level. The order was gracious, reasonable, and its spirit represented the middle way. One side of the French character is inclined to extremes in religion, as the affair of Port Royal demonstrates quite clearly. Francis de Sales, the solid Savoyard, was just sufficiently different from the French to have much to offer them without ceasing to be one of themselves or estranging them by a foreign idiom and a wholly different cast of mind. Just as he had tempered Madame de Chantal's over-eagerness while giving her even greater ardour for complete self-sacrifice, and had in this manner taught her a way of freedom and joy, so his order opened up new religious possibilities in the whole of France: the contemplative life in a fresh and vitally new framework. By its very nature this order released untapped spiritual resources in France. Had circumstances been different in England, it would also have made an immediate appeal of affinity to the English temperament. After the easing of the penal laws at the end of the eighteenth century the Visitation was in fact the first order to be established as a formal foundation in England,[1] while the rule of one of the first anglican communities for women, Dr Neale's Society of St Margaret, founded in 1855, was closely modelled on the first rule of the Visitation. The spirit and the achievement of this sisterhood, the whole history of its later development along the lines laid down by a remarkable founder, illustrates in a striking way how St Francis's original idea of a real compromise between contemplation and action can be put into effect and adapted to English attitudes.

Every good Visitation nun trained in the spirit of Annecy who went out on foundation, showed France what this new order was like, but the greatest ambassador of all was Madame de Chantal herself. She was, as has been said, administering a legacy; in a very real sense she was herself that legacy, so that wherever she went people could say: 'So this is what the Visitation is really like.'

They knew very little, of course, except by its effects, about her hidden life of prayer and mortification which is the normal course of any religious existence. Her long years of training had brought her closer and closer to God. Without knowing what it was that drew them, the people she met sensed this and yielded to its attraction in a way they could not explain. They simply felt that she was holy. When they began to call her a saint, when even high ecclesiastics knelt to ask for her blessing and made speeches of welcome in her honour, she was really shocked: 'For the love of God', she said in Nancy to her travelling companion who saw all the riot of her first triumphal tour in Lorraine, 'let us get away from here. These people are under some misapprehension; they just don't know who I am.' (1, 231)

During her visit to Châlons in 1628, she took to standing with

---

[1] The first English Visitation was founded in Acton, Middlesex, as early as 1804. This community quickly attracted postulants from the great recusant families and established a strongly English tradition in the course of the nineteenth century. The same community was later moved to Westbury-on-Trim, then to Harrow-on-the-Hill and is now at Waldron in Sussex. See *Saint Francis de Sales and the Order of the Visitation,* by Elisabeth Stopp, Waldron, 1962.

her back to the wall in the reception room of the bishop's palace, while for two days on end, people filed past her to be introduced. When she stood clear of the wall, the visitors at once took out their pocket scissors and began to snip little pieces from her veil so as to have a relic of her. In deep mortification, and distressed by the waste of one perfectly good veil after another, she protested to the bishop against the people's crude way of showing what they thought of her. But the bishop happened to be Jacques de Neufchèzes, her own nephew whom she had helped to bring up after her sister's death. He shared the general veneration for his aunt and did not disapprove of his enthusiastic flock.

Although she said little in public, she seems by her very presence to have had an extraordinary personal influence over all who came in contact with her. Simple and direct herself, without a trace of conventional stiffness, she at once put others at their ease. Thinking of them and not of herself led her to establish an immediate personal and human relationship with her visitors. No one felt rebuffed by her. People would call at the convent to talk of their spiritual difficulties, families came to have disputes settled, nuns of other orders consulted her on problems of organization, would-be postulants discussed their vocation. They had the impression that she read their hearts, quite simply, and that there was no mystery about it. She did not have to impose her point of view; people just found themselves calmly accepting it as a matter of course. She had the true courtesy that springs from love.

'He loved God in man and man in God' she wrote of her director, 'and he said he did not want to mean anything to other people, or others to mean anything to him, except in God. He was full of love (*"dilection"*), a true and manifold love (*"amour"*) for souls.'[1]

She too had the quality of universal love, and as the heritage of both founders, one particular form of God-centred love, *'la courtoisie Visitandine'*, 'Visitation courtesy', became a proverbial expression in France.

Her journeys as the envoy of her order cannot be told in detail, but a little episode here and there, or a comment the biographer makes in passing while hurrying on to the real business of the

[1] Deposition for the cause of St Francis de Sales, Article 27; 3, 126.

next reception, the next foundation, can suddenly make these years in the service of the order spring to life.

Generally she was received in state but whenever it could be managed she liked to travel simply and always light: never a pack-horse to follow her, no heavy luggage even when she went away for years on end. All she took was a little *'cassette'*, or leather covered box, that went into the litter next to her and contained her books, papers and clean linen. When a more luxurious method of travelling had been proposed by her daughter on some occasion, she said to Jacqueline Favre:

'I so much like to jog along in my own small way. Just our litter with the blinds down, our ecclesiastic and the two muleteers.' (1, 474) She disliked any appearance of worldliness about her journeys, and though she disapproved of rushing, she was with little apparent effort always punctual and expeditious. When time pressed, as on her tour in Provence, and the great heat of the plains made early morning travel essential, it was she, at the age of sixty-four, who constituted herself the *'reveil-matin'*, or alarm-clock, of the others. Often she woke them before the summer dawn so that they had heard mass and were on the road by three in the morning. It was she too who kept up the joy and courage of the others through all the weariness of the journey. The inns were often poor down in the south: *'une certaine pauvre petite bicoque'*, a poor little shanty, was sometimes all they could find, hardly a bed to sleep on, just straw and leaves. Food was simple. Often she had to make do with a dinner of black bread, curd-cheese and milk, which sounds delicious but was evidently the biographer's idea of stark simplicity. (1, 278)

She was always gay while travelling; nothing could frighten or depress her. If they were going by river and the water was rough, she counselled confidence in the boatmen who were after all only the instrument of providence; when she crossed the Alps in the early autumn of 1638, and it poured with rain all day as they moved up the Mount St Bernard pass, she saw no reason for stopping to take shelter. On the way home, when the mules picked their way along narrow paths with a rock face on one side and a sheer drop on the other, her companion was trembling and white with fear. Madame de Chantal, completely unperturbed, tried to reassure her but could not help smiling at her alarm:

'No sparrow falls into the hunter's net without God's leave, so obviously we won't fall into that precipice unless he has decided on it. And if he has, what can we do about it?' (1, 534)

It was all so clear to her. How could one be afraid? Such faith is catching. On all her travels, cheerfulness reigned in her little company as it did in St Teresa's.

This is how she described the crossing of the Alps when she got home, an afterthought at the end of a long letter to an unnamed superior:

'We had a very good journey back from Turin, thanks be to God. We got out of the town at speed and just in time, for it was besieged almost immediately. We found a good escort in a company of French soldiers, very good men who had nothing but kindness for us. We had to go a long way round so as to avoid running into the armies, making detours and travelling a whole week by paths that led us along the most frightening precipices imaginable. The mule to the fore of our litter fell down on one occasion; had it stumbled towards the right side instead of the left we should have been lost without a hope. You see, dear daughter, what a strong call we had to rely utterly on that same divine providence which so greatly blessed this journey; and I hope that by God's mercy this new monastery will do very well indeed. We gave the habit to five girls and admitted three or four others.—You must really be my very dear daughter, and no doubt about it, for me to write you such a long letter, because I'm quite overwhelmed with correspondence now that I've got back; and besides, as one gets older, one doesn't get any better at hard work. May God make us very strong in his holy love, in which I am all yours.' (8, 140) From Annecy, 1639.

Before she set out, she would carefully scrutinize her much mended clothes and her habit. Ignoring all tactful suggestions about a new habit or a specially light-weight one for hot places, she would add a few more patches where the cloth seemed worn: beautiful mending was a special skill of hers, indeed, all needlework and fine sewing. 'Incomparable neatness and cleanliness simply shone from her and were reflected in all she did.' (1, 446) She gloried in poverty, and in a discreet way, she also used it to bring home a mark of her religious profession to those who gazed at her. 'Just look at the splendour of this foundress', said a courtier to the Princess Royal at the court of Turin. He was pointing to her shoes. Two or three patches adorned them right at the front and they were attached, if not held together, with leather straps. The princess was much struck by this sight and Madame de Chantal went up yet higher in her esteem. (1, 426)

When state apartments were prepared for her, or rooms as a rule reserved for royal visitors, she would sleep—not on the floor, which would have been unsalesian and extreme—but at least in the little bed placed for the servant next to the state bed. She and her companion covered themselves with their own habit while all the silk counterpanes and eiderdowns were carefully folded and put away for the night. (1, 433) In the same way she managed to evade, inconspicuously, the velvet cushions prepared for her to kneel on in church. It is always emphasized that there was no showmanship about her little austerities. By their very nature most of them actually went unnoticed, as St Francis had intended; only a few things here and there attracted her companion's watchful eye, and she in turn reported them to the biographer. It was known, for instance, that she always stopped short of satisfying her hunger and her thirst at meal-times, and that she systematically denied herself every kind of indulgence, especially little, inconspicuous things connected with extra warmth in the winter or coolness in the heat.[1] It was not until a few years before her death, however, that her biographer first began to collect information on a methodical basis, especially from the earliest of the Visitation nuns.

Françoise-Madeleine de Chaugy, who became Madame de Chantal's secretary in 1632, had actually met her briefly a few years before this. It was she, with her writer's eye for a characteristic incident, who left on record something that happened at this first meeting during the time of the great plague. It was in the spring of 1628. Madame de Chantal was on her way back from Paris and staying for a few days with her daughter Françoise near Autun where the plague had already broken out in the city. To catch the disease meant certain death and further contagion to others. No travellers were allowed in or out of the town, but the superior of the Visitation somehow prevailed on the authorities to let her go outside the gates so as to consult the foundress on important matters connected with the convent. Her plan was to stand in the middle of a big field and call out her questions to Madame de Chantal who was to be just within earshot on the road

[1] Canonization Process, Vol. 8, folio 128 et seq.

skirting the edge of the field. The carriage drew up, Madame de Chantal got out and surveyed the scene, the nun standing there alone and far away, preparing to begin the conversation. It would not do. She made the sign of the cross, remained for an instant in prayer and walked rapidly towards the middle of the field. 'Come!' she said, 'in God's name let us get together. He will be with us and keep us from all harm.' The superior dared not move, but Madame de Chantal pressed forward, took her in her arms, kissed her and reassured her.

Watching this scene from the carriage there was amongst others her future secretary and biographer, Mademoiselle de Chaugy. A niece of the Count de Toulonjon, she was at that time staying with Françoise and trying to recover from an unhappy love affair. She was undecided how to spend the rest of her life so as to mend her broken heart: in the world, reading and writing novels and poetry—for she had a ready pen—or else at prayer in some hidden cloister. These were the only alternatives which suggested themselves to her. Madame de Chantal watched her, talked to her and formed her own opinion. When the time came for her to return to Annecy, she suggested that a change of scenery and the mountain air might meet Mademoiselle de Chaugy's case. The invitation was accepted. The rest was only a matter of time.

The plague years which lasted from 1628 to about 1631 were Madame de Chantal's only real respite from travelling and from the parlour. Had the cause not been so dreadful, she would have been perfectly happy. Many of the monasteries in France were affected, and those that were spared suffered isolation and extreme poverty; her practical charity found a ready field of action within Annecy itself and far into France. To the superior at Autun, for example, whom she had met in the field and whose convent was practically starving because no one from the farms would risk bringing provisions into the plague-stricken city, she made the following proposition: her daughter Françoise at her castle some way out would buy a little flock of sheep, have them driven over to a pasture near the town. The nuns could then have them brought along to graze in the convent orchard. One sheep a week, according to her calculations, would just do to keep the community alive and in good health till the worst was over.

From behind the closed doors of her convent—no visitors were allowed and provisions only reached them from across the lake to the enclosure wall of their garden—she sent out a circular letter dated 6 December 1629, and addressed to all the houses in France.[1] In detail, she described how she had dealt with the situation when the plague reached Annecy. Much practical skill is revealed in this letter, showing how every activity of the day was arranged to avoid dangers of infection. It is full, too, of interesting medical hints coming from one who had not forgotten the skill of her Monthelon days, of her 'little village recipes' as she called them. A final paragraph of this letter told of the special prayers and penances undertaken for the afflicted all over the country, and was devoted to words of encouragement such as only she could write.

She spent a good deal of time during those years when, in her own striking phrase, she lived 'high above death in the midst of so much death' (6, 217), with her pen in her hand or dictating to one of her secretaries. Unlike her grand-daughter who was taught the art of writing and carefully cultivated it, Madame de Chantal became, as the years went on, a writer in spite of herself. In nearly all her utterances, whether spoken or written, her undivided attention went to the message or meaning she wanted to put across while the way in which this was done, the artistic shaping of the phrase, was less important. Much practice in the expression of clear thought automatically leads to an adequate style, and as it happened, hers was also naturally good. This seems to have been partly a gift, partly the result of her lawyer father's early training in clear speech and formulation, to some extent also the result of reading, though she was at the same time remarkably independent. She did not, for instance, assimilate her director's style, even superficially.

Certainly she was aware of the need for good presentation of all written matter. Her advice to her nuns always tends in the same direction: when you have to write, begin by asking God to guide your pen (4, 88), then go ahead, write simply, briefly, without any affected phrases, without repetition (7, 4). In describing a sister's life and character for her necrology—an account of every nun who died was sent round to the other houses—avoid

[1] 6, 362–371.

exaggeration, be truthful and not too general; a specific and characteristic action carefully selected from among many is worth more than any amount of pious generalization.[1]

These instructions accord well with her own way of writing and speaking which was always spare, concrete and selective. Argument, analysis and narrative were equally successful in her letters and in her discourses, though these last were written down by others and therefore not quite representative. She was, perhaps, at her most attractive in telling anecdotes. As a young woman, she had been much alone with children and in a solitary country-side. The winter evenings at Bourbilly and Monthelon were spent sewing or spinning and telling stories or listening to legends. Her letters bear the imprint of this. On suitable occasions, what she wrote was peppered with homely, even racy and amusing phrases and proverbial expressions. When she uses an image to drive home a point, and this is rather rare, it is generally one taken from the concrete realities which surround a country woman and a housewife. She draws, for instance, upon her observation of fields in harvest and beneath the plough, vineyards lying fallow, trees growing to slow maturity and shedding their leaves, the rhythm of the seasons, sheep at pasture, birds hiding in terror from the hovering hawk, rivers hurrying towards the sea, the lake, calm and transparent in the sunlight.

She speaks to her nuns of small children and their simplicity and frankness at work and at play, of 'a certain small candle' which God himself must put into their hearts as into a dark room to show them what wants doing there, of their need to be responsive and pliable. Let your soul be soft and supple as a glove, she said to them one day, be like a ball of warm bees-wax in God's hands to be moulded as he pleases, let yourself be fashioned like a piece of cloth that is cut out to make a garment, allow yourself to be folded as you would fold a handkerchief. Again and again she comes back to what was closest of all for comparison: her own hand, if the portraits are to be believed, a very beautiful hand.

'Look at this hand of mine: it couldn't be more bare, more simple. That is how we must be, serving God with no other thought except how to please him.' (2, 224)

[1] *Réponses*, p. 504.

And lifting her hands, cupping them like someone who is holding and carrying something infinitely precious, she said: 'This is how we must hold and carry our souls.' (2, 79) Without any deliberate manoeuvre on her part, the life she herself had so abundantly, communicated itself to all she wrote and said. This is the most characteristic quality of her writing—a kindling power.

'How I wish I had burning coals to set your hearts on fire!'

she called out to the sisters at Annecy one day. (2, 243) She seemed to be unaware that this is what her words really could do, for she added:

'But I am not worthy to render God and our house this service.'

Her best piece of writing, and really her only deliberate composition of any length, was her formal deposition on the life and character of St Francis de Sales, a work which she prepared during the spring and early summer of 1627 for the First Canonization Process at Annecy. Her contribution consisted of fifty-five articles or sections amounting to about 40,000 words, dealing with his manner of life and the characteristic way in which his virtues were made manifest. She was acknowledged to be the person who knew him best, but many knew him well; a glance at some of the other depositions in the archives at Annecy shows what a wide gap there may be between just having material about a person, and being able to distil it in a form that would carry conviction far beyond its immediate object as evidence. Rarely has a saint been so fortunate in his chief witness. It is written in the form of answers to the promoter's questions, the form in which she said she was best able to express herself: 'I can only find something to say if you ask me questions', she used to tell her nuns. Her mind worked best when faced with a definite issue and stimulated by a concrete situation; she made no claim to powers of abstract thought unrelated to a personal situation.

Her deposition, together with a long letter about him addressed to the saint's first biographer, remains the best brief sketch of St Francis ever written. On literary grounds alone it has won the highest praise of an exacting critic. Sainte-Beuve found her words on St Francis de Sales clearer, more penetrating and alive than even those of her fellow countryman from Burgundy, Bossuet. Of her letter, Sainte-Beuve said: 'There has never been a better portrait than this, and no one has ever made things that seem to lie beyond words more immediately intelligible.'[1]

No mere summary of either the letter or the deposition can do them justice: the content alone is not what matters. The unique quality of this work, her own particular accent and approach, results from the interaction of the subject matter, a saint's life, with the form itself in which it found shape, a saint's written word. Her intention was to create a memorial for him, but inevitably and without intending it, she made it into a memorial of them both, jointly. Only her eyes could have seen so much and only she could have picked out from among thousands the most telling of his words and actions to quote and illustrate. Her insight and selection reflect her spirit as much, almost, as his. In the *Treatise* he had written of her, indirectly, and this is what helped to make it the outstanding book it was while revealing his own spirit: a unique combination of abstract reasoning power with practical insight. She, as a woman, wrote a personal account, only of him; and yet it is of all her writings the document in which she reveals her own spirit most intimately, all her ardour, her intuitive wisdom, her clear judgement.

The only way to give some idea of this work is to attempt a translation of a typical article, showing her method of alternating analysis and description: detail realistically observed, the very rhythm of his speech for instance, is followed by summarizing statement.

'*How devoted he was as a Confessor.* (Article 42)

'I submit that our Blessed Father was altogether beyond compare in his charity and zeal in the confessional. He gave himself completely and unstintingly to this holy work, setting neither limit nor measure to his zeal except the need of those who turned to him; he used to abandon everything else for that, unless it were something still more important for God's glory, because he knew that souls profited greatly by this sacrament. Every Sunday and feast-day a great number of people used to come to him, men and women of noble birth, ordinary citizens, soldiers, servants, peasants, beggars, people who were diseased, full of sores, stinking, afflicted with every sort of abject suffering—he received them all without difference or distinction of persons, with equal love and gentleness. He never sent anyone away, however lowly; rather the contrary, I firmly believe that he received these people with even greater

[1] *Causeries du Lundi*, 'Saint François de Sales'.

love, and welcomed them even more tenderly than those who were in easy circumstances and good-looking; and he used to say that this was a chance of exercising real charity. Even children were not afraid to approach him; he made them feel so much at home that they took joy in coming to him again.

'He gave his penitents all the time and opportunity they needed to tell him everything that wanted saying. He never hurried people. Moreover, on all the days above mentioned, at whatever time people asked for him, he used to leave everything else, not even going to the cathedral to join in the office at times, and delaying mass, even when he was all ready and robed; he went as far as leaving his meals though his household did not like it and wanted to prevent him.

'On great feast-days, jubilees and other occasions of this kind, he often had to hear confessions day and night. I remember one day when I saw him completely exhausted: "Days like this", he said to me, "are worth their weight in gold to me because of the many confessions." To give his penitents confidence he used to say to them: "Don't make any difference between your own heart and mine; I'm all yours, our hearts are equal."

'With some he wept over their sins even as they wept, and he treated his penitents so lovingly that the ice in their heart was melted as he spoke. . . . When he realized that people had difficulty in speaking out in confession, and were held back by shame or fear, he tried every means of opening their hearts and increasing their confidence. "Am I not your Father?" he would ask, and then go on asking till one said "yes"; and then: "Now don't you want to tell me everything? God is waiting for you to pour out your heart to him, his arms are wide open to welcome you. Now, don't you see, I'm in God's place, how can you be ashamed in front of me? And after all, I too am a sinner, and if you had done every wicked thing in the world, it would not put me off." He even used to help you, very gently and kindly, to state your sins when he realized that you were finding it hard to explain things, either because you were too ignorant or else too much covered in confusion.

'After confession he used to say such warm and heart-felt things. "O how dear your soul is to me, and all you have said! And now the angels rejoice and are happy about your confession, and I can join in with them and congratulate you too. But now you must really promise our Lord not to start sinning all over again, and promise me too."

'When he saw there was no contrition, he made people say a few little words, such as: "You wish you had never offended God, don't you?" And sometimes he made you say over again something you had accused yourself of, so as to break down your dislike of saying it.

'He gave very short penances and used to say: "You'll do as I tell you, won't you? Now say this", which would be some easy vocal prayer, and he never made you meditate on a mystery, or things of that kind, as a penance.

'He said little in confession, but limited himself to trying to remove vain scruples and to make clear to his penitents what was and what was not a sin; what he said, however, touched the heart more than any long discourse could have done, and you came away from him with great courage and often with great recollection and a sense of God's presence.

'He very much liked you to be clear, simple and straightforward in confession and told his penitents to say precisely what had led to their sin; they were not to go to confession lightly but to explain clearly to the confessor what had prompted or induced the sin in question. He used to say that if you didn't do this, you could never be properly cured and cleansed. By insisting on clear confessions to purify the heart, he uprooted evil passions which others who did not use this method, might well have left untouched.

'With this incomparable kindness ("*débonnaireté*") he opened the most firmly locked hearts, he drew out all the evil that was in them and established them in solid resolutions and affections. He was extremely decisive, and he could clear up doubts and scruples at once, there and then, filling the heart with perfect reassurance and peace.' (3, 204–207)

The chief witness did not live to see her director's canonization, for in 1634 Pope Urban VIII put the whole matter of the church's official recognition of sanctity on a more formal and uniform basis with his decree '*Caelestis Hierusalem*'. Official beatification, a preliminary stage, was to precede any petition for canonization; a process at that time already pending on the older system was declared void if certain conditions had not been observed. Thus, the judgement of the church was not to be presumed in advance by a public cult to the person concerned. But how was this suddenly to be imposed in a place like Annecy and with a man as beloved as Francis de Sales? Pilgrims filed past his tomb in the Visitation church all day, and there was a blaze of candles that never went out. In 1662 he became, in fact, the first saint to be officially beatified in a public ceremony at St Peter's in Rome, and this was followed by his canonization three years later.

These new measures were still a part of the Counter Reformation and aimed at clearing up ancient abuses. Though the delay was a blow to Madame de Chantal—she said, briefly, that it was the greatest disappointment of her whole life and then never referred to it again—she realized that what affected Annecy and her naturally had to yield to the common interest and ultimate welfare of the church. When Francis de Sales' second process was opened it was Françoise Madeleine de Chaugy, then superior at Annecy, and also her Franciscan priest brother, who saw to everything as the foundress would have wished it done. Madame de Chantal's statement was again read out as the most important, and that at a time when her own sanctity, though far from being as yet officially recognized, was hardly in doubt.

She contributed, too, to the founder's cause by the help she gave to the editors of his letters, sermons and spiritual conferences. Impartial study of the circumstances suggests that Madame de Chantal's share in this work, especially the more negative aspects of it, has been exaggerated. As a result of this exaggeration, much of the censure that a scholar would nowadays pass on seventeenth-century editorial policy with regard to original texts, is passed on her alone. In this as in all other aspects of her work, she regarded her part as ancillary in the true sense of that word: she was the 'ancilla' or handmaid, influencing policy but not dictating it. Her influence went towards keeping private what was in fact private, an instinct strong in the social milieu from which she came, and also inherent in her own particular temperament. She was reserved by nature.

Her aim, which was also an incidental one when she destroyed her own letters to St Francis, was to avoid publishing in the letters anything which might, however unjustifiably, give cause for scandal, and in the *Conferences* collected and written down at the convent, anything of domestic interest to the convent alone. Even though critics arrogate this right to themselves, she herself was surely the best judge of what was, and what was not, suitable for publication. She saw no reason for pandering to public curiosity which then, as now, fastens avidly on every detail of life behind the bars of an enclosed convent. In the case of the letters, she had to consider the fact that many of St Francis de Sales's correspondents were still alive. The actual editors of the letters, his cousin Louis, his brother and successor, Jean, and the Jesuit fathers at the college at Chambéry, were moved by the same motives of discretion. Where they differed from her—they thought, for instance, that if too many affectionate expressions were cut out of the letters, they would no longer be characteristic of the saint—she at once gave way and willingly revised her own opinion (5, 590). Her point had been 'that the world was incapable of understanding the purity of his love' (5, 538). To judge by much that is written on this subject, even now, she may well have been right.

When an unofficial edition of the *Conferences* was published in 1627, entitled '*Les Colloques*', and taken from a manuscript copy borrowed from one of the convents, Madame de Chantal at once set about organizing an official edition: '*Les Vrays Entretiens Spirituels*' which came out the following year. These talks, mainly given at Annecy, had circulated in manuscript copies all over France. They had been copied and recopied, mistakes and all, over a period of many years, the material was often set out in a confused way, details or little asides of St Francis which charm the reader now, but in the spirit of the times seemed irrelevant in a spiritual book then, had remained in the text. Jean de Sales and the Fathers at Chambéry had the last word in this new edition and they prepared a text which eliminated all direct personal references, also questions which only concerned Visitation customs. The main object in view was, after all, the good of souls and the increase of Francis de Sales' accidental glory.[1]

In all that concerned publication, Madame de Chantal remained consistent from the first: family affairs were to be kept within the family. Even when the *Constitutions*, *Rule* and *Book of Custom* had all been printed for circulation in the convents, questions continued to pour in concerning details of procedure and asking how this point or the other was to be understood. '*Les filles ne*

[1] The *Colloques* are now a bibliographical rarity because the edition was seized as unauthorized. The Annecy edition (Vol. VI) of the *Vrays Entretiens*, however, gives all the important variants so that most of the original MS material, though not all, can now be reconstructed. One of the main charges against the *Vrays Entretiens* was that St Francis' last talk to the nuns at Lyons, two days before he died, '*Ne rien demander, ne rien refuser*', was shortened and sections of it inserted into other conferences, as seemed appropriate. This was not Madame de Chantal's doing, and she herself found it distressing (see her letter to Lyons, 28 July 1630; 6, 467). In a talk of her own a month before she died, she refers to St Francis's comments on confession which were in one of his *Entretiens* and were cut out, 'I don't know why' (2, 480), she adds.

peuvent jamais assez demander', 'they have never done asking questions,' she said. She found herself answering the same things over and over again, so in time, a book of her answers, *'Les Réponses'*, was put together, largely by Jacqueline Favre. When the complete manuscript was ready, Jacqueline asked her to read and correct it, which she did, spending a considerable amount of time over her revision and writing a typical preface.

With this book she wanted, she said, to help her sisters concentrate on essentials in the religious life so as to preserve that *'sainte et très-aimable simplicité'* which their founder intended for them. If only he had been in their place to answer all their questions, they would soon have won their way through to complete inner clarity and satisfaction, but now they would have to make do with a poor second best. She will try to answer everything simply, as the Holy Ghost prompts her and in accordance with what her Blessed Father taught her. And at the end of this long book which contains some of her most characteristic and tender writing (St Vincent de Paul said he could never read it without tears), she begs the sisters to be content now and not go on asking so many questions. Too much instruction stifles the spirit of devotion and can harm even vocation itself. We *know* enough; all that remains is to *do*, and simply to keep our rule.

In 1628, without her knowledge, the book which she had thought would circulate in manuscript copies only, was printed. This was a source of great mortification to her. Bishop Jean de Sales decided, to her relief, that the book even now it was printed should only be read within the convents, unless by express permission and for an adequate reason. Apart from certain extracts which have been printed in anthologies, the book is unknown outside the Visitation and is not, in fact, in St Chantal's *'Works'*. Her wish has been respected. She never, of course, explicitly forbade the publication of anything she wrote, because it would hardly have occurred to her that the contingency would arise. The sight of her complete works in seven large volumes of which five contain letters up to the number of two thousand, and two give occasional writings, would have filled her with astonishment, if not complete dismay.

Her own ideas about herself as a writer cannot be taken as a final criterion; all the same, they are bound to influence a reader's attitude, the more so the better she is known. Her writing and speaking filled a large part of her life during its final phase but it never ceased to be a means to an end, an incidental activity; she wrote because she had to, and not, like St Francis de Sales, because it was not only a duty but a pleasure to express things in writing. In a letter she said:

'Speaking naturally, I find it disconcerting and distasteful to write in this way', that is, authoritatively, 'because it has some indefinable air about it of being in the know'—'*je ne sais quoi de maîtrise*'. (5, 551)

She had an almost modern shrinking from speaking and writing *ex cathedra*, or as one 'in the know'; but most of her writing, except for her deposition and some of her letters, necessarily had to be of this kind. In spite of her unusual ability in this field, Madame de Sévigné's grand-mother remained, when all is said and done, a writer in spite of herself.

Madame de Chantal's written and spoken word had one subject only: the personal and spiritual formation of the women in her order. She was a great teacher and educator of women. Her school was an enclosed convent, her subject the life of religious perfection in so far as it can be taught. She had qualified for her work by her own spiritual training and development under the guidance of the greatest director of her time; all she ever did, learnt and suffered went into the work which filled the last part of her life and gave it its unique character and power. The unusual combination of circumstances, the fact that she had been a married woman, a mother, and knew the life of a lady of the world, gave her influence as a religious educator a further interest and distinction.

How did she set about her work? No differently from any other good superior; the distinction came from what she was in herself. She taught her charges to live by the rule and the constitutions, that is, the founder's spirit, and she herself set the example of how this could best be done. She laid no claim to original teaching or method. Her special strength as a teacher lay, perhaps, in her simplicity and directness when she addressed the sisters, and in the resulting economy of words, the brief and memorable formulations which carried conviction. She had, moreover, much shrewd insight into the workings of a woman's

St Chantal in 1636. The Turin Portrait
Visitation, Turin, Italy

St Chantal writes to St Francis de Sales about her son, Celse-Bénigne (see p. 199)

Visitation Archives, Annecy

mind, knowing how to help her use her positive qualities of loyalty, zeal, pity, her strong feeling within a limited sphere; she encouraged her to overcome her weaknesses, more especially the foibles which bedevil the pious. With clear-sighted compassion she explained in her conferences their subtle self-regarding and lack of simplicity, their little jealousies, their flattery, insincerity, emotionalism and tendency to exaggerate. She castigated the habit of continually asking for advice or confirmation, of fussing about little things without a due sense of proportion, and she made them aware how easy it was for a nun to slip into a certain narrowness of outlook, hard to distinguish from complacency.

Madame de Chantal made the sisters conscious of such failings by first of all describing them accurately; after that, like her director, she left the pruning hook in God's hands and all the rest to the Spirit's working.[1] By her own example she helped them to see how the religious life could be lived nobly, generously and simply.

Loving by nature, without however being demonstrative, she understood as a matter of course that the sisters needed to feel and find affection.

'Be all things to your daughters' she said to a new superior, 'mother, friend, sister. Win their hearts. If they find no friendship and love in us and in one another, they will have nothing to hold on to at all. Now that may be best of all, of course, but very few are capable of it.' (4, 450)

She herself was essentially motherly and had to make no special conscious effort to be a mother figure to the young and to the whole order. Like St Francis de Sales, she was there to be used as a channel for the love of God and was never afraid of it. Her motherliness was the essence of her being; to be motherly was as natural to her as breathing, and as simple.

This realistic and entirely un-Jansenist attitude to human nature and affection, the legacy of St Francis and the fruit of her own experience as a wife and mother, she carried into every department of convent life. Madame de Chantal taught her superiors that recreation is a very important time for people who live in isolation. All have to contribute unselfishly and someone has to lead and direct it if it is to be a success in the long run. Here again,

[1] *Selected Letters*, p. 276.

she taught by example. At Bourbilly she had been a good hostess; her husband was sociable, he liked to have guests about the house and made the winter months a continual round of parties. She had not forgotten the art of entertaining in the best possible way, that is, without anyone guessing that it was, in fact, an art, or something done deliberately. All the sisters at Annecy, or in whatever house she happened to be, were enthusiastic about her recreations. She was a good raconteuse, and like her son, was able to make people laugh, though her wit had no sting in it; her unusually conscious awareness of the springs of human action leads one to suspect that the sting might easily have been there. Conversation too is an art, and she knew its secrets: the greatest, according to her countryman, La Bruyère, being to draw people out and let them talk; looking back afterwards, they burst into praise and say you are a brilliant conversationalist while all the time you have in fact hardly opened your mouth. Madame de Chantal could talk, certainly, but she was also an excellent listener. This is nowhere stated in so many words, but there is a clue: it is a quality she herself specially noticed about St Francis de Sales. A cumulative impression of her ability to listen is formed as one reads her life and observes how charmed people always were with her conversation—so little of which has been reported.

Then again, realizing the special needs of an enclosed community, she laid great stress on tasks and reading carefully done, not as ends in themselves, but as a necessary adjunct to the contemplative's actual work and profession: prayer. Unlike teaching or nursing, this vocation brings no stimulus from without; and yet there has to be some sort of interaction of the material from outside the personality with the introverted world in which its time is spent, else there is nothing left for grace to work on. Minds will then become dull and sour, the personality narrow and, at the worst, 'melancholy'. This was a technical term of the time, roughly corresponding to a still vaguer designation, 'neurotic'. Madame de Chantal no less than Teresa of Avila had to grapple with the problem of melancholy nuns and with the general responsibility of keeping an enclosed community of women spiritually and mentally fit for their exacting profession.

Strict observance was again her chief answer here, for the rule and constitutions had been designed with precisely these needs in mind. Apart from that, she always emphasized how necessary it was for the superior and community to work consciously together to build a little world of their own which would faithfully reflect, within the conditions laid down for them, the best of what they had left behind: a mother in the superior, a family in the sisters, fatherly guidance, though not too much of it, from competent priests. The advice of skilled confessors and retreat-givers was as important to her as to St Teresa, and as a result of the religious revival, the supply of such trained men in seventeenth-century France was better than in sixteenth-century Spain. In France it was the members of the Society of Jesus rather than the Dominicans who were to the fore. Foundations were only made where the help of religious was available.

She arranged for the sisters to have plenty of food for mind and heart in spiritual or doctrinal conferences, and in planned reading which in accordance with the constitutions was discussed in common every day. Madame de Chantal continually advises the renewed study of fundamentals in the shape of the catechism, especially that of the Council of Trent. This work is little read now except by theologians; a study of its closely packed hundreds of pages increases one's respect for the assimilative capacity Madame de Chantal expected of her sisters, even though the version used may have been an abridged one. She wanted the sisters to remain aware, always, of a wider horizon, of their membership of the church as a whole and of their serious obligations towards it as contemplatives. They were to think of their profession, as she herself quite naturally did, in great-hearted terms, holding in their prayer not only their own nation, but the community of nations the world over, and the whole universal church. Otherwise the voluntary imprisonment of the contemplative nun might well turn into a prison of the mind.

Nor was the body to be neglected: there was to be plenty of good though homely food, no choice fare, but enough variety. She wanted the sisters to have fruit according to season (6, 516), a good supply of bread, though baked not more than twice a week (2, 462), which would constitute a real though harmless sacrifice for a Frenchwoman, used to delicious, crusty loaves, warm from the oven as often as twice a day. Wherever possible, convents were to be self-supporting for the things that could be grown in the grounds, even for wheat, where, as in a mountain valley near Annecy, a farm was available. Livestock for the supply of milk, cheese, eggs, was a matter of course. For this reason, if for no other, every monastery was to have a large garden or orchard, where the sisters could get fresh air and exercise. The position of the convent was to be as 'healthy, airy and spacious' as possible (5, 546), preferably with a good view over the surrounding countryside (7, 146). The wide landscape beyond the forest at Bourbilly and all around the castle at Monthelon lived on in her memory, and was to her an integral part of a sane and healthy life of prayer. Anyone who knows Annecy, knows that the spirit of the Visitation is as inseparable from the natural beauty of its mountain scene as is, for instance, the Benedictine spirit from its landscape setting.

All Madame de Chantal's care for the spiritual and concrete side of Visitation life was ultimately directed towards fostering the spirit of prayer and the contemplative's ever increasing union with God. The work that was done in the convent apart from the actual office assigned, such as assistant, infirmarian, novice-mistress and so on, varied with individual talent: all could sew in those days and embroider, while many could spin. Printing was still in its fairly early stages so that nuns with a good hand copied books when necessary, not ornamentally, but as a practical measure, and also for economy. Books were an expensive luxury. A nun who had a gift for writing kept the chronicles, told the life of any outstanding sister and wrote up the history of her own foundation, a piece of work of historical importance which Madame de Chantal, familiar with the idea of archives through her father's profession, had the vision to organize from the very beginning. The Visitation archives, the majority of them as yet untapped, contain manuscripts of considerable incidental interest to the social and regional historian.

The nuns did not, of course, pursue study as an end in itself, or even as a part of their vocation, as the Benedictines do; but the majority of them, who were, after all, the sisters and daughters of the women who made the salons of the *Grand Siècle* famous all over Europe, were well read and cultivated in the true humanist tradition. Reading was encouraged, but like St Teresa, Madame de Chantal liked the superior to be watchful about the kind of book that was introduced to the convent library shelves. This was the age of Jansenism though the actual controversy did not flare up till after the death of the foundress. On the whole, she liked the sisters to give first place in their reading to the works of St Francis de Sales and to get into the good habit of making them last a long time, their whole life for preference. 'This is our bread', she used to say.

Apart from the New Testament and the Psalms, constantly stressed in her letters as reading matter, she suggests among other things the works of St Teresa of Avila, Rodriguez and Alvarez. She knew St Augustine and St Jerome well in the few contemporary translations and selections that were available, especially the *Confessions* and the letters. The Lives of the Saints and of the Desert Fathers were special favourites, also the stories of more recent saints, such as Catherine of Siena and Catherine of Genoa, Francis Borgia, and also Madame Acarie. The amount of spiritual reading available to those who had no Latin was still very limited at the beginning of the seventeenth century. It was St Francis de Sales himself who had set the fashion for this kind of reading among lay people. As Madame de Chantal grew older, she herself found reading a trial, and not only spiritually: her eyesight was bad, and in her letters there are occasional wry references to her *'bésicles'*, or glasses, pressed on her by a saintly Jesuit in Paris whose eyes seem to have been rather different from hers. But in the days before consulting opticians, spectacles were cheerfully passed round among friends as an expensive and interchangeable commodity, or merely as a curious novelty.

Too much reading, she felt, was worse than too little: what was obviously just an itch to read, was to be restrained. Read slowly, she said, mortify your curiosity by stopping from time to time, and remember that in order to acquire true perfection you have to 'talk little, think little, desire little and do a great deal.' (5, 495) Her letters show that she had a disconcerting way of bringing every topic back to the main issue; as a superior, she had a fundamental simplicity which was like a breath of fresh air to those who came to her with their minds befogged by inessentials.

Some sisters who wanted guidance for their voting, asked her what she thought were the qualities essential to a good superior. She listed in order of importance first of all humility and interior mortification, then discretion and sound judgement without worldly wisdom, thirdly, zeal for observance and sincerity in profession. As an after-thought, she added that special skill in business affairs was the least necessary qualification, because the rule allows a *Soeur Économe* for that. Nor was actual experience of office essential.[1] The order in which the qualities were listed may have come as rather a surprise to the sisters, but on thinking it over, they will have understood how far-sighted her ideas were. They will also have realized that without intending it she had given them a good portrait of herself. She had practical competence and years of experience, it is true, and also the indefinable strength that comes of personal holiness, but the essentials fit her. Humility heads her list. Humility, simplicity, obedience—these are the key words of all her training as a superior. She never attempted to act in her own strength:

'Keep your eyes fixed on the Master, work together with him. Teach your daughters to look into his eyes too, till they forget their own ideas and learn to think, act and work in him, through him and for him alone.' (3, 340)

This was the secret of her influence on others.

[1] *Réponses*, p. 309.

Chapter 12

LAST YEARS
1637-1641

——————◦◉◦——————

In the democratic Augustinian tradition the sisters of the Visitation were free to elect their superior from outside their own community. Francis de Sales foresaw that this would lead to competition for the person of the foundress and might cause difficulties of organization. He therefore suggested that she should not hold office as superior except at Annecy. This did not, of course, put her outside the ordinary rules applying to superiority: the first appointment was for three years and could be renewed for another triennial, but never under any circumstances whatever beyond that period. After a further interval during which the deposed superior learned to live under authority again, she could be re-elected either to her own convent or to another.

This was one of the points of the rule on which Madame de Chantal insisted most firmly and where she sometimes met with opposition, especially in her own case. Some communities, or towns and bishops even, became so attached to a good superior that there was quite an outcry when the end of her term of office came. In his wisdom Francis de Sales had foreseen this and had laid down that there were to be no exceptions whatever, no hard cases. Madame de Chantal saw to it that all houses kept strictly to the letter of the law in this matter, and she herself looked on it as a too rare privilege to be subject to a superior who had once been her own novice. From 1627, when she left for her journey in Lorraine, to the second year of the plague in 1629, Peronne-Marie de Chastel was superior at Annecy. The same sister, one of the first to enter the Galerie, and now a woman of forty-nine with much experience of superiority elsewhere, was elected to Annecy

again in 1635. As during the last interval, this was Madame de
Chantal's signal for another long tour of the convents from which
she did not return till late the following year. But for a short
while before setting out she could still enjoy the company of
Jacqueline Favre who stayed at Annecy for a few weeks while
changing houses from Paris to Chambéry. This meant that for a
little while, a time of happiness for all of them, three of the earliest
Visitandines were reunited.

Peronne-Marie used her position of authority with tact, but she
was not above the occasional little manoeuvre to make Madame
de Chantal commit to paper some of the things that the sisters
thought worth recording and of which, as everyone at Annecy
knew, there was so very little record. One day towards the end of
May 1637, when it was Madame de Chantal's turn to give the
superior an account of her inner state, Peronne-Marie said that she
was pressed for time and asked her to write out on a scrap of paper
what she had intended to say. Transparent as this must have been
to Madame de Chantal, it is not recorded that she allowed herself
any comment on this somewhat unusual request. Obediently she
picked up an old letter that lay close to hand; on the blank page
at the back she at once wrote the following account of her inner
darkness:

'I write of God and speak of him as though I were fully convinced.
I do this because I want him and believe in him far beyond my pain
and affliction, as it seems to me; and because the only thing I want is
the treasure of faith, hope and charity. I want to do everything that I
know God expects of me.

'Since last Easter this anguish and the frequent evil thoughts have
left me from time to time; and I take a little more comfort and rest in
this simple looking upon God. But I never lose sight of the actual trial
though I only feel the anguish of it intermittently. So there is my soul
in its poor shelter while blows hail down all around it, and God just
keeps me there and will not let me look at anything whatever. My
spirit remains at peace but weary. Sometimes it takes fright and wants
to go searching round to find some remedy, but there is none; that is,
not till I cast myself upon God and into his merciful arms, without any
act, for I cannot make one.

'One of the hardest things is to stop myself thinking about all this;
but in the end I do get the better of myself when there is some little ray
of light to help me. It is a torment I cannot explain but which does not

stop me from applying myself to whatever I happen to be doing—writing, talking of the business of the day and so on; and this in spite of the fact that when the pain presses me greatly I never really lose sight of it. This makes me want to die, because I'm afraid that if the pain goes on, it might make me stumble and sin. I should like to be in purgatory so as not to offend God and to be assured of him for ever.

'Not that I put my will behind this desire. For provided that God is not offended by all this, and if it is his will that I'm to suffer like this all my life, I'm happy to suffer as long as I also know what he wants me to do and can do it faithfully.

'Sometimes, indeed often, my whole mind is just a confused turmoil of darkness and helplessness, casting up feelings of rebellion, doubts and every other sort of horror. When things are at their worst, this process is almost continual and gives me inconceivable anguish. I don't know what I would not do and suffer to be rid of this torture. On the one hand the torment besets me and on the other I so much love my holy faith that I long to die for the least article of it.

'When I see all the people round me enjoying the happiness of their belief, it tortures me to feel deprived of it and not to be able to taste the confidence and rest I once had in giving myself up completely to God and to the arms of his providence. When I stop to look at this loss, however briefly, I find myself in a labyrinth. If God were not holding me, I should think myself on the very edge of despair and yet not free to despair, and not wanting to be rid of this torment as long as I am told that it is God's will for me. I am powerless to consent to the evil which temptation puts before me; not that I actually know and realize my inability to consent, not until afterwards, when the worst is over. Then I see that God has been holding me all the time, and sometimes a certain sense of peace comes over my spirit and a very small spark of inner sweetness. And then I long ardently not to offend God and to do all the good I possibly can.' (1, 520 f.)

This account was dashed off in haste, with scarcely a full-stop. Self-analysis and observation of spiritual symptoms was one of the things she most earnestly discouraged in others, and she herself was not given to it after the early years of her contact with St Francis. This document is then exceptional; apart from her biographer's description of her trial of doubt, and passing references in letters or talks, this is the only time she wrote about it at length in later years.[1] She wrote under obedience.

[1] The three letters 'À une grande servante de Dieu', dated 1637 (7, 586, 708 and 733) will be disregarded. They purport to be a personal statement from

Her trial of doubt became worse in her later years but it had been with her ever since she had first become spiritually conscious as a young woman. All the work and activity of her life within the order is set against a background of incessant doubt; she was working against the grain all the time as far as her feelings went. She herself chose the image of the labyrinth to describe her state. In her account to Peronne-Marie, she sees her spirit cowering as it were in a frail shelter at the centre of this labyrinth while a fierce hail storm threatens to destroy it, but somehow never quite does. God will not let her run out into the storm and look more closely at the destroying hail stones, or try and find other help. For real help is close at hand. She just has to sit very still in the darkness of her shelter and then she finds herself at peace, however exhausted.

In another image she sees herself standing in spirit at the very edge of a precipice, feeling that at any minute she will freely choose to plunge down into the darkness below. Yet she never does. Or when, as she thinks, she has yielded, she finds she has cast herself yet again, wordless, into God's arms. Suddenly she knows that he had been holding her all the time. Then the spark of light by which she had seen this fades once more. She finds herself in darkness again, hardly able to remember what the little flash of vision was like.

For many years this was her daily bread. She was never portentous about it and did not think it worth discussing either with herself or with others, or even with God. She did not fuss about her inner trials. They were not, and never had been matter for

Madame de Chantal and in some quarters are said to have been addressed to Angélique Arnauld at Port Royal. The possibility of this second claim, fantastic as it is to anyone who knows Madame de Chantal, need not even be taken seriously, because the first claim, i.e. that the letters were actually written by St Chantal, is not now capable of proof. These letters have been disregarded, then, for the following reasons:

1. In their present form as they now stand they are of highly doubtful authenticity.
2. They have been the subject of acrimonious controversy which can never now be finally settled because all the original manuscript material has disappeared.
3. They in any case add nothing significant to the portrayal of Madame de Chantal which is not already clear from her own authentic statement translated above.

confession, which she called 'the great place of simplicity and truth.' She was not conscious of ever having consented to them and so there was no sin. Nothing else mattered. If she had had her way, no one would ever have known anything about her inner state except those few to whom she was bound to speak of her conscience. Then her personal trials, instead of being singled out and emphasized, would have remained simply a part of her hidden life, like those of the least of her sisters. She herself looked on this suffering in a matter of fact, realistic and very French way, though the terms used to describe it may perhaps make her attitude appear more dramatic and certainly more self-conscious than it actually was. As a rule it was without her knowledge that the things she happened to say about her trials were written down. A phrase, for instance, like 'the martyrdom of love' used in a conversation recorded on St Basil's day some years previously, was quite simply in accordance with the language and concepts of the spirituality of her time, and of course she really was, in the terms of the account, a martyr to love; that is, she steadfastly endured the spiritual torment of doubt without assenting. She loved God, and like the martyrs was prepared to prove her love and bear witness to it in all she did. But the occasion of the conversation, with all its spiritual significance, was quite an everyday one: a recreation. This simple setting helps to keep the 'martyrdom of love' in its right place and proportion: this martyr's stake was the hidden and unspectacular one of her ordinary, everyday life.

'On the feast of St Basil in 1632 our Blessed Mother experienced a very great access of divine love so that she could not talk at recreation; she shut her eyes and her face was flushed; she tried to bring herself back to reality by spinning but had to stop short when her spindle was only half full. When she realized she could not do anything about it, she got us to sing to her, and tried to join in the singing herself. It was a song that Mother de Bréchard had written for her on some other occasion. It helped her a little, and she tried to talk to us because she wanted to hide the grace working in her. Her words were words of fire, faithfully noted down there and then.

' "St Basil, my dear daughters, was not a martyr, and neither were our holy Fathers, the pillars of the church. Why was this, do you think?"

'After each one of us had had her say, she went on:

' "I think it is because there is such a thing as a martyrdom of love: God keeps his servants alive to work for his glory, and this makes them martyrs and confessors at the same time. I know this is the sort of martyrdom the daughters of the Visitation will suffer, that is, those of them who are fortunate enough to set their heart on it."

'A sister wanted to know just how this martyrdom worked out in practice.

' "Give God your unconditional consent", she said, "and then you will find out. What happens" she went on, "is that love seeks out the most intimate and secret places of your soul as with a sharp sword, and cuts you off even from your own self. I know of a soul cut off in this way so that she felt it more keenly than if a tyrant had cleaved her body from her soul."

'We knew, of course, that she was speaking about herself. A sister wanted to know how long this martyrdom was likely to last.

' "From the moment we give ourselves up wholeheartedly to God until the moment we die", she answered. "But this goes for generous hearts and for people who keep faith with love and don't take back their offering; our Lord doesn't take the trouble to martyrize feeble hearts and people who have little love and not much constancy; he just lets them jog along in their own little way in case they give up and slip from his hands altogether; he never forces our free will."

'She was asked whether this martyrdom of love could ever be as bad as the physical kind.

' "We won't try to compare the two and look for equality; but I think that there is not much difference, because 'love is strong as death', and martyrs of love suffer infinitely more by staying alive to do God's will than if they had to give up a thousand lives for their faith and love and loyalty." ' (1, 355 ff.)

One sister wanted to have precise time and value indications. Her superior and the others knew, perhaps, that she was the sort of person who liked to have everything neatly docketed, and spent energy on spiritual arithmetic when she might have been more generously employed. In spite of the 'words of fire', the comment about feeble hearts who go along at a cautious jog-trot—the phrase used is *'rouler leur petit train'*—can hardly have been said without a look and a smile in this sister's direction. The sisters were sitting in a circle at recreation and their Mother was doing her best to bring the talk back to a more general level, to join in the singing herself, to go on spinning. She was anything but sententious about her suffering: *'un saint triste est un triste saint'*, 'a sad saint is a sorry saint', was a phrase, after all, coined by her own director. Another look at her portraits should also help to dispel the idea that she was a long-faced saint.

1637 was a year which brought Madame de Chantal great losses. She herself was sixty-five, her health seemed reasonably good though she was now '*bien pesante*', rather heavy, and found it hard to keep active all the time. All her life, judging by frequent references in her letters, she seems to have been subject to bronchial troubles and to catarrh, rarely completely incapacitating, but nevertheless a continual nuisance. There had been a time about seven years earlier when she was convinced her death was imminent; now she never mentions it. She got used to being, as she put it, the rotten and mildewed fruit that stays on the tree, or possibly the green fruit that never ripens at all, while the really good fruit is harvested. (1, 283)

Within a few months of one another, her three earliest companions, all of them younger than herself, died suddenly. The loss that affected her most deeply was perhaps that of Jacqueline Favre who died in the June of that year, aged forty-eight. She died as superior at Chambéry where as a young girl she had had the ball-room vision of death which had decided her vocation; and the illness she died of, the terrible, unrelieved pain of gallstones, at that time inoperable, was of the kind she had made a point of watching in her younger days when in need of a striking subject for meditation. Jacqueline had made a good nun and a very reliable superior. She was, to judge by the special warmth that speaks from every letter Madame de Chantal wrote to her, her closest and most beloved friend.

Peronne-Marie de Chastel died suddenly in October the same year, when she and Madame de Chantal had just begun their annual retreat together. It was the foundress herself who wrote her superior's necrology. This letter, with a summary of Peronne-Marie's religious life and particular qualities, an account of her unexpected illness and of the way in which she met death, is a model necrology and character sketch. It is a well written, unadorned account and narrative, characteristic of the writer herself, of her close yet detached way of observing things, her strong feeling that was never mere sentiment:

'. . . and then, fortunately, she seemed to rally again, and like a child who comes from far away, she put her arms round me once or twice, very tenderly. After that she folded her hands, smiled serenely and spoke with love and trust to our Lord and our Lady, and also thanked those of us who were standing round her bed . . . then quite gently, when her lips could no longer move, she closed her eyes herself and died without a sigh and without any contortion of her face, so very gently that we could hardly tell the precise moment of death, though we were watching her intently.' (7, 701)[1]

Less than a month later, news was brought from Riom of the death of Charlotte de Bréchard, her oldest friend of all, who had shared her life at Monthelon some years before the beginnings of the order. Her close association with her family, her husband and all her children, formed a bridge for Madame de Chantal which reached back by memories and shared experience to her earlier life. After 1637 she was left in increasing isolation and practically every link with the past was now broken.

When Peronne-Marie died, the superiority at Annecy fell to her again, but she made it clear to the sisters that this was to be the last time; she asked the bishop whether her name could now be removed from the register of superiors eligible for re-election. This was granted. Her name was replaced by that of Marie-Aymée de Blonay of Lyons, one of the last surviving companions of the early times at the Galerie. This sister was elected in May 1641; Madame de Chantal welcomed her with what the chronicle calls 'a little fire of joy in her heart.'

The arrival of the sister whom she and St Francis had always called 'la cadette'—she was the youngest of nine and had something of an eternal child about her—marked her final retirement from office. At the last chapter she conducted, when all the sisters were standing in order of rank, she embraced each one of them in turn, a thing she had never done before at a chapter meeting; it was to bid them a formal farewell in her capacity as superior. Not that she was now going to leave them, she said, or feel any differently about them, nor would she allow the meeting to be marked by any demonstration of sadness. A certain formality and a courteous regard for the ritual of social relationships formed part of her personality, but she considered emotional display on such occasions

[1] Circular Letter, 23 October 1637.

as positively unchristian. She was not stoical in the wrong sense, and though reserved in showing her feelings, she too had had to learn in this matter. In the past she had told the sisters that when she was saying good-bye to Francis de Sales on some occasion, and he took one road while she took another, he would not allow her to say how sad she was. This hurt her. 'Simply want what God wants, and let us go where he calls', he had said to her (1, 319). She had never forgotten this and had tried saying his words when it came to any parting. If you thought of it like this, how could you possibly be sad? For her, this last chapter in 1641 was a conscious rehearsal for a greater leavetaking. By her attitude and by formally enacting the actual gestures of a farewell, she was trying to prepare the sisters for the parting which she felt could not be far distant now.

A few days later news came from Paris telling Madame de Chantal of the death of her brother André. He had been living in retirement near the Paris Visitation for some years now and it was there, in the vaults beneath the round church of Sainte Marie, that he was buried. His niece Françoise, and also his nephew Jacques, Bishop of Châlons, were with him when he died. André's life had not turned out quite as he had hoped. As a result of political intrigue, his archbishopric, won for him in the first place by his father's valour and not by his own merit, had been taken from him and he had had to be content with a lesser charge. Then he had been seriously ill and this had led, as can be seen in the letters, to a complete change of heart which he discussed in detail with his sister. The postponing of the cause of his friend, Francis de Sales, the proceedings for whose canonization he financed largely out of his own pocket, was a great personal disappointment to him. Everything that happened served to drive home the lesson which he still needed to learn: that there was no abiding city here. He looked increasingly to his sister for help, encouragement and even direction. Her letters gave him all he looked for and were written so carefully and affectionately as never to make him feel humbled. While advising him, and in the very gesture of giving, she some-how managed to make it appear that he was the giver. At the news of his death which did not come as a surprise to her (the chronicle implies that she had a prophetic knowledge of it beforehand) she wrote round to all the convents asking for prayers for his soul and told them at the same time to pray for her to 'dispose herself happily for her own last passage'. (1, 302)

When the summer was at its hottest at the end of July, Madame de Chantal left Annecy for the last time. She had hoped to enjoy her retirement in peace but circumstances had arisen which made another journey essential, even in her own judgement. She admitted that it 'might be for God's glory.' The bishop was careful not to give any hint of his own opinion in the matter but put it to her quite impartially, asking her to tell him what she felt. Knowing what any response of hers to a call upon her goodness was likely to be, this procedure seems almost unfair, but the bishop was himself in a difficult position and subject to pressure from outside his own diocese and from France. The matter in question was one of state. It concerned a relative of the royal house of France, Princess Orsini, the widow of the Duke of Montmorency and a cousin of the reigning monarch, Louis XIII. This princess was such a well-known tragic figure in seventeenth-century France, and her story so celebrated, that Madame de Chantal's biographer takes knowledge of the circumstances for granted. But without this knowledge and some idea of the personality of the princess, the reason for Madame de Chantal's last journey and much of what led up to her death away from home at the end of that year, remains obscure, or at any rate, unsatisfactory.

The Duke of Montmorency was executed for high treason in 1632 when he took part in the march on France instigated by the king's younger brother, Gaston of Orléans. This attack was directed against Richelieu, the king's chief minister, rather than against Louis XIII himself. The plan miscarried, there had to be a scapegoat for the royal offender and so the duke was beheaded. His wife, an Italian princess, childless, frail in health and given to piety, was imprisoned in the Bourbon castle at Moulins in central France. At this time when no one else dared to befriend her, the superior of the Moulins Visitation showed her kindness. An outsister went up and down the little hill between castle and convent every day carrying food, comforts and messages. In time her health returned, her relatives in Italy were allowed to send her money (all her husband's property had, of course, been confiscated) and she was able to live a more human life. She chose to move to a house near the Visitation and to follow the community exercises as far as she was able. Though Richelieu remained her enemy, the royal house had always been disposed in her favour. She was, in fact, rather an embarrassing commitment for the king, and remained on his conscience; no one seemed to know quite what to do with her. He visited her at Moulins from time to time, and so did his wife, Queen Anne of Austria. As the years passed, her reputation for personal holiness grew, and at the age of forty she was considered to be living at Moulins in an honourable retreat, free from the disgrace which had attached to her name.

The princess venerated both the founders of the Visitation. When she was young she had been in Lyons with the French court the Christmas that St Francis de Sales died. A woman of considerable learning in the Italian humanist tradition, she was a constant reader, even a mathematician and also a Latinist, looking upon devotional and doctrinal works as a subject of study as well as food for the soul. She appears to have had an exceptionally close knowledge of all that St Francis wrote, and this formed an immediate bond between her and Madame de Chantal when they met at Moulins in 1635. As a mark of this friendship the foundress gave her one of the things she herself most valued and always carried with her, a miniature portrait of St Francis. The letters the two women exchanged prove that this was a relationship of real affection, not just a formal bond between pious royalty and saintly subject, as one might at first be inclined to suppose.

There were a number of parallels in their lives which even touched at certain points: Celse-Bénigne had been a member of the duke's immediate circle; a close mutual friend, the Easter Day duellist of the Porte Saint Antoine, had been the occasion for Chantal's disgrace and had himself later been executed; Duke Montmorency had also fought at the Isle de Ré. Had Celse-Bénigne lived he might perhaps, in a fit of despair at his hopeless position, have cast in his lot with the duke and shared his fate. Both women moreover, though the cases were in no way comparable, had had to learn to forgive where forgiveness was hard: Richelieu was responsible for the final death penalty that was exacted. Both had been really in love and had valued their marriage, not by any means the rule at court. Madame de Montmorency was a foreigner, alone in the world as people in her high position can well be, and this in spite of the uneasy royal favour which now surrounded her. She was also rather an invalid so that any long journey, for instance to Annecy, would have been impossible for her.

In 1641 she was given her confessor's sanction to enter the Visitation as a novice, a plan to which she had given long consideration. There were still a great many difficulties in her way which she felt she could only solve if she could discuss them with Madame de Chantal herself. Though she left it to others to judge whether the request should actually be put, she made no secret of her longing to have her friend's personal help. Her position was so exceptional that all who knew of her desire considered it reasonable. The bishop of the diocese wrote to the bishop at Annecy.

In mid-August, travelling by very easy stages and stopping for a while in Lyons, Madame de Chantal arrived at Moulins. This town which has little to recommend it, lies on the edge of a marshy plain in central France, the countryside is flat and featureless except for a wide, slack river, along which barges travel slowly. The heat there is oppressive even early in the year. It would be difficult to imagine a place more depressingly different from Madame de Chantal's real or adopted home towns, Dijon and Annecy. As far as she was concerned it had all the anonymity of death.[1]

[1] The Visitation at which Madame de Chantal died is now a state Lycée, established in the convent buildings since the time of the French Revolution when the nuns were expropriated. No trace of the room in the novitiate where she died, and which was made into an oratory, is now left: the corridors and cells have been rebuilt into class rooms. Next to the school there is still the Visitation chapel, and that too is much altered since the seventeenth century. The visitor can, if he likes, pay to go in and see the astonishing baroque marble monument which Madame de Montmorency erected to her husband's memory. The concierge who sells the entrance tickets does not know that the foundress of the Visitation died in what is now the school building; he assures you that you are misinformed and that what you really want to see is the duke's tomb next door. But in the new Visitation, a nondescript nineteenth-century building in a suburban street on the other side of the town, the sisters know all the details of the architectural layout of their former home, and will talk about the death of their foundress as though this event had just taken place in their own house a week or two ago.

The farewell at Annecy had been a tumultuous affair. The whole town turned out to see her go, she was in excellent health and spirits, even buoyant, looking vigorous and well. Her doctor congratulated her on her good mien and promised her another fifteen years of life, at the very least. She just smiled. Everything seems to have been a smiling matter that day; in the end her cheerfulness infected even the most tearful nuns who insisted on voicing premonitions. She had her way, and no lugubrious face was left in the convent, or indeed in the whole town when she was ready to leave. For the first time that anyone could remember she gave up her desire for secluded travel through the town. She had the leather blinds of the litter rolled up as she passed along the streets, giving her hand to all the people who lined her immediate path and reached out towards her to say good-bye. Nor did she forget to greet the sick who had had themselves put close to the windows to see her pass and call out their farewell. The whole journey proceeded in a spirit of '*allégresse*', or gladness.

At Moulins, days before, Madame de Montmorency posted up on a large pillar the note announcing the arrival, and the sisters kept going there to look at it. At this point even the biographer's ready flow of words gives out and she simply writes: 'No need to say with what great joy our Blessed Mother was received at Moulins, especially by the excellent Madame de Montmorency.' (1, 313) For the next five weeks the foundress devoted herself entirely to the community, especially to the novitiate, helping the princess, discussing everything with her as thoroughly as she could wish, and also advising her on her complicated temporal affairs. She was now a wealthy woman again who had expectations of still greater riches in the future; Madame de Chantal's chief concern was to prevent her pouring her whole fortune into the Visitation and to insist that all monetary affairs connected with her patrimony from Italy should be sorted out before she was professed. This took some years, mainly because she remained absolutely loyal to her instructions. Many years later she was elected superior of Moulins after proving an exemplary nun. She died in 1666, soon after the canonization of Francis de Sales and after herself organizing the local celebrations connected with this event.

As soon as it was known that the foundress was in Moulins,

insistent calls for her came from Paris, not only from the Visitation but from the queen herself, Anne of Austria, who wrote personally to the Bishop of Geneva asking if he could make it possible for Madame de Chantal to visit her. One of the queen's own travelling litters was sent to Moulins, and late in September, accompanied by her daughter Françoise for a short part of the way, she set out for Paris. The queeen rode out along the forest road from Saint Germain to meet her, taking her two children, the future Louis XIV and his brother. The boys knelt to receive Madame de Chantal's blessing. She blessed them, and seeing that any protest on her part would have been useless, she allowed the queen herself to kiss her hands. The confusion she had felt in former times at such signs of veneration had given place, in the course of this last journey, to a simple acceptance of the part God was asking her to play in the lives of those she met and in the whole life of her country. For two hours the queen spoke to her in private, asking her counsel and commending her family and herself to her prayers. The queen's life was not a happy one.

In Paris the number of people who poured into the convent parlour to see her was so great that she used to get up at three or four o'clock in the morning in order to fit everything in, her own prayer, the convent routine as well as the needs of her neighbour. She felt well and strong. Our Lord, she said, gave her new staying power, or in her own characteristic phrase, '*un estomac tout nouveau*' (1, 317), for all the talking she had to do. Her inner desolation, too, seems to have vanished during the last three months of her life, and for the first time for almost as long as she could remember, her doubts ceased to torment her.

After a long talk with St Vincent de Paul and a general confession in which everything was fully discussed for the last time, he helped her, according to her wish, to prepare for death. Complete peace filled her. Of the many letters that are known to have passed between them in the twenty years during which he was her director, only two or three have survived. It may have been an agreed arrangement between them; in any case, each would have thought it better so. His opinion of her is laid down in the deposition he made for her canonization, where he says that though she had all virtues, the greatest of them was undoubtedly her faith, the virtue against which she had been tempted all her life. Peace and tranquillity of mind were hers, he said, in spite of her state of inner darkness, and characteristically for this saint who himself so much loved cheerfulness, he made a special point of stressing the unfailingly serene expression in her face. This serenity he had seen in her always, not only during the last interviews in Paris. She for her part wrote of him without further ado in her last letter from Paris to Annecy: *'Monsieur Vincent est un saint.'* (8, 525)

Early in November she left the capital, excusing herself from a second invitation to Saint Germain where the whole court was in attendance on the king, now resident again at the palace. Instead, she visited three more convents, the last being Nevers where she stayed for some days and where her last illness began to declare itself. It appeared at first to be just another of the recurrent bronchial attacks from which she suffered every winter.

On the feast of St Andrew, the last day of November, she spoke to the community on the subject of suffering and gave the sisters plenty of time for questions afterwards. All was recorded (2, 481 ff.). Her message was what it had always been: humility, simplicity, exact observance. There was nothing new except her manner of saying it, and the expression in her face which remained unforgettable to those who were listening. Right at the end, when her daughter Françoise had already arrived to take her the short last stage of her journey to Moulins, she spoke again:

'Good-bye once more, my very dear sisters. I don't know whether we shall meet again in this life; we must leave that to providence. If it is not in this world, it will be in eternity. I shall often visit you and I shall be looking at you with the eyes of my spirit—not that I really know what this means, but I do know that I know all of you very well.' (2, 489)

For the first week after her return to Moulins, though she was already very ill, she refused to give in; she shared in the life of the community as usual, putting apart a little time every day for Madame de Montmorency. Her last appearance at mass was on Sunday 8 December, the feast of the Immaculate Conception. This was the thirty-first anniversary of the day when, by St Francis's permission, she had begun to receive holy communion daily, an almost unheard of concession at that time. It was a very cold day, there was a long period of prayer and office before mass.

Though she was, of course, fasting, she even made the effort of visiting a sick nun who was afraid of death and stood in need of comfort.

Hardly was mass over when she broke down and had to take to her bed. The doctor diagnosed pneumonia and pleurisy, making no secret of the fact that he considered her illness fatal. On Monday she was still dictating a long letter to the superior at Annecy, by Tuesday she admitted to her travelling companion, the same who had so feared a sudden end on the rocky Alpine pass from Turin, that she felt her death was near. By midnight on Wednesday 11 December, when her temperature was very high, the doctor thought that the Viaticum should be brought to her. She pleaded for the community not to be disturbed till the morning and this was granted. In the meanwhile the chaplain, Père de Ligendes, a Jesuit, stayed beside her, heard her confession and marvelled at the extraordinary lucidity of her mind and judgement in spite of her high temperature. On the Thursday afternoon she sat upright in bed and with her eyes closed, but in a calm, unfaltering voice, dictated a farewell letter for the convents all over France. It was taken down word for word, just as she said it, and when it had been read back to her, she signed it in her usual firm hand, in the manner customary to her: 'Soeur Jeanne Françoise Frémyot, De la Visitation Sainte-Marie. Dieu soit béni.'[1]

The letter itself was simple. She asked the sisters to stay loyal to all that the founder had wished, and especially to preserve complete unity while looking towards Annecy in a spirit of concord, humility and exact observance. No sister need be distressed about any letter she had written which could now no longer reach her: all such correspondence was going to be burnt unopened. Finally, there were a few words concerning Madame de Montmorency who had been a most devoted nurse throughout her illness and had hardly stirred from her bedside:

'She thinks you will blame her for my death. But it is providence, my dear daughters, that disposes of our days, and my life would not have lasted a quarter of an hour longer for all that. The journey has been very useful for the houses we visited and for the whole institute.'

Realizing that even though her tragic history was familiar to them

[1] Circular Letter, addressed to the whole Order of the Visitation, 12 December 1641; 8, 527.

the sisters did not know the princess as she did, and that there might be a general prejudice against the person who had been the occasion of her last journey, she remembered even at this extremity to say something about her to help them see her in a truer light. Have confidence in her, she urged, and thank God for her:

'She lives among our sisters more humbly and simply, with more lowliness and innocence than if she were a little peasant woman', high tribute indeed for a princess.

That night when she was unable to sleep, she asked a sister to read aloud to her. She chose to hear St Jerome's letter on St Paula's death in Bethlehem. Then as the night wore on and she still remained sleepless, she asked for the account of her own director's death, for Chapter Six of the Ninth Book of his *Treatise*, and finally for St Augustine's relation of his mother's death at Ostia. The whole course of her life, the bent of her mind and heart, are revealed in what she chose to ponder during her last night on earth.

First of all she heard one of St Jerome's most moving letters, describing the life and death of his beloved friend and disciple, a Roman widow. Paula left her own country to make a pilgrimage to the Holy Land which cast its spell on her so that she 'hid herself away in the small town of Bethlehem.' And there, in time, she founded a religious community to which many widows were drawn. Madame de Chantal loved especially St Jerome's epitaph for Paula, this 'first of Roman ladies, who hardship chose and Bethlehem for Christ.'

> '*Seest thou here hollowed in the rock a grave,*
> '*Tis Paula's tomb; high heaven has her soul.*
> *Who Rome and friends, riches and home forsook*
> *Here in this lonely spot to find her rest.*
> *For here Christ's manger was, and here the kings*
> *To him, both God and man, their offrings made.*'[1]

It was Advent when Madame de Chantal lay dying, the thought of Bethlehem and Christmas was in her mind, and brought closer still by the story of Paula and her love for the Holy Places.

Then followed the last chapter in the life of St Francis de Sales,

[1] Quoted from St Jerome, Vol. VI, *Library of Nicene and Post Nicene Fathers*, Oxford and New York, 1893, Letter CVIII, p. 212.

written by his nephew. It set before her the example of his death in the gardener's cottage at the Visitation in Lyons, away from his own beloved Savoy and from his people. The dying woman heard again about his patience in the face of suffering, his effort to his very last breath to acknowledge gratefully the kindness of the crowds who came to see him at a time when, like St Charles Borromeo, he would have preferred to close his eyes and be left in peace. This reading was followed by the chapter 'On serving and loving God without any choice of our own' from the *Treatise*, the book which marked their complete unity of spirit and which she considered a perfect portrait of him, and he of her. When the nun who was reading came to the passage:

'My mother is ill in bed, or else I'm ill myself, it comes to the same thing; perhaps, and only God knows, death may be the end of it. If she dies I will accept her death with all my love in my heart of hearts, however unhappy I may feel. Yes, Lord, I will say: I want this because you want it, for what am I but the very humble servant of your will?' (A, V, 125.)

Madame de Chantal looked compassionately at the princess, in tears at her bedside, and pressing her hand, she said:

'That is meant for you, Madame.'

Finally there were the pages from the *Confessions* in which St Augustine, son of many tears, tells of the ecstasy which he and his mother shared after his conversion and just before St Monica herself died:

'But the day approaching when she was to depart out of this life, it happened that she and I alone were standing, leaning in a certain window, which had a prospect upon a garden of the house where we then lay, at Ostia upon the Tiber; where being sequestered from the company after the labour of a long journey, we were preparing ourselves to pass over by sea into Africa.'[1]

There follows the description of their common ecstasy. This brought the convert his great moment of understanding and led to a final synthesis of his new belief as he and his mother spoke of the nature of God and of the Word Incarnate. These pages contain one of the greatest affirmations of Christian faith ever conceived or written.—When, a little further on, the sister read about Monica's

[1] From St Augustine's *Confessions*, translated in 1620 by an English contemporary of St Chantal, Sir Tobie Matthew, Knight and Priest.

death away from home, those listening heard how, in the past, she had clung to her desire to be buried close to her husband in her own home in Africa where she had built a tomb for them both; but now, at the moment of death, this desire no longer weighed with her:

' "Nothing is far off from God", Monica said, "neither is there any cause to fear that, at the day of judgement, God will not know well enough from what place to raise me up again." '

Thinking of her own monastery at Annecy and perhaps, too, remembering the tomb at Bourbilly and that other distant grave on a beach-head in the Atlantic, Madame de Chantal said as if speaking to herself:

'And that is meant for me.'

The following day, Friday 13 December, she asked to be anointed, and herself said all the responses in a clear, distinct voice. She was conscious almost to the very last minute and in full control of all her faculties in spite of her anguished breathing. Her eyes rested often on a crucifix at the foot of her bed and on a picture of Our Lady of Sorrows. After the chaplain had asked the community to withdraw for a while because the dying woman was exhausting herself still further in her attempt to speak, every sister came in turn to her to say good-bye. As each one knelt to kiss her hand, she looked at her with motherly compassion and whispered a last word of personal comfort and advice to every sister in turn. Père de Ligendes also knelt by her to kiss her hand while she thanked him and his Company for all they had done for her. He stayed beside her, and in the course of the afternoon he prayed with her and said over the Profession of Faith according to the Council of Trent, while she expressed her firm assent. Last of all he read the account of the Passion, to which she listened in a state of rapt attention, making a great final effort of love.

Her agony was long, and for a time she was profoundly disturbed, calling out to the chaplain:

'Oh Father, how terrible are the judgements of God!'

But gradually as death drew nearer, peace returned. When it came to the end, between 6 and 7 o'clock in the evening, and the community was standing round her bed for the final prayers: 'Help her, saints of God, make haste, O angels of the Lord, and receive her soul and bear it up into the presence of the Most High', she was holding her crucifix in her right hand and a candle in the other, as on the bridal day of her profession. Slowly and distinctly, pronouncing the name of Jesus three times, with a sigh, she died.

In death her face wore the same serenity it had always had in life.

Madame de Montmorency arranged for the body of the foundress to be transported back to Savoy, as she had promised, secretly and by night through France, for fear that her remains might be claimed in her own native country. The fear, it seems, was justified, especially at Lyons where the sisters heard too late that the funeral carriage had passed through the city while they were at midnight mass that Christmas. At the end of December, the body was received in state at Annecy and laid to rest in the Visitation chapel close to that of St Francis de Sales. In the new basilica of the Visitation the two shrines are still, as they were from the beginning, one on either side of the high altar. St Francis lies to the right of the altar, St Jane Frances to the left, next to the choir grille.

While Madame de Chantal lay dying, Monsieur Vincent knelt in prayer for her in Paris where the news of her illness had been received. In the deposition he made for her canonization, he wrote an account of what then happened to him. His great love for her soul and his admiration for her holiness might perhaps, he said, cast doubt on the authenticity of what he was about to relate; but against this was to be set the fact that he was not a man given to visions, and that this was the one and only experience of this kind he had ever had in his life. The vision of a man himself a saint, who knew her as few others did, may serve as an ending to the story of Madame de Chantal's life.

As he prayed, there appeared to him as in a vision a small globe of fire which rose from the earth to join a larger, more luminous globe, the two together then soaring up higher to mingle and lose themselves within an orb infinitely great and shining. He knew then that the souls of the two saints he had known on earth had been reunited in death, and that together they had returned to God, their first and last end.

EPILOGUE

There are fashions in saints as there are in poets and philosophers. This is not, as a rule, chance, though in the case of saints who were themselves writers and whose works are only accessible in translation outside their own country, much may depend on the skill of those who interpret them. In England, for example, the vogue of the Spanish Counter Reformation mystics owes a great deal to the work of Professor Allison Peers.

St Francis de Sales and the great spiritual writers of the French seventeenth century have found no interpreter of comparable insight and skill. Except for St Francis' *Introduction to the Devout Life*, his works are still, in the main, only available in a Victorian guise or disguise, a hundred years old and more. The favour enjoyed by St Francis in the nineteenth century in both anglican and catholic circles is based to some extent on an affinity of temper and attitude, but even so, the Victorian translator presented his author with far more rhetoric than was actually there. He also revelled in sheer length; the readers of three-decker novels and of Dickens took the two volumes of the *Treatise on the Love of God* in their stride, and thought nothing of tackling six hundred pages of St Chantal's Spiritual Conferences in an accurate but pedestrian translation. To some extent the Edwardians too were still capable of such an effort. Now, however, the more general trend in taste is reflected in the popularity of comparatively short spiritual works and of translations like the New English Bible.

The older Bible translations, Authorized and Douay, date from 1611 and 1609, and coincide in time with St Francis's literary work; St Chantal herself can only be understood if she too is seen as a representative of this particular epoch in European civilization. It was an age of transition from the old patriarchal forms which had not yet completely vanished, to the new, more complex and self-conscious forms of the age of Louis XIV. Though

Madame de Chantal died towards the middle of the century, both she and her director belonged by birth and natural affinity to the late sixteenth century, especially as both of them, though they had contacts with Paris, came from provincial centres where attitudes changed more slowly than in the capital. A mass of baroque rhetoric in spiritual writing flooded seventeenth-century France and came naturally to the Victorian pen in translation, but it is far less kindred to the writings and certainly to the temper of both saints than would appear to anyone who does not read them in their own language. Both of them, however different their style, wrote rather in the manner of Montaigne than of Bossuet, and their literary expression was essentially flexible and fluid in the old manner. It had little of the elaborate balance and the interplay of carefully rounded periods in a later oratory. Yet this is how nine-teenth-century English translators tend to present both saints, especially perhaps St Chantal who had less skilled interpreters. The general view of her has no doubt also been influenced by the fact that the only English translation of her life by Françoise-Madeleine de Chaugy dates from 1852 and was in any case based on a rather defective, earlier French text.

To a greater extent than is often realized, the portrait of a saint left in people's minds is conditioned by the language in which the saint is presented and made to talk. St Chantal comes to an English reader at a double remove: in translation from her own vigorous, simple and natural speech and style, and also in the literary presen-tation of a younger contemporary who was a nun trained in her own convent. All her early life, her marriage, her widowhood are seen from behind the cloister grille, for though the biographer did consult a handful of lay people, there were very few witnesses left who were not directly connected with the convent. Even her own daughter never made a formal deposition about her. A few peasants were called in to give evidence at Bourbilly more than eighty years after she had left it, and a very small number of lay people at Annecy and in Burgundy also made depositions.

Her biographer, Mère de Chaugy, was a competent, honest and vivid writer, but she can hardly be called an objective observer of her subject who was herself the person who had so largely helped to form her judgement. She wrote with great facility, her style bears some of the characteristic marks of the more popular variety of prose narrative in the French seventeenth century: she already belonged to a different age. In later years her official style as the laureate of the order was to degenerate to a baroque welter of word and sentiment, but in 1642 when the biography was composed she still wrote more simply. Nevertheless, the baroque tendency is there and occasionally obtrudes itself, especially in the stylized use of epithets and adjectives, in a rather self-conscious emotionalism and certain sentimental affectations, also noted on more than one occasion in her behaviour by Madame de Chantal and roundly censured by her.

The chronicle, written up by Mère de Chaugy but to some extent a joint official effort on the part of all responsible at Annecy, was composed with a double purpose: to serve as written evidence of holiness, and to give the nuns of her own order a record and an example to follow. The account was the main document in the saint's canonization process. Although it remained unpublished for two hundred years, it was the only source for all the earlier lives of St Chantal. Its position is therefore one of outstanding importance, and by its unique authority and sheer volume, has rightly conditioned all other attempts to portray the saint. While one recognizes its excellence and also its charm on its own merits, it is perhaps as well to try to see it in the round, and also critically, as a literary form producing a certain definite effect.

There was at this time a standard pattern for hagiographical writing, or a life written for a canonization process. It had to follow a threefold division, describing the candidate under different aspects: first the outline of his life and actions, which was usually the shortest section, then evidence for the practice of the main virtues and finally, evidence for the theological virtues of faith, hope and charity. This rational but inartistic arrangement, based on the known requirements of the Congregation of Rites, easily led to an unwieldy accumulation of anecdotal material in the later sections. Mère de Chaugy's chronicle was marshalled roughly along these lines, though she devotes rather less than half her book to the virtues as against the life. All the same, she naturally paid particular attention to all the moral and ethical points which were known to be stressed in the ecclesiastical inquiry, and which do not necessarily have any great individual and biographical interest. For a saint who was not a martyr everything in the canonization

253

process really hinged on proof for the heroicity of the virtues; for fear of misunderstanding, which was natural enough, hardly any-thing—if there really was anything—in the least negative, was allowed to enter the account.

If one bears these special requirements in mind when reading the biography, much is explained about the sometimes rather wearisome emphasis of certain qualities to the exclusion of others. It is also clear why a modern reader unused to thinking of charac-ter along the hard and fast lines of a hagiographical scheme cannot easily get a really definite impression of a personality in the round from such an account. So often the saint seems to be acting like a type, not an individual, because for the purpose of the judicial inquiry the saint really does have to be systematized and has, as it were, to conform to a type. But this is only a stage. In some ways, a life written for a canonization process may tend to prolong this stage unduly. Rightly read, the final canonization documents themselves may help to restore the balance, though in summary form.

Whereas Mère de Chaugy started out from the point of view that her subject was a saint, the Congregation of Rites began from the other end: Madame de Chantal was to them no more than an ordinarily pious person until she could be proved a saint. Jane Frances Frémyot de Chantal was canonized on 16 July, 1767. The pope who had most to do with her canonization, Benedict XIV, was the author of the standard post-tridentine work of reference on the principles and procedure connected with the official recog-nition of sanctity. Quite apart from his expertise as a law-giver in this matter, he had a great personal veneration for St Chantal and also for St Francis, and an unusually profound insight into her spiritual development. He entrusted the inquiry for the cause to Henry Benedict, Cardinal Duke of York, the last of the House of Stuart, who in the documents is actually referred to as James III of England.

The pope did not himself live to pronounce her official canon-ization—this was left to Clement XIII—but in 1751 he wrote the brief for her beatification, that is, for the preliminary stage of her cause. The ultimate findings of the official body which recom-mends canonization have every chance of being foolproof, even humanly speaking. The final judgement is the end-product of long research into evidence and of jealous cross-questioning by means of a carefully systematized process of inquiry into the life and virtues of the person concerned. All that the outsider knows is that this process takes years, perhaps even centuries, but if one actually has occasion to look through the folio volumes of a handwritten canonization process, one may gradually form some idea of its exhaustive thoroughness. The amount of evidence sifted and weighed, the number of witnesses questioned, the documents searched, the objections put forward and countered—all this forms an overwhelming mass of material and confirms one's impression that the claim to final infallibility is not made to serve as an excuse for slip-shod work.

It follows that the two main informatory documents which are in the end published, the Brief of Beatification and the Bull of Canonization, both as a rule quite short, should be revealing in themselves as well as noteworthy for their power of summary and synthesis. No attempt is made to include everything or to show the steps by which the final judgement was reached, but the most impressive circumstances of the life concerned, the virtues to be specially stressed for the encouragement and imitation of the faithful—the ultimate point of the whole procedure—are clearly set out for all to learn and understand. These documents reflect on the one hand the timelessness of the Christian principles on which their judgements are based, and on the other, the epoch in which the saint lived and in which he was finally raised to the altar. They provide ultimate criteria in a historical perspective. They have never, perhaps, been sufficiently considered in trying to sum up Madame de Chantal, possibly for the quite simple reason that the only available text is in Latin.

The first document in this case is less personal than the second because the pope decided to put the main emphasis on the historical situation. St Jane Frances, he said, was born at a time of fierce religious strife in her own country and all over Europe. God led her into the way of sanctity under the direction of a man himself a saint; both together were instrumental in restoring the good estate of the church in Counter Reformation times, he by his planning of a new religious order, and she by her co-operation in carrying out his plans. Between them these two saints whom he compares to St Jerome and St Paula of old, helped to vindicate for the church the idea of the monastic life which had been attacked as invalid and useless at the time of the Reformation. Of her virtues he singles out her 'most bright and shining charity', of her outstanding actions he mentions only that she made and kept the vow of always following the most perfect course of action.

The actual Bull of Canonization is a longer document with an introduction leading to an outline of her life (based on Mère de Chaugy), an account of some of the greatest and most fully attested miracles of healing attributed to her intercession, and finally a summary of the unique way in which the saint can serve as an example to women in every state of life: girls may ponder her obedience to her father and her good relationship with him, married women can look to her great love for her husband and her children, her goodness to the poor and sick, her domestic virtues in general. Widows can model their life on hers at Monthelon, nuns can see in her a great religious who shows them 'a way to evangelical perfection which is in itself arduous and yet made plain to them with great sweetness'.

In his introduction the pope mentions the great women of the Old Testament, Judith, Deborah, the mother of the Maccabees, and says that in the Christian era the weaker sex can show manly strength in ways perhaps not so spectacular but none the less valid: they can offer themselves as a living hostage to God by a perfect giving up of all things. In this way they too can render heroic witness to the faith. St Jane Frances acted heroically in that she allowed God to accomplish in her the change from one state of life to another. From being wholly a wife and mother, she became in the course of time dedicated to an existence informed by a supernatural ideal of chastity for Christ and resulting in a different kind of fruitfulness: she was made the mother of many daughters leading a life of perfection in the religious state. Because of her spiritual suppleness and strength, God was able to use as her greatest asset what, on the face of it, might have seemed to be her greatest bar from the religious and monastic life.

After reading this document one is left with a strong impression of her outstanding capacity for development and of the intimate suffering which this gradual change in orientation caused her. The pope stresses precisely that which to the modern mind seems to fly in the face of nature: we are made to realize that it was just because she had been a wife passionately in love with her husband and attached to her children that God was able to use her ultimately for a work above nature, in which her own womanly heart was the first and most complete sacrifice. The outward development of the Visitation for which she worked '*Salesio enim velut architecto*' ('with de Sales as architect'), was spectacular in its success; but more striking still in the eyes of the church was the inner development of the foundress, 'greater than anything that appeared to the outside world': her kindling charity, her humility, her utter self-abandonment to God's designs for her at every stage. It was because of her hidden interior life as a contemplative that 'bishops, monarchs and saints' came to consult her and commend themselves to her prayer.

While a papal document serves to stress essentials, it remains open to every age to single out more especially those elements in a saint's life and personality which it finds most significant and most relevant to its own needs. Organizing activity, good works, courage and endurance are always in fashion for saints, but perhaps they are now too easily valued on a purely natural level while their supernatural motive force may no longer be as self-evident as it once was. Striking mystical phenomena are not now in fashion: they were largely absent from St Chantal's life and scarcely one was mentioned in the document. In obedience to her director she did not practise great austerities though she may have been temperamentally drawn to them. Except on very rare occasions her life of prayer was not marked by anything extraordinary: she had darkness and aridity as her daily bread. By far the greater part of her life was spent in a simple routine of rather dull and very hard work. But in our own day the canonization of a saint such as Teresa of Lisieux has sharpened the general perception for what is not immediately obvious as an ingredient of sanctity: the hidden heroism to be found in the commonplace life, the steadfast practice of simple virtues, and an unquestioning, childlike trust.

When we now think about the life of Madame de Chantal, we will perhaps be attracted precisely by these apparently unspectacular things about her and by what lay behind her obvious greatness: the gradual process of spiritual formation through which a married woman and a mother who had fully assented to her role in life eventually reached a high degree of holiness; her extraordinary readiness to respond to spiritual guidance without ever losing her own individuality and her own particular womanly approach; the paradox by which a great foundress was able to live an essentially hidden life in the limelight of an ever growing publicity. In the same way, there is an appeal for us in the apparent contradiction between her life-long interior suffering and her growing outer serenity, in her burning love growing and feeding upon what seemed to her, and to her only, the treachery of continual doubt—a trial that we may be tempted to consider as a modern prerogative. We should like to think too, that we can understand the wordless prayer which sprang immediately from this dilemma or out of this paradox, and how in this prayer she yielded herself up completely, remaining to the end as simple as a child.

'Kindle in our hearts the fire of love which
burned so brightly in her heart, consuming it
with undying charity.'

Secret from the Mass for the Feast of
St Jane Frances de Chantal,
21 August

SAINT JANE FRANCES
DE CHANTAL

CHRONOLOGY

1572, 23 January	Jeanne-Françoise Frémyot born at Dijon
1592, 28 December	Marriage at Bourbilly to Christophe, Baron de Rabutin-Chantal
1596–1601	Birth of their children: Celse-Bénigne, Marie Aymée, Françoise and Charlotte
1601, October	Christophe killed in a hunting accident. Madame de Chantal goes to live with her father-in-law at Monthelon
1604, March	Francis de Sales, Bishop of Geneva, comes from Annecy to preach the Lenten sermons at Dijon where Madame de Chantal is on a visit to her father
1604, 25 August	She meets the bishop again at Saint Claude in the Jura and puts herself under his direction
1609, October	Marriage of Marie-Aymée de Chantal to Bernard de Sales at Monthelon
1610, 6 June	The Visitation founded at Annecy when Madame de Chantal enters the Galerie
1615	First French foundation at Lyons
1617	Death of Bernard and Marie-Aymée
1618–23	Madame de Chantal away from Annecy, making foundations in Bourges, Paris and Dijon
1620	Marriage of Françoise de Chantal to Count de Toulonjon
1622, 28 December	Death of Francis de Sales at Lyons. Last interview with Madame de Chantal early in December

1623	Marriage of Celse-Bénigne de Chantal to Marie de Coulanges
1624	First General Chapter of the Visitation at Annecy
1626	Tour in the Lorraine Birth of Celse-Bénigne's daughter, the future Madame de Sévigné
1627	He is killed in battle at the siege of the Isle de Ré Madame de Chantal makes her Deposition for the Cause of Francis de Sales
1628–31	Years of the Great Plague
1635–37	General tour of the Visitations in France
1637	Death of her three earliest companions at the Galerie
1638	Madame de Chantal crosses the Alps to make the foundation at Turin
1640	Death of her brother André, Archbishop of Bourges
1641, 28 July	Madame de Chantal sets out on her last journey and visits Moulins and Paris
1641, 13 December	Death at Moulins on her homeward journey
1767, 16 July	Canonization

BIBLIOGRAPHY

I MS SOURCES

Canonization Process; Procès fait par autorité apostolique sur la réputation de sainteté, vertus et miracles de la vénérable servante de Dieu, Jeanne-Françoise Frémyot de Chantal. 19 vols. folio, 1710–1767. Archives of the First Monastery of the Visitation at Annecy.

Fondations manuscrites de nos monastères. Copy in a later hand of St Chantal's own accounts:
1. Fondation de la Galerie, 6 juin, 1610. Archives of the Monastery of the Visitation at Angers. 23 pages.
2. Fondation du premier monastère de Paris, 1 mai, 1619. Archives of the First Monastery of the Visitation at Paris. 36 pages.

II PRINTED SOURCES

Ste. Jeanne-Françoise Frémyot de Chantal. Sa Vie et ses Oeuvres. Édition authentique publiée par les soins des Religieuses du Premier Monastère de la Visitation Sainte-Marie d'Annecy. 8 vols., Paris 1874–79. 2nd and 3rd ed., 1893 and 1910.
Vol. 1, *Mémoire sur la Vie et les Vertus de Ste. Jeanne-Françoise Frémyot de Chantal*, par la Mère Françoise-Madeleine de Chaugy. Appendix, Latin text of the Brief for the Beatification and the Canonization Bull; Vols. 2 and 3, *Oeuvres Diverses*; vols. 4–8, *Lettres*.

English Translations. *The Life of St Jane Frances de Chantal, Foundress of the Order of the Visitation.* From the French. Faber's Series: Saints and Servants of God, London, 1852.

The Exhortations, Conferences, Instructions and Retreat of St Jane Frances de Chantal. Translated from the French edition of Paris 1875. Clifton 1888.

The Exhortations, Conferences and Instructions of St Jane Frances de Chantal, Chicago, Loyola University Press, 1929.

Selected Letters of St Jane Frances de Chantal. Translated by the Sisters of the Visitation, Harrow-on-the-Hill. London 1918. Revised edition, *The Spirit of St Jane Frances de Chantal as shown by her letters.* London 1922.

The Spiritual Life. A summary of the instructions on the virtues and on prayer given by St Jane Frances Frémyot de Chantal. Compiled by the Sisters of the Visitation of Harrow-on-the-Hill with a preface by Cardinal Bourne. London 1928.

Oeuvres de Saint François de Sales. Edition complète d'après les autographes et les éditions originales. Par les soins des Religieuses de la Visitation du Premier Monastère d'Annecy. Annecy 26 vols., 1892–1932; especially Vols. 11–21, *Lettres,* and Vol. 25, *Opuscules: La Visitation.*

English Translations. *Library of St Francis de Sales.* Translated and edited by H. B. Mackey, O.S.B., London, 1883–1910, 7 vols.; especially Vol. 2, *Treatise on the Love of God* and Vol. 6, *Depositions of St Jane Frances de Chantal in the Cause of the Canonization of St Francis de Sales.*

St Francis de Sales. Selected Letters. Translated with an Introduction by Elisabeth Stopp. London and New York 1960. (See also full bibliography on St Francis de Sales in this volume.)

L'Âme de S. François de Sales révélée par Ste Jeanne-Françoise de Chantal dans une de ses lettres et dans sa Déposition au Procès de Béatification du Serviteur de Dieu, 1627. Annecy 1922.

Année Sainte des Religieuses de la Visitation Sainte-Marie. 12 vols. Annecy 1867–1871. (Lives of the sisters, accounts of foundations, and much anecdotal material from the Visitation archives. The collection was begun by Françoise-Madeleine de Chaugy.)

CHAUGY, FRANÇOISE-MADELEINE DE
Les Vies de quatre des premières Mères de l'Ordre de la Visitation Sainte Marie. Paris 1852 and 1892.

MENTHON, LA COMTESSE A. DE
Les deux filles de Sainte Chantal. Paris 1870 and Annecy 1913.

III SELECTION OF WORKS ON ST CHANTAL

ANON

La Retraite du Monde de la bien-heureuse de Chantal. Poème dramatique en 5 Actes. Avignon 1758.

Vie abrégée de Madame de Chantal. Paris 1697. (Attributed to the Marquise de Coligny, a descendant of the saint.)

BEAUFILS, G., S.J.

La Vie de la Bienheureuse Mère Jeanne-Françoise Frémiot de Chantal. Annecy 1751 and 1826.

BOUGAUD, ÉMILE

Histoire de Sainte Chantal et des Origines de la Visitation. 2 vols., Paris 1863 and later editions.

St Chantal and the Foundation of the Visitation. Translated from the eleventh French edition by a Visitandine. London 1895 and 1923.

BREMOND, HENRI

Sainte Jeanne de Chantal, 1572–1641. 2nd ed. Paris 1912.

CIONI, R.

S. Giovanna-Francesca, Baronessa di Chantal. Rome 1947.

DU JEU, VICOMTE EMMANUEL

Madame de Chantal, Sa vie dans le monde, sa vie religieuse. Paris 1928.

FICHET, ALEXANDRE, S.J.

Les saintes reliques de l'Erothée. La sainte vie de la Mère Jeanne-Françoise de Frémiot, Baronne de Chantal, excellent original de sainteté et vrai pourtraict de l'épouse de Jésus. Paris 1643 and Lyons 1662.

HÄMEL-STIER, ANGELA

Das Seelenleben der hlg. Johanna Franziska von Chantal. Ein wissenschaftlicher Beitrag zur Psychologie weiblichen Heiligkeitsstrebens. Würzburg 1937.

Johanna Franziska von Chantal. Ein Lebensbild aus der Wende des 16. Jahrhunderts. 2nd ed. Eichstätt, Vienna 1950.

MADELEINE-LOUISE, MÈRE

Physionomie d'une Sainte. Jeanne de Chantal. Paris 1950.

263

MARDUEL, M.
L'Âme ardente de Ste Chantal. Paris 1955.

MAUPAS DU TOUR, HENRI DE
Vie de la vénérable Mère Jeanne-Françoise Frémiot, Baronne de Chantal. Paris 1644.

MÉZARD, DENYS, O.P.
Doctrine Spirituelle de Ste Jeanne-Françoise de Chantal. Paris 1928.

MÜLLER, MICHAEL
Die Freundschaft des heiligen Franz von Sales mit der heiligen Johanna Franziska von Chantal. Regensburg 1928.

PERRENET, PIERRE
La Maison Natale de Jeanne Françoise Frémyot, Baronne de Chantal. Revue de Bourgogne 1916 – 17, pp. 65–88.

SACCARELLI, CARLO ANTONIO
Vita della Beata Giovanna Francesca Fremiot di Chantal, descritta in compendio da C. A. Saccarelli, Postulatore della Causa. Rome 1751.

IV GENERAL WORKS

BAILLON, JEAN, COMTE DE
Madame de Montmorency. Marie Félice des Ursins. Paris 1880.

CALVET, MGR. JEAN
La Littérature Religieuse de François de Sales à Fénelon. 2nd ed. Paris 1956.

CHABEUF, HENRI
Dijon à travers les âges. Dijon 1897.

DONCIEUX, SCIPION
Le Président Frémyot et la Ligue en Bourgogne. Dijon 1865.

ÉVERAT, EDUARD
Vie de Jeanne-Charlotte de Bréchard. Clermont-Ferrand 1938.

FABER, FREDERICK WILLIAM
An essay on beatification, canonization, and the processes of the Congregation of Rites. London 1848.

FRANQUEVILLE, COMTE DE
Histoire de Bourbilly. Paris 1907.

GAUCHET, CLAUDE
Le Plaisir des Champs. Paris 1583. (ed. with notes by P. Blanchemain, Paris 1869.)

GRIVOT, DENIS, and ZARNECKI, GEORGE
Gislebertus: Sculptor of Autun. London 1961.

GÜNTER, HEINRICH
Psychologie der Legende. Studien zu einer wissenschaftlichen Heiligen-Geschichte. Freiburg 1949.

HENRY-COÜANNIER, MAURICE
Saint François de Sales et ses Amitiés. 6th ed., Paris 1958.

KLEINCLAUSZ, ARTHUR
Histoire de Bourgogne. Paris 1909.

LE COUTURIER, ERNESTINE
Françoise-Madeleine de Chaugy et la Tradition Salésienne au XVIIᵉ siècle. 2 vols. Paris 1933.

MAGNE, ÉMILE
La Vie Quotidienne au temps de Louis XIII. Paris 1942.

MILSAND, PHILIBERT
Bibliographie bourguignonne, ou catalogue méthodique d'ouvrages relatifs à la Bourgogne. Dijon 1885.

PRUNEL, LOUIS N.
La Renaissance Catholique en France au 17e Siècle. Paris 1921.

ROELKER, N. L.
The Paris of Henry of Navarre as seen by Pierre de l'Estoile. Harvard U.P., Cambridge 1958.

ROUPNEL, GASTON
La Ville et la Campagne au XVIIᵉ siècle. Étude sur les populations du pays dijonnais. Dijon 1922.

RUPPERT, J.
Histoire du costume de l'antiquité au XIXe siècle. Paris 1931.

TROCHU, MGR FRANCIS
Saint François de Sales, d'après ses écrits, ses premiers historiens et les deux procès inédits de sa canonisation. 2 vols., Lyons and Paris 1946.

UZANNE, OCTAVE
La Locomotion à travers le temps, les moeurs et l'espace. Paris 1912.

VAISSIÈRE, PIERRE DE
Gentilshommes campagnards de l'ancienne France. Paris 1904.

VERMEYLIN, ALPHONSE
Ste Thérèse en France au XVIIe siècle, 1600–1660. Louvain 1958.

WATSON, F.
Vivès and the Renascence education of women. London 1912. (A selection and translation from Juan Luis Vives, *De Institutione feminae christianae*, 1523.)

INDEX

Relationships, unless otherwise stated, are to St Chantal.